# GUILT
# AND
# GRATITUDE

Recent titles in
Contributions in Philosophy

The New Image of the Person: The Theory and Practice of Clinical
Philosophy
*Peter Koestenbaum*

Panorama of Evil: Insights from the Behavioral Sciences
*Leonard W. Doob*

Alienation: From the Past to the Future
*Ignace Feuerlicht*

The Philosopher's World Model
*Archie J. Bahm*

Persons: A Comparative Account of the Six Possible Theories
*F. F. Centore*

Science, Animals, and Evolution: Reflections on Some Unrealized
Potentials of Biology and Medicine
*Catherine Roberts*

The Philosophy of Human Rights: International Perspectives
*Alan S. Rosenbaum, editor*

Estrangement: Marx's Conception of Human Nature and the Division
of Labor
*Isidor Walliman*

The Concept of Ideology and Political Analysis: A Critical Examination
of Its Usage by Marx, Lenin, and Mannheim
*Walter Carlsnaes*

Soviet Marxism and Nuclear War: An International Debate
*John Somerville, editor*

Understanding: A Phenomenological-Pragmatic Analysis
*G. B. Madison*

# GUILT
# AND
# GRATITUDE

## A Study of the Origins
## of Contemporary Conscience

JOSEPH ANTHONY AMATO II

Foreword by Thaddeus C. Radzialowski

Contributions in Philosophy, Number 20

Greenwood Press
Westport, Connecticut • London, England

BJ
1471
.A468
1982

**Library of Congress Cataloging in Publication Data**

Amato, Joseph Anthony.
    Guilt and gratitude.

    (Contributions in philosophy, ISSN 0084-926X ; no.
20)
    Bibliography: p.
    Includes index.
    1. Conscience.  2. Guilt.  3. Gratitude.  I. Title.
II. Series.
BJ1471.A468      170'.42        81-6991
ISBN 0-313-22946-5 (lib. bdg.)      AACR2

Library of Congress Catalog Card Number: 81-6991
ISBN: 0-313-22946-5
ISSN: 0084-926X

First published in 1982

Greenwood Press
A division of Congressional Information Service, Inc.
88 Post Road West, Westport, Connecticut 06881

Printed in the United States of America

10 9 8 7 6 5 4 3 2 1

To my parents, Ethel and Joe

Live possessed by powers we pretend to understand.

W. H. Auden

# Contents

Foreword                                                                      *ix*

Preface                                                                       *xiii*

Acknowledgments                                                               *xxiii*

Introduction:   A New Guilt                                                   3

1   The Old Man's Gratitude                                                   22

2   Progress, The Making of a New Conscience                                  48

3   The Transmission of the New Conscience
    from the Philosophers' Ideal to Mass
    National Sacrifice                                                        81

4   Humanity, A Failed God: Intellectuals in Search
    of a Moral Way in a Guilty Era                                            116

5   The Test of a National Conscience: From
    Philosophers' Republic to World Empire                                    144

Conclusion:   A Conscience for This Time                                      186

*Selected Bibliography*                                                       *205*

*Index*                                                                       *213*

# Foreword

Joseph Amato is a historian and a philosopher, and, to our profit, he unites these two areas in this work. It is the essential marriage of history and philosophy that makes this work a unique explanation of contemporary conscience.

There is a strong continuity between *Guilt and Gratitude* and Amato's previous writings. The continuity is especially marked between *Guilt and Gratitude* and his earlier *Mounier and Maritain: A French Catholic Understanding of the Modern World*. There he examined the attempt of interwar French Catholic intellectuals to find moorings in the crises of the twentieth century. Under the banner of personalism they sought a philosophy for our times that combined the most generous aspects of Christian tradition with a progressive political response to events. In *Guilt and Gratitude* Professor Amato extends his examination of the contemporary crisis in civilization to the crisis of contemporary conscience.

What is distinctive about Amato's approach is his insistence on grounding his ethical reflections firmly in history. His reflections are never a free-floating and disembodied, and hence a sterile, body of prescriptions. This characterizes, and separates, his work from those studies of ethics that purport to examine "eternal verities," with only scant reference to the historical context in which men and women make ethical choices. Amato shows a historian's care for fact, objectivity, and method, but he does not shy away from moral judgment.

There is another interesting combination that characterizes his work. He joins abiding philosophical concerns of ethics with the most fertile and productive themes of the "new history." In fact, this work places him among the ablest practitioners of the new history.

The new history combines an interest in economics, class interaction, social psychology, and social mobility, with a concern for the mentalities, the world views, the popular beliefs, and the rituals by which peoples create, regulate, and value their worlds. It focuses on symbols, meanings, and identities, as well as the contexts in which moral choices and social options occur. At its best, the new history seeks out an understanding of the existential consequences of being a member of a particular culture, class, ethnic group, or gender. It does not ask about this or that event, but it seeks to understand the interconnections of history and culture that form particular moral realities. In this ecological approach to the study of human experience Amato has found an ideal instrument for illuminating the dilemmas of our culture and seeking the fundamentals of a new ethics.

What gives *Guilt and Gratitude* its power as a study of the development of modern conscience is the author's tragic optimism. Amato believes that all human endeavors, given enough time, can—and often do—go wrong; that, despite the best efforts of men and women, good intentions sometimes result in great evils. Conversely, Amato affirms that human spirit, will, and intelligence are capable of resisting, and even triumphing over, evil and adversity. It is with that tragic optimism that he explores the historical dimensions of conscience and seeks to find authentic inner roots for ethics for our times.

Amato bases his study of the crises of conscience in our time on an analysis of the transition from the older, rural order to a bureaucratic, urban, industrial society in the Western world during the last two centuries. His work, however, gives us no simple juxtaposition of the traditional world versus the modern world. There is no call to return to the warm community and ethical simplicity of the village, nor is there an uncritical acceptance of the benefits of progress. Amato shows us the crushing burdens, fatalism, and narrowness of the traditional world, while he enumerates its enduring strengths. And while he appreciates the fundamental advances of the modern order, he exposes the demonic forces underlying the contemporary search for an earthly paradise.

The central focus of this study is the fracturing of the traditional roots of conscience. In the name of progress the forces of the modern world destroyed the autonomy of all past cultures, and at the same time, modern institutions (especially, for Amato, the nation-state) have come to deny the very humanism, liberation, and hope that spawned them. Amato shows us correctly that only when we understand this subversion of conscience and its consequences, which leave us children of neither traditional nor modern worlds, can we begin to have an ethics for our times. *Guilt and Gratitude* is the thread by which he seeks to lead us into and out of the moral labyrinths in which we find our individual and collective selves.

On the eve of the 1848 revolutions, the priest-revolutionary Lamartine spoke for all of us who have lived in the Western world during the last two centuries, when he observed plaintively that "the World has jumbled its catalogue." In *Guilt and Gratitude* Joseph Amato has unscrambled a part of that catalogue.

Thaddeus C. Radzialowski
Special Advisor on Ethnic and Social History
to the Chairman of the National
Endowment for the Humanities

# Preface

Every year in the springtime when the flowers are in bloom and the trees and shrubs are most beautiful, citizens of the Union celebrate Memorial Day. Over most of the United States it is a legal holiday. Being both sacred and secular, it is a holy day as well as a holiday and is accordingly celebrated.

Memorial Day is an important occasion in the American ceremonial calendar. . . . Memorial Day is a cult of the dead which organizes and integrates the various faiths and national and class groups into a sacred unity. It is a cult of the dead organized around community cemeteries. . . . The cemetery provides them [the community] with enduring visible symbols which help them to contemplate man's fate and their own separate destinies. . . . The symbols of death say what life is and those of life define what death must be.

The Memorial Day rite is a cult of the dead, but not just of the dead as such, since by symbolically elaborating sacrifice of human life for the country through, or identifying it with the Christian church's sacrifice of their god, the deaths of such men also become powerful sacred symbols which organize, direct, and constantly revive the collective ideals of the community and the nation.

W. Lloyd Warner, "An American Sacred Ceremony," *The American Life, Dream and Reality* (Berkeley, 1962), 5, 6, 8, 18, 19.

In the small village of Cottonwood in southwestern Minnesota, there occurred in 1970 what was known locally as "The War of the

Cannon." This study has its origins in my reflections on that war.

The war began when the local legionnaires decided to establish a war memorial in order to honor the village's war dead and make manifest their patriotism in that troubled time. They took advantage of the army's offer to donate a free obsolete howitzer for placement in a veterans' memorial, then purchased a downtown corner lot and ordered an appropriately inscribed marble marker. The legionnaires then proudly announced their plans for the memorial in the local paper. To the shock of the ninety legionnaires, as well as the majority of the eight hundred residents of the village and the one thousand readers of the paper in the surrounding countryside, the next issue of the paper carried a letter protesting the use of the cannon in the memorial. The letter, written by a local college professor, argued that it was wrong to commemorate the war dead with a cannon, which was an instrument of killing; instead it would be more fitting, he argued, to adopt a symbol of the peace for which the war dead had striven.

In the legionnaires' eyes, by the very act of commenting on the memorial, the professor had committed a multitude of sins. It was as though in one single act he had transgressed hallowed ground, polluted graves, mocked burial customs, and disrupted religious services. These were the legionnaires' war dead. Together, they and the dead were, in some real but mystical way, comrades in arms. It was they who remembered the dead. This memorial was their sacred ceremony; they were its priesthood. Was not the professor, they angrily asked, presuming to tell the priests about their own sacraments, lecturing friends about friendship, and explaining the meaning of a shared ordeal, the value of honor, and the proprieties of affection?

Abundant materials stored in the local mind helped fuel the legionnaires' anger, not just against the professor who wrote the letter, but also against the other four professors who lived in the village and were assumed correctly to share his sentiment. The professors worked thirteen miles to the south in Marshall, that growing city of ten thousand. There they taught at the new four-year college, Southwest Minnesota State, which housed blacks, war protestors, and long-haired youth, and which was rumored in Cottonwood and throughout the region to be a haven for drugs. With one exception, the professors and their families did not attend church—and the one family that did was Catholic in a town that traditionally had been Protestant, most distinctly Norwegian Lutheran. The professors all refused invitations to join the one important local service group, the Lions Club. Further, if there was a vet among them—there was one—not one of them had joined the Legion.

Also not to be forgotten was the fact that these professors were strangers. They came from cities. They made their livings with words, not by labor. They were often seen around the village, in the restaurant, at the post office, and working in their gardens at the very time when the villagers were hard at work—for less pay, too. Some villagers even reasoned that since the professors were paid by the state, they were, in fact, the employees of Cottonwood's local taxpayers. Indeed, the legionnaires had no trouble going to war against these impious professors who had moved into their midst during the past two years.

For that matter, the professors held equally unflattering images of the legionnaires. The professors judged the legionnaires to be "red necks" who measured the world with the moralism of a bad World War II movie. In the professors' opinion, the legionnaires' greatest wrong was sacrificing this generation to the misconstrued meaning they gave to yesterday's military deaths. They, with their myths, ignorance, angry gods, and American Legion, were to be held responsible as much as anyone for the Vietnam War. In attacking the legionnaires, the professors had no trouble believing themselves to be engaged in noble combat. The educators began with the assumption that they were missionaries of enlightenment in a dark land where love of guns abounded and where the majority, still imprisoned in their grandparents' fear-filled memories, had visions of Indian braves raiding, looting, burning, and raping. For the professors, fighting the legionnaires was a noble war; it was to do battle against the dark side of America. Their objective was to try to save the sons from having the sins of the fathers visited upon them.

The accusations and insinuations unleashed by the war swirled in village hearts long after the cannon had been ceremoniously but uneventfully installed. My wife, four children, and I, one of the professors, continued to live in the village for the following eight years, and during that time I found myself reflecting on the ethical principles and sentiments embodied in the war. These reflections raised fundamental questions of conscience about loyalty: loyalty to the old or new ways, public or private lives; loyalty to self, community, nation, or humanity. Further, they led me to consider, on the one hand, abstract matters regarding the nature of human exchange and the obligations and rights that accompany it. On the other hand, questions were raised, which were more personal but not as easily answered, questions about what gifts we have been given and what we owe in return for them. At almost all points my reflections revealed not only a self but, so to speak, a world divided in its conscience.

Of all the ethical polarities that underlay the war and captured my reflections, none seemed as elemental and intriguing as the opposition between a kind of gratitude that requires obedience to a specific established order and a type of guilt that demands the universal realization of human potential. In fact, this opposition, which can be considered to form an elemental ethical antinomy for all modern people as they choose between past and future, appears to be at the heart of the divided condition of contemporary conscience. To fathom this division and its ramifications—its hold upon our feelings, sensibilities, assumptions, language, and thus consciousness itself—is to help free conscience from debilitating contradictions that deny clarity to its power to survey and judge human experience.

Therefore, it is my reflection upon guilt and gratitude that produced this work: a work which, I hope, embodies not just a personal search for ethical clarification, but proves to be an enlightening inquiry into the condition of contemporary conscience. As in an earlier work dedicated to Emmanuel Mounier's Personalism, in which I sought to explore the nature of "a philosophy for our times," so here in this work I seek to examine more precisely the conditions of an "ethics for our times."

From one point of view, the village debate was like so many of those exchanges that characterized the nation during the late 1960s and early 1970s. It was another expression of the perennial American rite of moral self-examination. Professors and legionnaires were, in effect, debating the essence of America with different myths. The legionnaires' view was based on the myth that America since its founding has meant freedom, opportunity, progress, and hope. America's cause, they contended, has always been the good; its purposes always those of humanity. It deserves universal gratitude. Any criticism of America, therefore, seemed to them not only to be a sin against the truth but, worse, an expression of the most impious ingratitude.

Although the professors shared the legionnaires' ideal of America as servant to humanity, they expressed this myth in the secular language of America, the enlightened republic. Though this faith was older than the republic itself, the professors used it to focus not on the good that America has done, but on the good it should do. Influenced by the severe criticism of the United States that pervaded the late 1960s and early 1970s, the professors asked, to the sheer incomprehension of the legionnaires, whether America was in the process of transforming itself from being a friend into becoming an enemy of humanity. The professors were certain that America was failing its universal mission and that somehow they, like all its citizens, bore responsibility for this failure. For the legionnaires, America was unquestionably an enduring object of gratitude, but for the professors America had become a pressing matter of guilt.

From another point of view, the conflict between the legionnaires' cult of gratitude and the professors' sense of guilt was not exclusively an American affair. Instead it expressed the standing twentieth-century struggle between nationalism and internationalism. The legionnaires voiced a nationalism particularly common to this century of war, a nationalism that enrolls the whole nation into "the church of the fallen soldier." No blood is held to be as innocent, no sacrifice as noble, and no community as moral as that of the martyred soldier. He is the founding hero. He is the measure of the good. He is the reason for our limitless indebtedness.

The professors, in contrast, voiced an internationalism that conceives no national cause, however exalted, to be of real worth when measured against humanity's cause. No greatness, no sacrifice, no martyred heroism of a national past, in the professors' eyes, could equal the innocence of human potential. For them, the universal promise of the future was the greatest good.

Beyond rehearsing the obvious ideological conflict of nationalism and internationalism which, so redundantly and so tragically, fills this century, the professors and the legionnaires set forth irreconcilable claims to conscience. The legionnaires defined the good by the value of past heroic sacrifice. They asked that the ethical world, the world of the good and the right, be structured around gratitude, that is, thankful recognition for what has been given to us. The legionnaires assumed that we would be less than we are—or perhaps we would not even be at all—if it were not for the gifts the heroes had given us. Gratitude alone, in their opinion, properly recognized the gifts and assured the succession of the benefits. Like traditional, preindustrial humanity, the legionnaires assumed that the good was established by the heroic acts of founders and was renewed by the commemoration and imitation of those acts. In accord with the oldest ethical teachings, the legionnaires assumed gratitude was the primary source of piety. Gratitude should determine our obligations. It should be the cornerstone of our ethics. Without it the family, the society, religion, conscience, indeed all authority itself would come undone. Ingratitude puts all in jeopardy.

The professors constructed their moral universe around different sentiments. The cult of gratitude was alien to them. They looked at the past not as a sort of communion of saints, a sacred chain of grace extending across time, but instead they viewed the past as something to be overcome. In their opinion, the past at its best contained lessons on how contemporary men and women could surpass their ancestors. At its worst, the past was a flawed inheritance, composed of failed revolutions, limiting superstitions, and tragically self-destructive assumptions. In opposition to the legionnaires, the professors would have us measure the good by the promise they perceived in the present. Their focus was the universal human potential. As the legionnaires found judgment in their "fathers' eyes," so the professors were judged by their "imagined children's eyes." Violence for the professors was the denial of possibilities; the greatest sins were those against the innocence of the history yet to be made.

The legionnaires' and professors' debate reflected not only such perennial questions of ethics as what is the good and what is its source, but it also revealed the divided condition of contemporary conscience. In contrast to traditional society, in which guilt and gratitude mutually fulfilled the conservative function of defending the established order, in modern society guilt and gratitude have become, at least in two of their essential forms, conflicting modalities of human obligation. Gratitude, when serving either private or public purposes, points backward in time toward first gifts. It forms exclusive attachments involving, even demanding, trust, affection, obedience, and subservience. Almost inevitably, gratitude

serves the authorities of established tradition. Even when manipulated, as it often is, gratitude affirms the worth of maintaining
present relations. On the other hand, guilt—at least the sort that
calls one to serve mankind at large—opens the person to a changing
world and the new responsibilities it suggests. The guilt is inseparable from a progressive view of existence that binds all
humans in a mutuality of problems and potential. This culpability
values change more than permanence, experimentation and reform
more than tradition, imagination more than memory, and child
more than ancestor.

Because in measure we are all both legionnaires and professors,
we live divided between the claims of guilt and gratitude. This
book is about that division. It is intended to examine the contemporary conscience, which is caught between the conflicting claims
of guilt and gratitude and lacks elemental answers to such absolutely preliminary ethical questions as what has been given to us
and what we owe in return. Divided conscience, it is assumed, is
itself the condition of being a contemporary.

The more I reflected on the professors' and legionnaires' debate,
the more I came to believe that contemporary conscience was
formed around the division of guilt and gratitude. Gratitude is one
of the well springs of human justice. It is one ethical axis of conscience. We build our moral world out of gratitude: We take ethical
measure of ourselves in relation to gifts received and gifts given.
We cannot value ourselves without knowing what we have given
and without acknowledging our indebtedness to family, friends,
community, and God. Gratitude reminds us that so much of what
we are and what we have depends upon the gifts of others. When
we are moved by gratitude, we admit that our abiding source is
what we have received from others—their service, example, legacy,
love, sacrifice, heroism. We even take the very good of our existence to be the sum of gifts we have received. We find reason for
gratitude, the acknowledgment of the gift, in our birth; the inheritance of our ancestors; those countless acts of abnegation (great
and small) that our parents committed for us; and in all the wonderful things of God, nature, and men and women that have provided us with a home and a homeland. We find gratitude, and the
loyalty it calls forth, as the way to be true to the good that has been
and is, and any possible good that could be. We measure all things

human—our daily transactions, our family, friends, colleagues, associations, communities, and government—by the gratitude we feel and expect. Gratitude is at the ethical–moral core of ourselves.

In our contemporary world, the claims upon us are manifold; the claims to our gratitude alone are many, diverse, subtle, and complicated. Every institution (real and imagined, local and universal, political, social, economic, and religious) claims to have given us an indebting gift. No doubt there are times—a great number of them, indeed whole periods of our lives—when we hunger for a simpler era when our conscience at least could start with confidence about established conventions for the recognition and the exchange of gifts. How much simpler an ethical existence is in a small, traditional village where one knows the community face-to-face, and rights and obligations are part of a traditional transaction of goods and services. However, for us, no such simple system of ethical accounting is possible. Gifts cannot be entered simply into some double column ledger marked "accounts received" and "accounts owed." Constantly the public world (that vast collection of institutions, ideologies, and forces of state, market, and world politics) imposes itself and its claims into our local worlds and conscience. It encompasses us with its facts, events, explanations, structures, hopes, and values. Nothing of ourselves—even our very projection of our most intimate and personal selves—is free of the realities and ideals of the public world.

In the contemporary world the claims of humanity at large cannot be escaped. Both humanity as real and humanity as ideal, which we now conceive for the first time as interconnected by the possibilities of our power, gain an ever larger place in our conscience. No longer can we treat the diverse multitudes of the world with sheer indifference. We cannot simply dismiss them as being outside the pale of our responsibility and assign them to the mercy of some kind god, for in some radical sense we humans—especially those of us in powerful states and with education and wealth—have transformed ourselves into gods. As failed and cruel as we are, we cannot shake, however distant and absurd it might be, the sense that we are responsible for this humanity, this earth. We hear the cries (sometimes our own) for justice and right, and we hear all those plans, usually so coarse, bizarre, impossible, for realizing a more perfect individual and collective humanity. With such awesome responsibility—no doubt created in measure by the official ideologies of nations, progressive technology, business, and radicalisms, as well as the undeniable power we have—we experience a guilt about the humanity that is and the humanity that should be. This guilt can arise before all that is wrong, for all that is not yet perfect.

No doubt this guilt belongs mainly, but not exclusively, to the secular, educated, liberal citizens of the West. By conscious citizenship in a democratic industrial nation, and in a way that has never existed before, we accept humanity as its own artificer. We are not free to exempt from ethical consideration any part of our own or our nation's givings and takings. By virtue of our knowledge, power, and benefits we are required, if we are to save our conscience's integrity, to account for our actions to humanity. In a new sense the whole world has become a stage and we the players upon it.

We, therefore, cannot fix the boundaries of our guilt and gratitude. The limits of old selves have been broken. If we are to give and take with justice, which is a first condition of our dignity and an essential element of our ethics, our conscience must be open to the universal effects of our actions. This is, in all its bewildering perplexity, a duty of contemporary conscience.

Although I do not seek to formulate an ethics here, I do hope, after elucidating fundamental terms by which we define the good, to examine the divided condition of contemporary conscience. Further, I hope to diminish, in some cases to dispel altogether, the power of many of the ambivalences, dichotomies, and contradictions that confuse our conscience, and thus impede us from valuing the world. Of course, attention will be given to the conflicting obligations born out of guilt and gratitude, with special attention also directed to the matters of diffuse guilt and institutionally manipulated guilt and gratitude. The guiding premise of this work is that of traditional humanism: Knowledge is good and those willing to bear its discipline will be freer and, therefore, more human.

I have striven consistently to keep this work popular, accessible not just to academic philosophers and historians, but to all readers who reflect upon ethical obligations in the contemporary world. In addition, although I have drawn heavily here from all the major social sciences, especially anthropology and sociology, I have sought to fuse my interest in ethics and cultural history in this work. That fusion has been effected in the crucible of a moderate historicism, which, while not denying transcendence to the truth, affirms that in great measure we are our past, and therefore we understand ourselves best by critically reflecting upon our inheritance.

The only other assumptions that I consider worthy of special attention here are these: I have joined European and American history believing that they are treated best as a unity for our purposes. I have paid particular attention to the nation-state, for it represents mankind's most generalized form of power. Nothing significant can be embodied that is contrary to it. The nation-state thus is a first issue of conscience. As legionnaires and professors show, this is especially the case for Americans whose nation was the boldest of eighteenth-century Western philosophers' dreams.

Finally, I should point out that guilt and gratitude are used here as a typology, a kind of idealized dichotomy similar to Eliade's definition of the relationship between the sacred and the profane. Guilt and gratitude express the radical difference between the ethics of modern man and traditional man. This difference serves to measure the ethical distance traversed by traditional men and women en route to modernity; in the passage from a past formed around small, isolated, static rural villages to a modern order dominated by massive, individualistic, and changing urban society. It must be noted at this point, however, that the passage from the world of gratitude to that of guilt is never entirely completed by any one individual or group. Within the conscience of the vast majority of us there reside both the values of the traditional rural man and the contemporary urban dweller. Furthermore, none of us, individually or collectively, advances in our understanding of this world by preordained rhythms, at measured paces, with calculated consequences. Our cultures, traditions, and conditions make us too varied for such spiritual uniformity. As we have all come to learn (some tragically from the war in Vietnam), the process of modernization itself is not singular, uniform, and inevitable. The very concepts of "traditional" and "contemporary" are themselves abstractions, regardless of how necessary they are in order to define ourselves and our experiences.

So we pursue the truth with approximations. On such matters as ethics, we should not expect more than insightful generalization. Yet to the extent that we can understand the peasant and the contemporary man, the legionnaire and the professor, who quarrel within us, we free our conscience.

# Acknowledgments

This long study has left me in debt to many. May those whom I have forgotten forgive me.

My wife Catherine and my children Felice, Anthony, Adam, and Ethel have supported this work in many ways. The joy they give me is not the least of the ways. My parents Ethel and Joe, to whom this work is dedicated, have taught me by word and by example much of what I know about conscience. My wife's parents, who have always generously supported my work, have also taught me about the nature of gifts, exchange, reciprocity, and class and ethnic warfare in the Pennsylvania Anthracite region. That is where my grandparents from Sicily first met America and, more importantly, each other.

My fellow historians at Southwest State University in Marshall, Minnesota, Maynard Brass, Thaddeus Radzialowski, and David Nass, have provided me with over a decade of friendship and scholarship. Maynard Brass, who died last year, was a scholar and friend of wide interests who gave me more than one idea, and put more than one of my sentences into English. Thaddeus Radzialowski, who wrote the foreword to this work, and I started talking to each other in Detroit in 1961 at Wayne State and have not stopped yet. David Nass and I know what we have shared in community this year. I hope, in turn, this work will add to my continuing dialogue with Michael Kopp, our new historian.

Phillip Dacey in our English Department is a teacher, friend, and poet who inspires me. Also to be thanked are my colleagues in the Social Science Division: I have not without reason nicknamed anthropologist James Hayes "*la petite Bibliothèque Nationale*"; and political scientist Loren Tesdell and psychologists Robert Riedel and William LaFief have provided me with interesting material; and sociologists Robert White and Charles Grubb have taught a great deal to me about the left in contemporary America.

David Monge and Steven Wiener labored in earnest to understand what I meant and helped me to say it so others might understand it.

Friends and colleagues elsewhere have also been vitally important to this work. Professor Don Martindale, in the Department of Sociology at the University of Minnesota, proved to be a truly keen and encouraging guide during this work's long labor. Professor Jeffrey Russell, of the Department of History at the University of California in Santa Barbara, also was directly responsible for improving the work and strengthening my resolution to complete it. Professor Alfred McClung Lee, former President of the American Sociological Association, also was generous with insight and encouragement, as was *World View* editor Richard Neuhaus. Professors Jerre Mangione and David Noble took some interest in this work, and there is an abiding debt owed to Professor A. W. Salomone, whose encouragement and influence were at an earlier period decisive in my intellectual development.

In addition, I would like to extend my gratitude to colleague-participants in a one-year National Endowment for the Humanities seminar on European Culture held at the University of California in Los Angeles, 1975-1976. It was there that this work received its first outline and some of its inspiration. Special thanks are owed to the National Endowment for the Humanities for granting me the year-long fellowship; to Professor Eugen Weber who chaired the seminar with a guileful charm and a spirited intelligence; and to President Ivan Hinderacker, librarian Ronald Baker, Chairman of the History department Edwin Gaustad, and the History faculty of the University of California in Riverside who generously welcomed me back to the university where I once taught. They truly made me feel like a prodigal son.

Here I recognize a sense of debt to SSU President Jon Wefald, Vice-President Judith Sturnick, and Dean Christopher Eismann, who are good leaders. Also, faculty leaders Mary Hickerson and David Simpson have helped maintain rights and traditions essential for scholarly work.

Our library staff—Donald Olsen, Mary Jane Striegel, Frank Shindo, Betty Zupfer, and Margaret Schultz—has furnished me with intelligent help on this project, and on more than one occasion the staff at the University of Minnesota reference desk furnished me with important help. The many drafts of this work have left me indebted to Arlene Schoephoerster, Director of the Word Processing Center, typist Linda Dieken, and two master Social Science secretaries, Gloria Peters and Dorothy Frisvold. The latter have summoned to their aid many fine students, numbered among whom were Mary Warner, Myra Ricketts, Gail McPherson, Paul Wentzlaff, Karen Hoffman, Judy Noyes (whose indefatigable labors on this manuscript may leave it indelibly set in her memory), and Teresa Treinen, who has a good ear for good English. Lauri Fox, our paraprofessional, and our aide Shirley Carlson also were pressed into important service on the manuscript. Also particular thanks are owed to Janice Louwagie and Nancy Shearer for their work on the index.

Each contact with Greenwood Press has increased my appreciation for the press and its personnel. Margaret Brezicki could not have been any more generous and supportive. Also not to be forgotten at Greenwood is Director James Sabin who established the press's initial interest in this work, and Production Editor Louise Hatem and Copy Editor Sarah Helyar Smith, whose diligent efforts radically improved this work.

# GUILT
# AND
# GRATITUDE

*Introduction*

# A New Guilt

It is true that benevolence and sympathy are essential to morality, even if they do not exhaust its entire nature. It is true that to serve mankind is a worthy ideal, even if humanity be no god.

Morris Ginsberg, *Essays in Sociology and Social Philosophy* (Baltimore, 1968), 275.

The notion that man is his own maker, responsible collectively and individually for his own happiness, is a modern world view. This world view took form in the high culture of Western Europe two centuries ago during the Enlightenment and has come to dominate all others in the contemporary era. It constituted a new ethics, a new conscience, and a new guilt. Its ethics, secular in essence, made man's earthly happiness the highest measure of the good.

The new ethics, so closely tied to faith in progress and the spreading commercial, industrial, social, and political revolutions, contrasted dramatically with the older ways of valuing the world. Its assumption that man is his own maker challenged not just essential dogmas of Christianity, but all hierarchical, political, and social notions based on the concepts of inherited right and limited good.

When less than a century old, and hardly having begun its penetration of the traditional rural order, the new ethics encountered

awesome obstacles. As discussed in later chapters, these obstacles
first came in the form of mass politics and states and then appeared
in the guise of violently irrational, totalitarian societies that denied
the central tenet of all humanisms: that man could master the evil
within himself. Before considering institutions and ideologies in
conflict with the new ethics, however, we must define this guilt that
is in the service of mankind. In our era, in which so many are preoccupied with the pursuit of untroubled happiness, we engage in
the untimely and unpopular task of defining a guilt worthy of having and suffering.

At the outset, two initial assumptions should be set forth. First,
specific forms and amounts of guilt are not considered to be a constant element in human nature, even though admittedly there are
always differing and varying kinds of guilt connected with families,
law, and morality.[1] Guilt cannot be separated from the culture,
era, and situation in which it is experienced. If a choice needs to be
made, history, it is assumed here, better explains psychology than
psychology explains history. Second, there will be no explicit effort
here to distinguish between guilt and shame beyond the suggestion
that, although guilt and shame often are interrelated psychologi-
cally, the former implies some sort of wrongdoing (be it legal,
ethical, or moral), whereas the latter implies that the person is out
of place by virtue of situation, condition, action, or by his very
body and person.[2] Shame, therefore, can range from relatively
superficial and momentary embarrassments caused by a slip of the
tongue to the profound sense that one's existence is an ugly, un-
justifiable, and humiliating condition.[3]

## "GUILTLESS MAN," "GUILTY MAN," "THE MAN OF GUILT"

A sense of guilt clings to this age and is diffused throughout it.[4]
Twentieth-century high culture testifies to contemporary man's ob-
session with guilt. Freudian-inspired psychology, existential literature and philosophy, as well as many theologies are predicated
upon the assumption that guilt is a fundamental reality of the human condition.[5] The Freudians argue that guilt is a result of irre-
ducible conflicts between the basic drives of human sexuality and
the needs of human social life.[6] Existentialists conceive of guilt as
having its sources in inalterable disjunctions that exist between human consciousness and existence, values, and actions.[7] Even "reformers," who contend that guilt is the fundamental barrier to

human liberation, assume the central place of guilt in twentieth-century experience.[8]

Seeming to contradict the important place occupied by guilt in the twentieth century is the existence of countless numbers of people who appear to be utterly without conscience. These "guiltless men" have been considered the most toxic waste of contemporary society. As a type, the "guiltless man" seems to have one common attribute: He is without empathy. He has neither charity, sympathy, nor pity. His spirit is not extended to others. His horizons exclude others both by habit and by will. He recognizes only his own worth, security, needs, and desires.

Guiltless man can be horrid in both his individual and collective guises. The guiltless individual is the bomber who bombs because it is his job; and it is the anarchist who kills simply to satisfy his sense of logic. But for all the guiltless types of the individualist variety, there are similar numbers of the collectivist variety. Modern sociology provides us with examples—the crowd, the mob, the teen-age gangs, the indifferent passersby, or those apartment dwellers who did absolutely nothing (not even telephone for help) as they listened for over half an hour to the pleadings of a woman who was pursued in their courtyard and stabbed to death. Studies of the factory system, the bureaucracy, the suburbs have suggested (with the use of such concepts as the organizational man and the outer-directed person) that we are in the presence of a new breed of man who is without conscience, whose existence is limited to conforming to the requirements of the status of self, work, and community.[9]

Twentieth-century political reality parades before us community after community composed of guiltless man. Above all others, the supporters of Nazism are taken to be the symbol of the twentieth-century man devoid of conscience. In *Escape From Freedom*, Erich Fromm depicts the lower-middle class Germans of the 1920s who flocked to Nazism in order to escape their insecurity.[10] Hannah Arendt argues in *Eichmann in Jerusalem* that Nazi Adolph Eichmann's most terrifying characteristic of his brutality was his prosaic normalcy.[11] The very "banality of his evil" he manifested indicts the civilization that produced him. With such varying concepts as "mass man," "the crowd," "the internal proletariat," or "the *Lumpenproletariat*," social critics from all parts of the political spectrum have sought to identify that vast group of immoral people who, they believe, reside dangerously within contemporary civilization.

Nevertheless, the further we proceed in conceding the contemporary existence of guiltless man, the more we must postulate an absolutely opposing type, "the guilty man." In contrast to guiltless man, guilty man anguishes over everything. It is as if anything that comes to consciousness is a matter of conscience, a matter of choice, hesitation, anxiety, judgment, and guilt. It is as if he, like T. S. Eliot's J. Alfred Prufrock, stands defenselessly open before all. He, who says, "Do I dare? Do I dare?" hesitates before everything; he suffers all that he experiences. His integrity is easily violated. His mind is fraught with do's and don'ts. His conscience is always awake and threatened. His guilt and shame are joined. Fear of embarrassment and ridicule are always present for him. At every step into the world he feels himself the subject of another's gaze. Sometimes he wants to cover his face, to shrink into the ground, to be invisible. Like one of Chekov's petty officials, the slightest social faux pas becomes a life-and-death matter. The world for the guilty man is a "moral" mine field. Feeling without validity, he is forever turning back upon himself. It is as if his whole existence is tethered to his anxious conscience; his life is spent hopelessly warring against closing circles of self-doubt.

To offer yet another characterization of guilty man, his mind is a tribunal before which he always stands as defendant. Cross-examining him is his mother, his father, some friend from childhood, a boss, or just a pair of eyes he recently glimpsed along the street. What he pleads makes no difference. His trial continues but sentencing never occurs. This agony drives the defendant out into the world to do something, anything, that will rid him of those damning voices. But there are always the same voices, the same accusations. Consequently, his boldest actions to free himself fail. Invariably they lead him to embarrassment, scandal, and then a remorse that first pacifies and then leads him back to the prison of his guilt. Over decades this vicious cycle wears the guilty man down. Often he can survive only by reducing his life to a familiar set of habits or by making himself laughable, more humiliated than his worst imagined persecutor would have him.

Joseph K., the protagonist of Franz Kafka's The Trial, is contemporary literature's best known depiction of the guilty man.[12] Joseph K., bachelor and minor bank official, woke up one morning to discover his room being searched by two men. They were looking for evidence. He was indicted. Why? For what? He never found out.

His attempts to find out about his case led him to a sick, perverse lawyer, a loving girl, a wealthy relative. They couldn't help. The final counsel of a priest—offered to Joseph K. in a dark, empty church—only baffled him. It was a senseless parable: Each person has a door and he can pass through it only when he asks to pass through it.

Later, Joseph K. was taken away and stabbed to death in a desolate spot, on the outskirts of the city. Was he guilty of violating a secret ritual, of offending hidden gods, or simply of being born Joseph K.? There is no answer, only the charge, the anxiety, and the punishment.

As Joseph K.'s guilt comes from the sense of being personally condemned in an impersonal world, so there is another form of guilt in our collective world that comes from the sense of being guilty, if by knowledge alone, of all the evil in the world. This guilty man feels ashamed of existing and being conscious in a world that is less than perfect.

To be conscious of twentieth-century historical experience is to realize how even those significant few who wield power do not feel in control of the world they supposedly rule. Hannah Arendt wrote of action in twentieth-century public life:

> He who acts never quite knows what he is doing, that he always becomes "guilty" of consequences he never intended or [sic] even foresaw, that no matter how disastrous and unexpected the consequences of his deed he can never undo it, that the process he starts is never consummated unequivocally in one single deed or event, and that its very meaning never discloses itself to the actor but only to the backward glance of the historian who himself does not act.[13]

What Arendt indicates can be terrifying insofar as it implies that the good is a child of time or yet, even though man causes what happens, he does not control it.[14] Consequently, man is guilty for being the cause of his actions and guilty for not being able to direct their consequences. Man scandalizes himself as he encounters the senselessness of being his own god.

There are three other general types of explanations why guilt is so pervasive in twentieth-century experience. First, the twentieth century has been comprised of a succession of awful events such as wars, revolutions, depressions, and purges that have affected entire peoples.[15] Events like these make people feel guilty simply because

they happened. No doubt these events fill the atmosphere with accusation and counteraccusation, creating a hostile climate of victimizers and victims. Events linger in the human heart long after
they have happened. They live on in the minds of those who have
initiated them, and in those who have participated in and suffered
from them; they irreversibly affect those who know about them. In
the form of memories, events propagate and breed, defining senses
of right and wrong and separating the sensibilities, passions, ethics,
and values of generations. Interpretations of events can form the
core of political rhetoric expressing, intensifying, and even creating
the division between those who have power and those who want it.

Events, therefore, for contemporary man are the landmarks of
his existence. They form his experience, shape his mentality, and
furnish his justifications. They make *collective guilt* real. Events
put individuals, classes, nations, cultures, economies, and whole
epochs on trial. In this era of mass communication, these trials,
rendered in the form of ideology and propaganda, define collective
consciousness; they initiate radical social change and commit
armies. The chain between event and guilt is unbroken in our era.
Its ultimate source is found in the human affinity to fuse value and
memory.

Often, especially in developing societies, collective events indoc-
trinate individuals into the public world. Such major events as
wars, revolutions, and famines put them in contact with the national perspective. The events give individuals their places in it;
they establish relations, give identities, and offer opinions about
the public life. Individuals, upon entering the public life, take up
common sensibilities, prejudices, judgment values, and guilt, as
well as other emotions like resentment, anger, and hatred.

To a large degree, national societies exist by virtue of having a
mentality formed out of events experienced and valued collectively. In this manner, the citizens of a nation continue to live the
experiences of the past long after they have happened. By this reliv-
ing, guilts as well as gratitudes are passed on from father to son.

A second source of collective guilt is the vast change that characterizes contemporary life. First, increasing numbers of people in
the West identify themselves with the consequences of changes
associated with the dominance of the urban, scientific, industrial
society over all traditional societies.[16] The victims of progress have
produced a guilt that shapes twentieth century Western political

life. This guilt implicates Westerners in the crime not only of having destroyed the old way, but of having virtually annihilated whole groups of indigenous peoples in North America, South America, Africa, Southeast Asia, and the Pacific Islands. Refuge from this guilt is no longer easily found: progress is dubious justification for our behavior. In fact, we must ask if it conceals an awesome cultural ethnocentrism that incriminates us in advance with the greatest crimes of the future.

Also inherent in modernization is the guilt-producing process of constant judgment and change. As societies modernize, the mass of people must alter their concepts of self, family, community, and work. A society caught up in modernization poses agonizing, inescapable choices for all its members about one's allegiance to the old or the new way. Why and how one stays on the land, marries, raises children, saves money, and pursues pleasures are questions none can escape. Increasingly, individuals understand their lives and themselves to be tentative hypotheses, matters of self-invention, of choice, judgment, will, and responsibility. No doubt this awareness is accompanied by anxiety and guilt.

Daniel Lerner writes insightfully of the person in modernizing society: "The model for behavior developed by modern society is characterized by empathy, a high capacity for rearranging the self-system on short notice,"[17] which explains why modern man, in contrast to traditional man, is characterized by "increased psychic mobility."[18] Joined by mass communications to almost the entire world, modern man lives much of his life vicariously inhabiting the spirits of others. His mind is peopled with the desires, ideals, conflicts, and fantasies of others. This experience can be exhilarating, even euphoric at such times as when a person first learns to have "his own opinions," or to thumb his nose at past authorities and codes of conduct. Also, this experience can be shamefully degrading when one has to try to duplicate the customs, habits, and manners of the prevailing culture. A significant part of a person's mental life can be caught up in the tasks of mastering the basic etiquettes of proper eating, dress, leisure, and dating.[19] Still, great numbers today sense themselves to be guilty of being out of place "in the eyes of good society." "Transitionals," Lerner writes, "are making their way toward an unclear future via a path replete with hard bumps and unsuspected detours. Their voyage entails a sustained commingling of joyous anticipation with lingering anxieties, sensuous euphoria with *recurrent shame, guilts, and puzzlement.*"[20]

The children and grandchildren of transitionals are the ones who fully enter into the public world. On the one hand, Barrington Moore writes, this means they experience coercion:

> To maintain and transmit a value system, human beings are punched, bullied, sent to jail, thrown into concentration camps, cajoled, bribed, made into heroes, encouraged to read newspapers, stood up against a wall and shot, and sometimes even taught sociology. To speak of cultural inertia is to overlook the concrete interests and privileges that are served by indoctrination, education, and the entire complicated process of transmitting culture from one generation to the next.[21]

On the other hand, life in a modern society means the anxiety-creating business of constantly making up one's mind about a range of matters from such incidentals as the type of toothpaste and golf balls one should use to the more serious choices about career, marriage, and family.

"The contemporary experience of being lost, orphaned, disinherited, or alienated," Don Martindale notes, "belongs to men who have been recently specialized and whose feeling of a new efficiency in a small way is outweighed by a sense of loss of overall significance. Into this experience, contemporary men carry personality ideals which are increasingly difficult to realize."[22] The fragmentation of the self occurs increasingly as people have to adapt themselves to changing roles as family members, citizens, professional workers, and consumers, and this adaptation makes them conscious that their integrity hinges upon their own affirmation. Mass industrial society, materially structured around the division of labor and predicated upon the constant psychological adaption of the self, exposes all to new forms of shame and guilt as they venture into new realms of responsibility, obligation, and choice.[23]

To be modern, in effect, is to build one's life upon the process of making decisions. Always present are the fear, the guilt, and the shame of failure. In *The Hidden Injuries of Class,* Richard Sennett and Johnathan Cobb write of the guilt that afflicts the members of a society dominated by the myth of the self-made man.

> Even though we might have been born in different stations, the fact that he is getting more means that somehow he had the power in him, the character, to "realize himself," to earn his superiority. It is

in this way that a system of unequal classes is actually reinforced by the ideas of equality and charity formulated in the past. The idea of potential equality of power has been given a form peculiarly fitted to a competitive society where inequality of power is the rule and expectation. If all men start on some basis of equal potential ability, then the inequalities they experience in their lives are arbitrary, they are the logical consequence of different personal drives to use those powers—in other words, social differences can now appear as questions of character, of moral resolve, will and competence. The lesson of this historic flaw is that once respect is made, the reward for human ability, no matter if the ability is seen potentially in all, the stage is set for all the dangers of individualism: loneliness for those who are called the possessors, a feeling of individual guilt for those who do not come off as well.[24]

A person's conscience is formed by a myriad of collective notions, impulses, and ideals. "Social conscience loading" is the phrase Jules Henry uses to describe the process by which a conscience is shaped to the morality of the collective, the stereotypes, and other idealizations and taboos.[25] Ideologies, laws, and institutions form a collective identity; they give a person the perceptions, moralities, and values of his society. His sciences, for instance, define the rational and irrational, his courts and prisons define the right and wrong and his asylums tell him what is sane and insane. In mass society this process of establishing collective identities is sufficiently generalized to make a person, to a degree, the sum total of these identities.[26] Every person, in a sense, becomes every other person; their consciences are interchangeable.

Yet it is important to understand that all collectivities within a society do not conform in values to one another and that the conscience of the contemporary citizen of literate, urban civilizations reaches far beyond the societies' borders. No longer is any country entirely independent of the commercial, industrial, and political activities, or of the economic, social, and cultural revolutions of other societies. Zbigniew Brzezinski perceptively writes: "For the first time in human history, inequality is no longer isolated by time and distance. One experiences spatial immediacy to every suffering."[27]

Conscience awakened to the suffering of the world produces a new kind of universal guilt. René Du Bos expresses one form of this universal guilt, which is so prevalent throughout the West:

Our collective sense of guilt comes from a general awareness that our praise of human and natural values is hypocrisy as long as we practice social indifference and convert our land into a gigantic dump. . . . Tagore wrote of man's active wooing of the earth, and stated that "love and action are the only media through which perfect knowledge can be obtained." Saint Exupéry urged that we can know and enjoy only that which we tame through love. From a sense of guilt at seeing man-made ugliness, and also for reasons that must reach deep into man's origins, most people believe that nature should be preserved.[28]

This guilt, which arises from the existence of world-wide inequality, the destruction of nature, or the awesome spread of weaponry, has the profoundest primitive religious resonances.[29] It fills one with the awesome sense of being joined to an accursed evil force, a force that contaminates, negates, and destroys all that is good. In his study of soldiering entitled *The Warriors*, J. Glenn Gray writes how this guilt can penetrate right to an individual's awareness of his membership in humanity itself: "The awakened soldier will be driven to say in his heart: I, too, belong to this species. I am ashamed not only of my nation, but of human deeds as well. *I am ashamed to be a man.*"[30]

The diffusion of this universal guilt in the twentieth-century consciousness is not tied just to an awareness of evil perpetrated by man on nature and on one another, but is also joined to the growing recognition of the increasing good that men could, but do not, do for one another. The belief in progress, as we will see throughout this work, brought with it a sense of unprecedented responsibility. Man is considered not to be responsible just for loving mankind as a matter of general attitude and immediate charity, as all the high religions prescribe; he is now expected to be responsible universally and specifically for all men and women alive. This responsibility exists both in regard to the present conditions and wants of humanity as well as the general potential as human beings. Moral obligation, therefore, includes human improvement if not perfection; conscience is now joined to the imagined good.

Like the Christian doctrine of sin by omission, faith in progress holds its believers responsible for working for the best of all possible worlds. Here, as never before, ethics is joined to the dimension of the possible. Conscience now deals with what should be and what eventually could be. Every person who is inadequately "fed, clad, and sheltered" calls for a moral accounting; every failure, all waste, all potential left unrealized, every dream unfulfilled can indict.[31] No aspect of the human condition is exempt from ethical judgment. Everything about man, his society, past, present, and future, has become a matter of conscience. In this conscience only bad faith would permit one, either in the name of God, nature, history, or human weakness, to surrender man to being less than he could be. Walter Lippmann voiced this new conscience when he wrote: "Resignation may have been an appropriate attitude for mankind to assume during the long centuries when the world was posed uncertainly on the edge of starvation. But in the midst of plenty, the imagination becomes ambitious, rebellion against misery is at last justified, and dreams have a basis in fact."[32] In a radical new way, this modern conscience repeats the mystical ethics of saintly Father Zossima of Dostoyevsky's *Brothers Karamazov:* "Little heart of mine, my joy, believe me, everyone *is responsible to all men for all men and for everything.*"[33]

This new conscience, with its bold concern for the present plight and the future improvement of mankind, can be considered contemporary man's ethical reaction to the truly increasing interdependence of all civilization. This conscience, idealized, can be said to belong to a new kind of person, "the man of guilt." In contrast to the guiltless man and the guilty man, the man of guilt is an ethical being. He does not deny the fact of evil in the world. He is not satisfied with the right of either traditions or authorities to define what is good. His conscience is not still. He asks at whose expense and with what consequences are our transactions undertaken. He knows, admits, and remembers that there are victims. He hears Abel's cry.

Furthermore, this man of guilt, signifying more the principles of a new conscience than the real existence of an embodied person, is restless for a better world. He thinks in terms of possibilities and potentialities, not in terms of inevitabilities. He knows, too, that those who prefer purity of conscience to the transformation of the human condition still condone untold amounts of suffering. He knows that resignation before what is wrong or imperfect is a form of violence. He is even aware that preoccupation with the guilts and anxieties of the inner self can impede human action. The man of guilt is alive to possibility. He will not let the dead bury the living.

The man of guilt, the new conscience, of course could also be interpreted critically. He could be understood to be a vanishing shadow of hopeful and progressive nineteenth-century internationalism. He could be understood to be merely the self-righteous conjuring of all those who presume to take humanity's destiny upon themselves. Obviously, the claim to serve humanity can be self-serving. Such a "noble dedication" is not, at least at times, without its callous political uses. No doubt it can serve as a dramatic self-sanctification for all those who wish to talk "seriously" about their times. High-blown causes are a common addiction in this era when powers are so strong and words so weak. Concern about universal causes also can be a way to seek escape from the monotony of everyday life.[34] The man of guilt, then, perceived critically could be understood to be the pretense of conscience in what seems to be a conscienceless era.

No amount of critical analysis of the man of guilt would succeed in denying the relevance of his conscience for contemporary mankind which, for the first time, approaches becoming universally interdependent. Man's ability to have a coherent understanding, indeed his very survival, might depend on a conscience aware of humanity's interdependence. Form must be given to this conscience.

Nurturing this new conscience of the man of guilt is a primary goal of this work. The analysis is not intended to praise the conscience as an ideal to be attained, but instead to assess its genesis, formation, authenticity, and possibilities. This means that we must grasp how much the consciousness of contemporary man is characterized by the conflict, division, ambiguity, and contradiction of ethical principles. Contemporary man is experiencing a veritable war over how he should value himself. At war within him, as discussed in the following chapters, are the competing ethical principles of the traditional way, the Christian way, and the secular progressive way. All three of these identities reside at the heart of contemporary consciousness and pose contradictory methods of valuing existence.

The development of a new conscience not only must be formed in a divided spirit but also must be shaped in a world made dichotomous by warring and broken interpretations. Contemporary man's fundamental ambivalence about his own technology, nation-states, economic systems (capitalist and socialist alike), as well as the uncertainty about progress itself, explains why he is so ethically divided. He is confused about his rights and obligations, unsure about his givings and takings, and altogether unclear about what is justly expected in his public reciprocities. In fact, this very divided condition makes all traditional ethical systems seem remotely academic—whether it be egoism, utilitarianism with its precept of "the greatest good for the greatest good," or some other formal ethical system.

To define the new conscience we must examine its genesis. What must be grasped initially, as shown in Chapter 2, is that the new conscience, with its ideals of humanity as rational, powerful, happy, and self-fulfilling, historically has its genesis with a small segment of the upper literate classes. More precisely, the new conscience has its primary source in the world view of eighteenth-century philosophers. These ideals, the essential argument of Chapter 3, were not transmitted to the majority of peoples in the form of intellectual truths. Instead, for the majority the ideals of earthly happiness, rationalism, and progress came as they were refracted through an experience shaped by the instrumentalities of market, class, state, nationalism, public education, and other institutions that resulted from the French Revolution and the Industrial Revolution. In the simplest terms, history taught the new conscience.

It should also be understood, as is pointed out in Chapters 4 and 5, that the ideals from which the new conscience is emerging are not free of distortion. The distortion is attributable not only to the realities of historical immanence, but also to the sensibilities, political language, and ideologies that incorporate the ideals. Abuse of the concept of humanity can take the form of either putting it to the exclusive service of one group, one class, one nation; or transforming it into the symbol of a sickly, secular piety, which (as Nietzsche argued) amounts to little more than a self-imposed, debilitating reverence before every supposed victim. To choose another example, the ideal of human improvement can be used to justify technological irrationalism or it can invite a vicious spirit that regards the past as a mere accumulation of error, failure, wrong, and evil; the present existing as simply a resistance to a will toward the future. Ironically, the ideals that can inspire a new conscience can help create a conscienceless person, a moral nihilist.

There are other limits to the formation of the new conscience. Humanity must be defined. Is it real or ideal, a matter of infinite existing individuals or some sort of universalized history—past, present, and future? Are the ideals of humanity and God antagonistic?

Does the worth of future man negate the value of man past? Similar questions could be asked of reason, philanthropy, or progress. Then there are questions of a different order: If the new conscience is real, it surely demands to be expressed in action, embodied in institution, powers, and experience. And this invariably raises the question: How? What communications can carry the truth of the new conscience in this era of mass propaganda and ideology? What agencies should carry out a struggle on behalf of mankind as a whole when international bodies are so feeble; and when nation-states, the most powerful concentrations of human power ever to exist, have caused a century of awesome war and now threaten humanity with nothing other than annihilation itself.

All this should convince us that the man of guilt, the new conscience, is far from being fully formed. Yet his formation becomes critical for a mankind rapidly becoming one in promise and tragedy. A new conscience is required for this world of interdependence. However, neither necessity, nor wish, nor volition will create the new conscience that alone can test humanism's highest hopes against man's most demonic creations. What is needed at the start is understanding, and I hope there is a little light to aid that understanding.

## NOTES

1. The six general definitions of guilt given in the *Oxford English Dictionary* (Oxford, 1933, reissued and corrected edition, 1961), 496, are: (1) A failure of duty, delinquency; offence, crime, sin. . . . (2) Responsibility for an action or event; the 'fault' *of* (some person). . . . (3) Desert (*of* a penalty); esp. in phrase *Without guilt*, without having done anything to deserve one's fate, innocently. . . . (4) The fact of having committed, or of being guilty of, some specified or implied offence. . . . (5) The state (meriting condemnation and reproach of conscience) of having wilfully committed crime or heinous moral offence; criminality, great culpability. . . . (6) In legal use: The state of being regarded as justly liable to penalty."

2. A recent and fine guide to guilt and shame is Gerhardt Pier and Milton Singer's *Shame and Guilt: A Psychoanalytic Study* (New York, 1971); for a classic from the earlier period, see Helen Merrel Lynd's *On Shame and the Search for Identity* (New York, 1958) which is summarized and put in perspective in Don Martindale's fine chapter "Personality in Mass Society," in his *Institutions, Organizations, and Mass Society* (New York, 1966), 537–62. The distinction between guilt societies and shame

societies produced a small corpus of social science literature a few decades ago, as efforts were made to distinguish between traditional and communal societies and changing and individual societies. See, for example, Ruth Benedict's *The Chrysanthemum and the Sword: Patterns of Japanese Culture* (New York, 1946); Margaret Mead, *Cooperation and Competition Among Primitive Peoples* (Boston, 1961); and as a useful, if only partial antidote, see Herbert Fingarette's *Confucius: The Secular As Sacred* (New York, 1972).

3. Shame can be either momentary or a deep state of humiliation, a violent condition of the whole corporal being.

4. For the particular phrase "guilt is diffuse in our times," I am indebted to Professor Eugen Weber of U.C.L.A. For a collection of essays on different forms and interpretations of guilt by such writers as Nietzsche, Freud, Buber, Mead, Arendt, and others, see Roger Smith, ed., *Guilt: Man and Society* (Garden City, N.Y., 1971). A recent set of essays on guilt is Herbert Morris's *On Guilt and Innocence* (Los Angeles, 1976), which I reviewed in *World View* 20 (April, 1977), 56–57.

5. Catholic and Protestant thinkers, influenced by and helping to give form to existentialism, have drawn upon nineteenth-century Danish Protestant thinker Søren Kierkegaard, and seventeenth-century Catholic Jansenist thinker Blaise Pascal. They have taught that man's abiding condition was one of limits, anxiety, and culpability.

6. Freud's adherence to the inescapability of guilt rests upon the premise that man must repress instinctual drives which recognize no familiar cultural boundaries. For Freud, repression and thus guilt, account for the fundamental content of human culture, symbols, and history. This he sought to prove in such works as *Totem and Taboo* and *Moses and Monotheism*. Useful for an introduction to Freud is Philip Rieff's *Freud: The Mind of the Moralist* (Garden City, N.Y., 1961). Followers of Freud have sought to elaborate upon the connection of culture and guilt. For instance, in *Myth and Guilt: The Crime and Punishment of Mankind* (New York, 1957), 41, Theodor Reik postulated "a free-floating guilt feeling in all men beyond the frontiers of races and nations, a collective guilt of mankind that only occasionally reaches the threshold of conscious feeling. Whereas Ernest Becker in *The Denial of Death* (New York, 1973), argued that guilt and anxiety are inescapably part of the condition of man whose symbols are predicated on an immortality that is contradicted by the body's mortality.

7. Discussions of Sartre and Camus in Chapter 6 will confirm the degree to which existential thought is involved with guilt. One useful guide to existentialism and guilt is found in John Macquarrie's *Existentialism* (New York, 1973), esp. Chapter 10 "Finitude and Guilt," 147–60. A recent work on guilt reflecting the influence of existentialism is Michael Gelven's *Winter, Friendship, and Guilt* (New York, 1972).

8. A host of popular literature makes guilt itself the enemy to be defeated if happiness is to be attained. An extreme example is Nietzsche scholar Walter Kaufmann's *Without Guilt and Justice: From Decidophobia to Autonomy* (New York, 1973). As the title suggests, Kaufmann puts aside notions of justice, God, and guilt on the grounds that they stand in the way of man's autonomy. Neo-Freudians also have joined the assault of "liberation" against guilt. Of recent note are Herbert Marcuse's and Erich Fromm's efforts to see modern social life as the cause of contemporary man's repression and guilt. See Fromm's *Beyond the Chains of Illusion: My Encounters with Marx and Freud* (New York, 1962) and Marcuse's *Eros and Civilization* (New York, 1962). As brilliant as they are insane, anticipating the work of such radical gay separatists as Mary Daly, are Norman Brown's *Life Against Death* (New York, 1959) and his *Love's Body*. His books advocate as an ideal that humanity return to the stage of life of guiltless presexual differentiation.

9. Suggestive of the effect of mass conformities on ethics is William Whyte's *The Organization Man* (Garden City, N.Y., 1957) and David Riesman, Nathan Glazier, and Reuel Denney's *The Lonely Crowd* (Garden City, N.Y., 1956). However, different groups, cultures, and classes within mass society have distinct senses of guilt as is nicely illustrated by E. Franklin Frasier's penetrating study of the black middle class, *Black Bourgeoisie* (New York, 1957), esp. 216–23, and Michael Novak's *The Rise of the Unmeltable Ethnics* (New York, 1973), esp. 85–136.

10. Erich Fromm, *Escape from Freedom* (New York, 1941).

11. Hannah Arendt's *Eichmann in Jerusalem* (New York, 1969).

12. For additional parabolic stories of Kafka involving shame, guilt, and judgment, see "The Judgment," "The Metamorphosis," "In the Penal Colony," all of which are conveniently collected in an edition by Philip Rahv, *Selected Stories of Franz Kafka* (New York, 1952).

13. Hannah Arendt, *Human Condition,* cited in "A Place Called Freedom," *World View* (June, 1974), 25.

14. For some a terror lurks in the affirmation of human historicity. Discovering that man is his own maker need not be a matter of liberation, but can mean discovering the awesome burden of assuming responsibility for human history. It is this insight into human historicity that led Hegel to speak of history as being a "slaughter bench" in his *Philosophy of History*. The meaning of historical man was the central issue at stake in Dostoyevsky's dialogue between Christ and the Grand Inquisitor in the *Brothers Karamazov*. More recently Mircea Eliade has argued in his *Cosmos and History* (New York, 1959) that history produces a terror that will either return man to religion or lead him to absolute nihilism.

15. Twentieth-century fiction and scholarship, so deeply involved with the meaning of the First World War and the Russian Revolution, the Second World War and the dropping of the atomic bomb, not only develop

around judgments of guilt and innocence but arise and take form in conjunction with these judgments.

16. In *Victims of Progress* (Menlo Park, Calif., 1975), John Bodley asks whether the industrial society can make any contact at all (even learned and disinterested) with tribal societies that does not lead to their destruction and hence the destruction of the global diversity of humanity upon which man's survival depends. Also beneficially consulted for the theme of "the victims of progress" are many sections of Kurt Glaser and Stefan Possony's near encyclopedic *Victims of Politics* (New York, 1979), which I have reviewed for *The Annals of the American Academy of Political and Social Science* 455 (Sept., 1979), 167–68.

There is, of course, ample evidence to argue that the West, since the Enlightenment, has been the source of its own most severe criticism. For instance, there is all the antiimperial literature, ranging from established Marxian schools to singular literary indictments of the "civilized" European among the "noble" savages, like Joseph Conrad's classic *Heart of Darkness* (1902; reprint ed., New York, 1970). For a study of that sort of self-hatred, cultivated and articulated among a certain type of intellectuals, see Victor Brombert's *The Intellectual Hero* (Chicago, 1960).

17. In *The Passing of Traditional Society: Modernizing the Middle East* (New York, 1958), 51, Daniel Lerner went on to say: "Whereas the isolated communities of traditional society functioned well on the basis of a highly constrictive personality, the interdependent sectors of modern society require widespread participation. This in turn requires an expansive and adaptive self-system, ready to incorporate new roles and to identify personal values with public issues. This is why modernization of any society has involved the great characterological transformation we call psychic mobility. The latent statistical assertion involved here is this: In modern society *more* individuals exhibit *higher* empathic capacity than in any previous society."

18. Ibid., 52.

19. Useful for examples and themes of a nation cleaning itself up is much of the second volume of Theodore Zeldin's *France: 1848–1945* (Oxford, 1977), which contains chapters on such guilt-inducing matters as "Eating and Drinking," 752–62, "Good and Bad Taste," 349–92, "Fashion and Beauty," 420–91 "Conformity and Superstition," 393–414, and "Happiness and Humor," 646–724. Also of use is Norbert Elias *La civilisation des moeurs* (Paris, 1973).

20. Lerner, *The Passing of Traditional Society*, 73. Emphasis is mine.

21. Cited in Irving Zeitlin's *Rethinking Sociology* (Englewood Cliffs, N.J., 1973), 32.

22. Martindale, *Institutions, Organizations and Mass Society*, 562.

23. Insightful about the changing roles of modern man is "Pluralization of Social Life-Worlds," Chapter 3 of Hansfried Kellner and Peter and

Brigitte Berger, *The Homeless Mind: Modernization and Consciousness* (New York, 1973), 63–82. There they write of the technological communications media: "Through mass publications, motion pictures, radio and television, the cognitive and normative definitions of reality invented in the city are rapidly diffused throughout the entire society. To be linked to these media is to be involved in the continuing urbanization of consciousness. Plurality is intrinsic to the process. The individual, wherever he be, is bombarded with a multiplicity of information and communication," 67.

24. Richard Sennett and Johnathan Cobb, *The Hidden Injuries of Class* (New York, 1972), 256.

25. Although the specific concept "social conscience loading" (SCL) is given on pages 35–38 in Chapter 2, "Personality and Aging," in Jules Henry's *On Shame, Vulnerability and Other Forms of Self-Destruction* (New York, 1973), also of interest are Chapter 5 "Vulnerability: Sources of Man's Fear in Himself and in Society," 82–105, and Chapter 6 "Values: Guilt, Suffering and Consequences," 106–19.

26. Some theorists carry this insight into the social determinants of ethics to the point of denying conscience altogether. Don Martindale wrote instructively of Riesman, Gerth, Mills, and Goffman: "[They] have rejected both the religious and the humanistic views of man and the theories that account for them. They presuppose a world of large-scale organizations concerned with the individual's external characteristic but indifferent to his inner being. In various ways they all insist that contemporary man is a sort of hollow shell: in place of shame or guilt, the operation of a diffuse anxiety (Riesman); instead of being viewed as the mainsprings of action, motives are treated as 'vocabularies' operative in strategies of deceit (Gerth and Mills); conscience and taste are not found in man's nature, only in appearances of morality (Goffman). The hypothesis that the world of large-scale organization has introduced a major crisis in contemporary man's self-conception and the theories of personality seems to be overwhelmingly confirmed." *Institutions, Organizations, and Mass Society*, 560.

27. Zbigniew Brzezinski, *Between Two Ages: America's Role in the Technocratic Order* (New York, 1970), 111.

28. René Du Bos, *So Human An Animal* (New York, 1968), 4, 198–99.

29. Talk of matters like the Holocaust or Hiroshima and Nagasaki or the awesome yet common starvations, deportations, or exterminations of millions return us to elemental issues of guilt as curse, contamination, diabolical evil, that is, our oldest languages of morality, which is examined in Paul Ricoeur's *The Symbolism of Evil* (Boston, 1969).

30. J. Glenn Gray, *The Warriors* (New York, 1970), 207. Emphasis is mine.

31. The phrase, "fed, clad and sheltered," is Jacob Hollander's classic 1914 definition of well being, cited in Robert Bremner's *From the Depths: The Discovery of Poverty in the United States* (New York, 1956), 125.

32. Ibid., 129.

33. Cited in Morris, *Guilt and Innocence*, 111. Emphasis is mine.

34. The sense of feeling utterly irrelevant to the public world was suffered profoundly by active resistance fighters in the post-world war period. Hannah Arendt wrote of them: "After a few short years they were liberated from what they originally had thought to be a 'burden' and thrown back into what they now knew to be the weightless irrelevances of their personal affairs, once more separated from 'the world of reality' by an *épaisseur triste*, the 'sad opaqueness' of a private life centered about nothing but itself. And if they refused 'to go back to their most indigent behaviour,' they could only return to the old empty strife on conflicting ideologies," *Between Past and Future* (Cleveland, 1965), 4.

# 1

# The Old Man's Gratitude

But while the issues of giving and getting are apt to be presented in Western Society in the form of dialogue between self-interest and religious principle, they can be set in secular as well as religious frame, and are so set in many societies. What is clear is that whether the concept of giving and getting be set in a frame of altruism and gratitude, or in a frame of obligation and reciprocity, the procedures in many aspects are symbolic instruments used for the maintenance or alteration of social relationships, in the interests of both self and society.

Raymond Firth, "Symbolism in Giving and Getting," *Symbols, Public and Private* (Ithaca, 1973), 402.

Max Beerbohm's remark that mankind is divisible in two great classes, hosts and guests, might be translated into terms of donors and recipients.

Firth, "Symbolism in Giving and Getting," 402.

As far as we can tell from eighteenth-century Languedoc, it was unusual to invite passers-by to share one's food or drink. Yet also (or perhaps therefore?) this is a world where the gratuitous gesture—kindness, selflessness is the greatest virtue (perhaps because there is so little to give, perhaps precisely because it is so rare).

Eugen Weber, "Fairies and Hard Facts: The Reality of Folktales," *The Journal of the History of Ideas* 42, no. 1 (January-March, 1981), 108–9.

## OUR DIVIDED SELF

The new conscience must seek to find a place in human spirit pervaded by diffuse guilt. Guilt goes with the human condition itself. It resides in the perennial human tasks of weighing one's interests against those of others; of assessing one's loyalties to parents, spouse, children; and of forever being forced to choose between the practical way and the honorable way in the conduct of one's affairs. However, what makes that guilt so diffuse and crippling are the confusions, ambiguities, and contradictions that surround contemporary man's transactions and leave him in doubt about his gifts.

The opposition between individualism and collectivism is one great ethical conflict confronting contemporary man. Individualism has become a commanding principle of contemporary sensibility, law, and culture. Whatever form it takes, individualism conflicts with the rights of the older communities as well as with the growing collectivisms that shape all facets of contemporary society.

Another profound opposition in contemporary society exists between private life and public life. In place of the relatively homogeneous and static communities of traditional society—which no doubt harbored inequalities and violence, and even at times underwent severe change—modern society is built around the dichotomous principles of the public and the private. This polarization invites, even demands, attempts at reintegration by the politicizing of the private or, conversely, by privatizing the public. The former always borders on being totalitarian and the latter produces a variety of ersatz world views, usually based on psychology or utopian communitarianism.

Social critics Richard Sennett, in his *Fall of Public Man*, and Christopher Lasch, in his *Culture of Narcissism*, have called attention to the dangers of the privatization of man. Both have argued correctly that the boundaries between the public and the private—which were so essential for the successful practice of eighteenth- and nineteenth-century constitutional politics—have been disastrously violated in the twentieth century.[1] The private has invaded the public in an unprecedented way and on an unprecedented scale. The unique person is declared sovereign over everything. He attributes no autonomy whatever to the public world; it has neither special value, nor knowledge, nor practice attached to it. He understands it only as an arena for the extension of the self.

However, the invasions of the public order into the private realm have proven to be even more deadly in this century. They include the dominance of mass values, which have been generated both politically and commercially, and the invasion of traditional, popular, and high cultures by perverted ideologies and pseudosciences intent on transforming contemporary humanity into their own images. The totalitarian state, the most awesome expression of this attack, presumes to make itself the commanding agent of all human existence, it allows no opposing authorities, cultures, or consciences to exist.

Adding to the guilt of contemporary humanity is the change that pervades all aspects of human existence. Carlo Cipolla describes what that change, which has overtaken humanity since the Industrial Revolution, has meant for contemporary conscience:

> Every aspect of life has to be geared to the new modes of production. Family ties are on the wane and give way to broader perspectives for larger social groups. Individual saving gives way to collective social services, undistributed profits, and taxes. The rounded philosophical training of the few is set aside in favour of the technical training of the many. Artistic intuition must give way to technical precision. New juridic institutions, new types of ownership and management, different distributions of income, new tastes, new values, new ideals have to emerge as an essential part of the industrialization process.[2]

Each of these changes raises the most serious questions about human relations, transactions, and integrity. To put this in a formula, industrialization in particular and modernization in general mean ethical revolution. It can be said that modernization makes common for the majority what Descartes once defined to be the unique starting point of his philosophy: the doubting of everything. The awesome accelerating change of our era—of which Henry Adams was so rightfully terrified—makes painfully ambiguous the values that men and women over centuries have assumed to be a fixed inheritance, namely the natural, enduring ways of sex, age, and family. Now subject to doubt for the first time are the most elemental assumptions governing marriage, child rearing, aging, suffering, pain, and dying.

The great majority of contemporary people who confront this novel situation are, in fact, a few generations away from a world, a mentality, and a conscience thousands of years old. Carlo Cipolla grimly reminds us of how recent our birth has been in the industrial world:

> Considering that the Neolithic Revolution diffused into Europe be-
> tween 5000 B.C. and 2000 B.C., and assuming for a generation a
> period of about twenty-five years, slightly more than 150 genera-
> tions separate each European from his "nasty and brutish" ancestor.
> Here, in fact, lies the great question. Because of a cumulative pro-
> cess, the technical progress of *homo sapiens* has been extremely
> rapid. Within a relatively small number of generations, man has
> come to control his environment and to master the most powerful
> forces of Nature. But how much has he himself improved in quality?
> There is no escaping man's origin—a carnivorous and cannibalistic
> animal—and disgustingly so. Man, the greatest of all scavengers,
> whether presapient or sapient, could cope with the flesh of any and
> every competitor—even if it happened to be his own flesh and
> blood. . . .[3]

Within contemporary man there exists an old man who measures the world by the reality of a limited good and the age-old struggle against scarcity. For the old man, the good—whether it was given by God and nature; won by work, discipline, and suffering; or was necessary and useful—has been understood to be limited. Fate, fortune, nature, the gods, all that was greater than man, have made the good a fragile possession. Scarcity taught man that the good was dependent on material things; to give abundantly was to be generous and noble, not to give was to be cheap and stingy.[4] Envy, jealousy, resentment, gratification, joy, hope, and all the other emotions out of which the old man has shaped his notions of the good and the bad bear the mark of a world of limited good.

This belief of the old man, taught by countless generations of ancestors, still resides in the heart of contemporary man. Yet another faith grows there too, which challenges the fundamentals of the old man's giving and taking. This new faith says that the good is not limited and, more radically, it suggests that happiness can be achieved on this earth. Implying new ethics, the good is not considered to be limited to what the gods have given or what man has set forth, but it depends solely upon the collective effort of humanity to improve its condition. This new faith, which makes humanity its own god, forms a new conscience and a new guilt.

So within contemporary humanity there exist old and new ways of valuing human existence. Often the old way forms our subconscious, habitual, and private exchanges whereas the new way defines our public reasoning. Exploring the duality of conscience is a goal of this book.

In this chapter the ethical modes that gave value to traditional man's transactions, such as gratitude, fair exchange, and sacrifice, are examined. Also in this chapter the ethical conflict between the old and the new way of valuing human experience is introduced, and an overview is offered of the fundamental forces that define contemporary man's giving and taking.

## THE ETHICS OF THE OLD MAN:
## GRATITUDE, FAIR EXCHANGE, AND SACRIFICE

Gratitude is among the first human measures of the good. What has been given, which need not have been given, is always appreciated. In a world of scarcity it is deeply appreciated, for the individual's survival depends upon the reception of goods he could not have controlled.

Like chastity, prudence, and patience, gratitude seems to echo the human spirit from an earlier period. Go just about anywhere and listen to people talk. Their conversations get most intense when they touch upon the subject of unrewarded labor and unacknowledged gifts. Speaking of gratitude and ingratitude is serious business, worthy both of the most elevated philosophy and of the basest gossip.

Classical authors confirm the importance of gratitude in human affairs. Cicero called gratitude "the mother of all virtue," and Seneca wrote: "He that urges gratitude pleads the cause both of God and men, for without it we can neither be sociable nor religious." A thankful heart was considered to be the source of piety. "In a heart replete with thankfulness," justice and love were thought to be nurtured.

On the subject of ingratitude the voices of antiquity were equally strong. Cicero declared ingratitude to be a cause of hatred: "Men detest one forgetful of a benefit." Seneca commented: "There never was any man so wicked as not to approve of gratitude and to detest ingratitude, as the two things in the whole world, the one to be the most esteemed, and the other to be the most abominated." Truly, *ingratitude is a universally powerful accusation.* It even undercuts the biological activity of the person. A Japanese proverb states, "Thankless labor brings fatigue." As if it was the key to basic civility, the Omahas say of the ungrateful man: "He does not appreciate the gift. He has no manners." Any human word and act, every slip of tongue, and even posture of body can be interpreted as a show of ingratitude. The charge of ingratitude often forms the sharpest edges of accusation, as when someone is accused of being stingy, cheap, niggardly, or petty, as well as the accusation of "welching" or being an "Indian giver."[5] Not to give is bad, to give begrudgingly is worse and to give falsely, with fickle heart, is worst of all. Beyond the law there exists a world of deep insults and resentments. Xenophon wrote:

> They go to trial on a charge on account of which men hate each other most, but go to trial about least, that is, *ingratitude*. . . . For they think that the ungrateful would also be most neglectful about gods, about parents, about country, and about friends.[6]

Gratitude defines different personality types. At one extreme there are those who seem almost devoid of a sense of gratitude; they do not acknowledge the gifts they receive. At the other extreme there are those who sense themselves perpetually indebted for everything. A customary inquiry as to how they are can elicit from them a profuse show of thankfulness. In the extreme this type of gratefulness becomes associated with the reprehensible people who are forever groveling before others.

Gratitude is evoked by different kinds of gifts, favors, and deeds.[7] The gift may be tangible or intangible, given once or repeatedly, recognized instantaneously or realized only in distant retrospect. The gift may come from a friend or an enemy, be willingly declared or reluctantly acknowledged, accepted as elevating or experienced as debasing. Eskimos have an adage: "Gifts make slaves just as whips make dogs."

A person's self-image—his status, race, sex, and so on—generally shapes his sense of gratitude.[8] For example, a homely female is commonly taught to be thankful for any male who comes her way; whereas the beautiful girl is taught to think of herself as a great gift to whomever she presents herself. In addition, receiving often involves the feigning of gratitude. As a wealthy tourist gives to the poor beggar to get rid of him, so the beggar repeatedly thanks the tourist to try to get more. Giving or receiving can become so ritualized and institutionalized that it is carried out in such a way that the giver expects no gratitude and the receiver gives none.

Nevertheless, with these observations aside, gratitude constitutes a fundamental element out of which all societies are formed. Perhaps gratitude is the first source of morality.[9] As exchanges of goods, services, and other favors belong to the external side of human interactions, so gratitude is the heart's internal tally of gifts and exchanges. Meeting obligations, saving face, maintaining honor, and other similar actions arise from an inner sense of duty rather than from fear of external reprisal or punishment. To use a Chinese expression, "Kindness is more binding than a loan."

Gratitude, we should note, is not a matter of simple materialism. It is not elicited only by tangible gifts and quantifiable services. The very presence of another person, like Beatrice's presence for Dante or Laura's for Petrarch, can occasion profound thankfulness. Gratitude, at least in a decent heart, is not like water from a faucet, to be turned off and on at will. Instead, to paraphrase Georg Simmel, gratitude is a kind of moral memory of mankind that binds together those who have exchanged gifts.[10]

Every community has beliefs, rituals, and myths, contracts and customs that join, tally, equate, and value gifts. In the preindustrial order, there were always patriarchs to whom one was indebted. They originated the people's ways and tied them by rituals to the gods. Today whole nations and their leaders try to take the place of these elders.

The power of gratitude as an element of social cohesion can be measured by its abuse. To have a person's gratitude is to have his loyalty. This means social control. Understandably, groups who try to control societies vie for their gratitude. Members of contemporary society are besieged daily by bids for public appreciation. Though there can be no doubt that freedom depends on conflict, only vacuous idealists, propagandists, and advertisement people deny how mad, shrill, abusive, and encompassing the choirs are that today sing for our gratefulness. Undoubtedly it was a din of all those contradictory voices simultaneously claiming our gratitude, that led Emerson to remark over a century ago: "The world is in a state of bankruptcy; the world owes more than it can pay and ought to go into the chancery and be sold."[11]

The argument over gifts given and gifts owed is at the heart of the contemporary political debate over justice. In the name of the people, states came almost simultaneously to give and to take all. Liberal democratic governments in particular preach that the people shape the common good, while they teach by daily example that public life is an ongoing struggle of self-interest. Always fueling conflict in modern society is the opposition between the satisfied and the dissatisfied, the haves and the have-nots. In fact, it can be suggested that two spiritual communities exist in all modern societies: *The party of gratitude and the party of expectation.* The former counsels thankful acceptance for gifts given, and the latter preaches discontent in the name of gifts promised.

Many social commentators, mistakenly I believe, hold the opinion that gratitude is a disguise for deeper interest. Epicurus cynically suggested that gratitude is a virtue that commonly has profit annexed to it. La Rochefoucauld's terse maxims pointed in the same direction: "We have to accept respectfully the harm done us by a person whose benefactions we have enjoyed," and "Not all those who repay debts of gratitude can flatter themselves that by so doing they are being grateful."[12] Surely, no one would argue for gratitude's importance in human affairs if to do so meant to deny the reality of self-interest in human exchanges. Furthermore, whoever wishes to maintain his individuality is wary of gratitude.

The lower social classes have known since time immemorial that to give is to express power, to be god-like; to receive is to admit vulnerability. Today's gifts are followed by tomorrow's insults. Gratitude is only for equals; it has no place among master and slave.[13] The poor and the weak also know that the charge of ingratitude is among the most frequently favored, yet the deadliest charge leveled against them by the rich.

The strongest argument against gratitude having an important place in human experience is that gratitude is derived simply from the human effort to secure fair exchange. On all levels of his existence, man is involved in types of exchange.[14] His personal world is developed around shared benefits and duties; in the public world he engages in the trade of ideas, goods, and services.[15] His mind is constantly preoccupied with equitable exchange. His emotions, passions, and memories register his transactions; he utilizes all his reason, imagination, and judgment to carry out his giving and taking.[16] Even the most superficial forms of etiquette can conceal the sternest demands for fair exchange. The depth of a bow and the length of a smile travel great distances in the human heart. Every gesture however delicate, every phase however subtle weighs heavily on the scale of human feelings.[17]

The demand for fair exchange shapes man's first senses of justice.[18] One aim of the law itself is to define and to effect fair exchange. A contract, for example, demands a promise or a set of promises involving consideration on both sides. Equity, although more elusive to define than contract, also pursues fair exchange: "He who seeks equity must do equity." "One who comes to equity must come with clean hands." Punishment also shows the law's pursuit of just balance in the community's equilibrium. When a serious wrong occurs, a threatening imbalance is understood to exist among members of the community and its moral status. Punishment must rectify that situation.[19]

These impulses to maintain a proper balance, a fair exchange in all things—impulses that are alive in us still—were boldly manifested in earlier codes of law.[20] The precepts made provisions for such different situations as compensatory dismemberment of the wrongdoer (an eye for an eye, and so on), revoking gifts because of a show of ingratitude, sentencing and hanging animals for the harm they caused, or supporting the right of blood-family feuds as a legitimate way to redress a wrong. Living in smaller groups, and closer to nature and its powers, traditional man was extremely sensitive to the village's moral-social equilibrium. As Henry Sumner Maine instructively pointed out, the moral state of the individual was a corporate matter:

> The moral elevation and moral debasement of the individual appear to be confounded with, or postponed to, the merits and offenses of the group to which the individual belongs. If the community sins, its guilt is much more than the sum of the offenses committed by its members; the crime is a corporate act, and extends in its consequences to many more persons than have shared in its actual perpetration. If, on the other hand, the individual is conspicuously guilty, it is his children, his kinsfolk, his tribesmen, or his fellow citizens who suffer with him and sometimes for him.[21]

In the traditional world every person, every action, every situation, every ceremony had its proper way, measure, and due; it merited a certain reciprocity of giving and taking. This "principle

THE OLD MAN'S GRATITUDE

of give and take," according to Bronislaw Malinowski, "pervades tribal life" and "reciprocity is the basis of social structure."[22] In his *Argonauts of the Western Pacific*, Malinowski argued that customary exchange, rather than contractual or monetary, is a fundamental distinction between primitive and modern.[23] The Trobriand Islanders' social life, the subject of his study, is developed around the continuous exchange of treasured shell armbands and necklaces (*vaygu a*) with their neighboring islanders of Dobu. The whole process of exchange (the *Kula*) forms not only a vital trade network, but also a way of life. As yesterday's receiving demands today's giving, so today's giving assures tomorrow's receiving. Individuals and families are known by their place in the *Kula*; every piece of jewelry tells the story of its exchange. In the islanders' values, the very acts of giving and receiving are good. "Generosity" is considered to be "the essence of goodness," whereas "meanness is the most despised." For the islanders, the process of giving and taking is fully engrossing—as in fact it is for so many members of contemporary society. From them Malinowski drew conclusions concerning all primitive societies: "Apart from any consideration as to whether the gifts are necessary or even useful, giving for the sake of giving is one of the most fundamental features of Trobriand sociology, and from its very general and fundamental nature, I submit that it is a very universal feature of all primitive societies."[24]

In *The Gift: Forms and Functions of Exchange in Archaic Society*, Marcel Mauss found the key to human exchange in the Maori proverb: "Give as much as you receive and all is for the best."[25] Mauss's intent, which was inspired by Malinowski's *Argonauts*, denied the importance of gratitude in human exchange and constituted an informal attempt to show that gifts served reasoned self-interest. Formally, Mauss's goal was to examine those gifts which "are in theory voluntary, disinterested and spontaneous, but in fact obligatory and interested."[26] Under the scrutiny of Mauss's functionalist analysis, gifts in primitive societies have such practical purposes as initiating the conditions of trade, establishing credit, serving as a down payment, clinching a contract, or performing additional functions which are now fully articulated and differentiated in modern economy. Also, the exchange of gifts in primitive society has additional noneconomic functions such as: (1) displaying power, wealth, status, and authority; (2) sealing marriages and

consecrating other important relationships; (3) obtaining peace by
the purchase of allies and the pacification of enemies; (4) maintaining internal order by a kind of damage payment to those who have
suffered injury by the loss of honor or goods.[27] Among the other
important functions of gifts is their use in seeking to establish beneficial relations with mythical ancestors, spirits, and other powers
which, in the primitive mind, are considered crucial to the group's
well-being.

At this point, the question arises whether gratitude has any
meaningful place in human affairs or is simply a secondary emotional reaction to the demand for fairness. Sacrifice—a fundamental way by which primitive man overtly, and contemporary man
inwardly, carries on many of his fundamental transactions with existence—can serve as a testing point of gratitude's importance as a
determinant of human value.

At first glance it seems that sacrifice is merely a calculated human
attempt to establish fair exchange with superior powers. This is
suggested by the countless ways by which people escape offering,
in sacrifice, objects of real value; how they manage to make the
time, manner, and situation of their sacrifices conveniently accord
with their own ends; and how they use their sacrifices for such self-
serving ends as an occasion for displaying wealth, averting a
disaster, curing illness, and so on. Sacrifice indeed appears from
this angle to be an attempt to effect a direct, beneficial, if not auto-
matic and binding exchange.[28]

In *Elementary Forms of Religious Life*, Émile Durkheim attributes a pragmatic social goal to sacrifice.[29] Sacrifice, he explains,
joins the individual to the group. At heart, Durkheim finds the
binding rule of group formation: "The rule *do ut des* [I give to you
and you give to me], which has been identified as the first principle
of sacrifice, is not a late invention of utilitarian theorists; it only expresses in an explicit way the very mechanism of the sacrificial
system and, more generally, of the whole positive cult."[30] In effect,
sacrifice is a gift to a superior recipient in exchange for the
guarantee of a gift in return. Examples of this are many. For instance, first offerings (first crops and first born) are made for the
purposes of future multiplication; thanksgiving (*Dankopfer*) is
often a mode to keep future favors coming; and requests for favors
(*Bittenopfer*) include a near limitless number of ceremonies that are
aimed at specific wants. There are even sacrificial sanctification

and desanctification rites concerned with the practical business of legitimating the use of certain land, animals, and so on. Perhaps even more suggestive of sacrifice as a matter of hard-headed exchange instead of gratitude are vows, fasts, ordeals, self-mortifications, almsgiving, and other acts of charity that aim at gaining merit.[31] Sacrifices that conveniently allow a group to offer prisoners, strangers, criminals, and "unwanted ones" instead of themselves as the victims of their sacrifices certainly manifest self-interested bargaining. Also, there are self-interested sacrifices joined to rites of passage, as well as those calculating actions that join magic and sacrifice in order to seek directly to regulate natural forces.[32] A great part of the horizon of sacrifice reveals man engaged in bargaining with the gods. From that perspective, *thankfulness seems but one posture in man's dealings with a superior power.*

Nevertheless, it is precisely at this point, when we stand most ready to exclude any reference to gratitude in our definition of sacrifice, that we realize we cannot omit this qualification. What is most obvious has now become least repressible: Whatever form sacrifice takes, it reveals man's awareness of his own inferior place in the order of things. Man's condition reaffirms his fragility, vulnerability, dependence, and especially his mortality. He lacks equal footing with his ancestors, the powers of nature, the gods, and spirits. Before them he must supplicate. He cannot hide from them, but they need never show themselves to him. Consequently, no matter how anthropomorphically man conceives the powers who are superior to him, he must carry on this commerce with them in a symbolic, ritualistic, and diffident manner—and never as if he were their equal.

With sacrifice, whether in the form of the old man's elaborate ritual or contemporary man's faintest inward plea, there exist varying orders of uneven powers, asymmetrical relations between giver and recipient. There is no equality between givers, no parity of gifts, and finally, no assurance that a successful transaction has been concluded.[33] In this hierarchical, changing, and fickle world, man knows himself to be inferior; his prayers can go unanswered, his offerings unnoticed. Even if an individual takes to cajoling, threatening, lying, and trying to bribe the spirits, he is compelled to do their bidding. In this existence, "man proposes and god disposes."

Men and women of all ages believe that they suffer for their failures to show gratitude. Even we contemporaries fear that neglected thanksgiving brings bad consequences. The old man feared his own ingratitude. He assumed that his whole moral-social-religious order depended upon a fitting display of gratitude. Sacrifice, homage, and other commemorations were all part of that display. As he himself wanted gratitude, so he assumed that his ancestors and gods wanted the same.

This point, in turn, yields another central characteristic of premodern man's mentality. His conscience was composed around gratitude and the various obligations this gratitude spawned. Invariably these obligations faced him backward toward those special times (*in illo tempore, ab origine*) when the primordial founding acts, whose repetition was believed essential for the group's survival, were performed. At the same time, gratitude reverently led him to the founding ancestors whose heroism, cunning, and wisdom initiated the group's moral-social order. Anthropologist Christoph von Furer-Haimendorf, in *Morals and Merit: A Study of Values in South Asian Societies*, remarks: "In all tribal societies investigated [here] we have found the belief that man lives in an ordered world of stable relations which has been unchanging since time immemorial. The founding ancestors can only be praised and imitated; that is sacred and essential business."[34] This belief is one of the fundamental sources of ancestor worship, which was so powerful in the ancient worlds of both East and West and is far from dead in the contemporary spirit.

So much of traditional man's religion, sacrifice, and elaborate cults to commemorate the dead can be explained only by the importance of gratitude. It is tempting to postulate that gratitude expresses man's primal recognitions of his beholden position in the universe.[35] He senses that he owes his birth and nurturing to his parents; his identity and well-being to the community; and his very existence to spirits and forces, to the land, water, animals, wind, plants, sun, moon, and so much else stronger and more lasting than he. In contrast to modernity's preferred philosophical formula of Descartes' "I think, therefore I am," I hear the old man dancing and singing out this proposition: "*I am, therefore I am thankful.*"

Thus sacrifice can be interpreted to support two opposite conclusions regarding gratitude's place as a determinant of human values. On the one hand, it can be understood to be derived from the fact that man, above all else, ethically values the world by the principle of fair exchange. Even at his most generous moments, he does not—at least for long—abdicate his insistence that justice requires there to be a gift in exchange for a gift.[36] On the other hand, sacrifice can be understood to show that gratitude is a fundamental source of human value. It acknowledges the reality of gifts that cannot be compelled; the need for services that cannot be commanded.

Here, of course, the latter interpretation is preferred, though there is no denial of the ethical importance of the demand for fair exchange, which is intimately tied to all human notions of justice. Gratitude is considered to be a fundamental element in forming conscience. It is the dutiful memory of the man who recognizes gifts. Traditional man, the old man, built his moral order out of the sense of gratitude.

## THE OLD MAN WITHIN US ALL

We still value much of the world as if the voice of the old man commands us. We build and explain our transactions in terms of gratitude, fair exchange, and sacrifice. Surely they serve as first measures of family, friend, neighbor, and work, and they judge all else. It is even tempting to say there is no contemporary man. From the point of view of ethics, contemporary man seems to be only the shell in which a very ancient peasant survives.

We might even wish this to be the case. Whoever has tried in this era to sort out conscience must, at least at times, wish to be a peasant. Pervasive throughout our world is a nostalgia for an imagined ethical wholeness, an existence in which man can declare himself to be sound and secure. This yearning might be expressed by the legionnaires' cult of the fallen solider, or the endless creation of religions, communities, and cults, or even the popularity of a movie like *The Godfather*. (The Godfather's world keeps the elemental laws of exchange ruthlessly intact, free of the modern tendency to legalize, bureaucratize, politicize, and, worse, psychologize and sociologize away primary human meaning.)

To have integrity, man must know his gifts and exchanges. Not to know them—what they are, who gave them and why, and what they require in return—is to lack an ethical center. It is precisely this condition that is threatening. Man's existence is made up of a vast, varied, and ceaseless array of transactions that give rise to a multitude of conflicting voices. This, in turn, creates immense dissonance which drowns conscience itself.

The old man is but one voice of many within us and he must contend mightily to be heard. Of all the voices contradicting him, there are two voices against which he must contend the most. The important spiritual voices are Christianity and progressive secular humanism, both of which will be examined at greater length in the next chapter. Christianity fundamentally contradicts the ideas of the old man. It defines the ultimate transactions as those which exist between the divine and the human. Christianity assumes mankind is one, and it teaches an unknown humility which counsels that it is better to give than to receive. Modern humanists, who contend against Christianity, also argue keenly against the old man within us. In the name of future possibilities, they contradict the old way; their ideal is the innocent child, not the founding patriarch. They side with the rebellious; Prometheus is their favorite god. In contrast to the old man's hierarchical view of existence—which conceives of all that is good, true, and noble as flowing from heaven downward and from earlier times forward—they propose a historical view of existence.[37] Man, they teach, grows cumulatively in knowledge, being, and happiness.

Progressive humanists challenge the most elemental ethical assumptions of the old man. They teach that men and women need not be strangers to one another, that their tolerance and affection should be universal. Additionally, they argue that gratitude is owed primarily only to those whose past sacrifices make tomorrow's possibilities. They teach that gratitude is expressed by preparing a better future; that guilt should not be incurred for a failure to imitate the old way, but for a lack of will in pursuing the new. In fact, the humanists challenge the old man's most fundamental assumption: They deny the principle of limited good and its correlative notion that scarcity, pain, suffering, and misery are inevitable. They argue against the old man's truth: *"Ce n'est pas le malheur, c'est le bonheur qui est contre la nature"* (It is not misery, but happiness, that is against nature).[38] The progressive humanists could not more fundamentally contradict the old man and the traditional order.

The old man's voice in contemporary conscience has not been attacked by the spiritual principles of Christianity and progressive humanism alone. It has been challenged—as shown in Chapter 3—by a whole new range of "material voices," forces that have produced radically changing environment. Two of these forces are the free market and the nation-state.

The free market was one of the great forces that hurried traditional man toward his rendezvous with the modern world. It taught no pure ethics. Yet it was not without profound ethical consequences, for it forced traditional man to reconsider almost all his exchanges. For the first time in history, it unleashed forces that the countryside—the home of traditional man—could neither disregard, nor, on any terms whatsoever, assimilate and adopt as part of its way. The market gave a new measure to almost everything in the family and village. Intrinsic to the revolution caused by the market—a revolution which occurred over several centuries—was the supremacy of cash; it became the omnipresent measure of all. Directly or indirectly, it judged all transactions. No exchanges, reciprocities, or traditions escaped the new calculations brought by the market.[39]

At the heart of the market's transformation was the divorce of land and labor. This spelled, as Karl Polanyi suggested, an attack on the entire moral-social order of the traditional world:

> Traditionally, land and labor are not separated; labor forms part of life, land remains part of nature, life and nature form an articulate whole. Land is thus tied up with the organization of kinship, neighborhood, craft, and creed—with tribe and temple, village, guild, and church. One Big Market, on the other hand, is an arrangement of economic life which includes markets for factors of production. Since these factors happen to be indistinguishable from the elements of human institutions, man and nature, it can be readily seen that market economy involves a society, the institutions of which are subordinated to the requirements of the market mechanism.[40]

The market radically transformed traditional man's fundamental conception of giving and taking. The market meant, first in England and then in the world, awesome social dislocation and thus mounting government intervention to respond to the dislocation. It created an encompassing environment where cash and contract, lawyer and police, corporate boss and bureaucrat prevail. Distant business cycles came to determine prosperity, and the actions of remote politicians, businessmen, and union leaders affected one's well-being more than one's own neighbors did. Gifts, fair exchange, and justice had to be computed across even greater spaces and through more intricate relations.

Although contacts with the market did not transform the traditional villagers instantaneously into modern urban dwellers, it taught even the least shrewd peasant new forms of calculation. Now to be computed were not only cash but the personal pleasure of the autonomous individual. This new middle-class calculus undid past figuring about giving and taking. Also, as the new guiding principles of equality at the market place took hold, poverty was denied a permanency. Indeed, it was understood to be wrong itself. Begging became repulsive. Money was lord at the market place. All were universally expected to exchange as equals. The old hierarchical society was denied.

The nation-state was another great vehicle that brought traditional man into the modern world and started a whole new set of voices speaking within man. During the early and middle decades of the nineteenth century, governments preoccupied themselves with society for the first time. The requirements of national productivity forced even the most reluctant government elites to try their hand at fostering economic growth. That posed in turn, as we see in retrospect, the insoluble problems of trying to maintain social stability while stimulating economic growth, and of seeking to retain legitimacy, while either violently repressing or cautiously assimilating the new ideologies of freedom, justice, and equality. These tasks were compounded further in the second half of the nineteenth century by intensifying nationalism, militarism, and colonialism. To win the loyalties of its citizens became the essential business of government. Accordingly, it had to put itself at the center of society's transactions. Government had to strive to become the primary source of justice, the final arbitrator of right, and the author of the most important gifts, which in this era are all the benefits associated with improved well-being.

World War I—the first prolonged, mass, technological war—led each government to seek to control society as it never had before. Conscription, mobilization, and mass propaganda were all elements of the state's increasing necessity to harness the hearts, the bodies, and the goods of its citizens. Nation-states, the newest political forms, thus renewed the oldest archaic myths of sacrificed warriors. In this way the state set to determining consciences.

The totalitarian governments of the interwar periods carried social control to unprecedented levels. Each defined itself as the nation and the nation as the greatest source of all value. Church, unions, law, political parties, and all groups competing for citizens' loyalties were swept aside. All opposition was judged to be divisive, treasonous, and parricidal. Neither gratitude, nor guilt, nor conscience was allowed to stand against the good of the society as defined by the ruler. Robert Conquest describes how the Soviet Union, to choose one example, made it a policy to praise sons who betrayed their fathers:

> In fact, there was a widely praised and celebrated Soviet example of sons denouncing their parents. During collectivization Pavlik Morozov, leader of his village group of young Communist "Pioneers" who were acting as auxiliaries in the attack on the peasantry, "unmasked" his father—who had previously been president of the village soviet but had "fallen under the influence of kulak relations." The father was shot, and on 3 September 1932 a group of peasants, including the boy's uncle, in turn killed the son, at the age of fourteen—thus as it were, anticipating Stalin's age-limit for executions. The killers were themselves all executed, and young Morozov became, and has remained, a great hero of the Komsomol. The Palace of Culture of the Red Pioneers in Moscow was named after him. The Soviet press lately celebrated the "sacred and dear" Pavlik Morozov Museum in his own village: "In this timbered house was held the court at which Pavlik unmasked his father who had sheltered the kulaks. Here are reliquaries dear to the heart of every inhabitant of Gerasimovka." (In 1965 a statue was set up to him in the village, as if to show that the principles he acted on are still considered admirable.)[41]

While democratic governments cannot go to such lengths in their quest for control, they too find it essential to win their citizen's gratitude, to find a means of defining, managing, and manipulating it. As part of efforts to win their citizens' loyalties are serious attempts by governments to be considered as impartial arbitrators of fair exchange and as agents for the progressive expansion of the common good. All governments seek to be the godfathers of their people. They give gifts and protection, and in exchange they demand unquestioning loyalty. In less ominous terms, governments, in order to succeed in a democratic era, must provide their people with a public identity. This identity, however narrowly defined, nevertheless carries with it a rudimentary ethical posture in the world. It defines a citizen's rights and duties in society, and a nation's rights and duties in the world. National identities are ethical identities.

The old man who lives within us does not hesitate to think of the government as a kind of personal moral entity, worthy of gratitude and other human emotions. He has known lords, seigniors, bosses, and patrons too long to do otherwise. The old man's residual sense of being bound by gifts is one of the most powerful sources supporting contemporary nationalism. He thinks of the nation as having both a personal nature and a transcendent worth. In his relationship to the nation, the old man, who still survives in the majority of us, senses himself to be the inferior party. Generations have taught him subservience; and the habit of paying homage is not easily suppressed.

Nevertheless, governments nearly universally fail to win and hold their citizens' loyalties. This is so for several reasons. First, governments must compete with older, more immediate communities for their citizens' affections. Second, for the sake of authority, governments inevitably take actions that are antithetical to those communities. Third, government policies cannot help but be perceived through the prism of classes and other groups locked in conflict with each other. Parties themselves thrive because of that conflict. Parties teach, even in the quietest of times, that government is power to be captured and goods to be distributed. In fact, politics incites suspicions and doubts, exposes corruption, undercuts the government's authority, and even makes loyalty to the nation itself questionable. All of this has enlivened the skepticism of the old man, whose survival since time immemorial has depended on a keen sense of judging exchanges.

There is a fourth reason why governments, no matter how effectively they pursue the commonweal, never really win the abiding thankfulness of their people. In an age of rising expectations, which has been the general condition of the West for the last two centuries and of the entire world for at least the past century, dissatisfaction invariably is more prevalent than satisfaction for the simplest reason: *While society increases goods arithmetically, imagination raises expectations geometrically.* The expectations, to develop further this "Malthusian law of satisfaction," have put increasing pressure on governments to try to increase the size and the variety of their gifts to satisfy their peoples.

There are still other reasons why governments fail to hold their citizens' loyalties. Powerful ideologies exist which teach resistance to government's authority. Conservative critiques of the modern democratic state focus on how it unjustly demands freedom in exchange for the security it provides. Radical critiques accent how the state invariably serves a ruling class, and therefore abets the unjust process of taking from the many for the benefit of the few. Also, an increasingly prevalent criticism of government, which has been articulated by anarchism, pacifism, and internationalism, argues that the nation-state, humanity's most powerful agency for establishing the good, fails the common destiny we all share. It shortchanges our promise of earthly happiness.

The nation-state, which has been so instrumental in creating the contemporary world, has not taught a new ethics however. Regardless of the advances identified with the nation-state, this centralized form of government has created a violent, abstract environment in which the human sense of fair exchange has been confounded and gratitude has been distorted and manipulated. The ultimate effect of the new politics' attack on ethics is the paradoxical situation it creates: While it has been instrumental in helping man realize new levels of well-being, the nation-state has threatened new forms of destruction. The nation-state, as Henry Adams feared of all contemporary technology, has proven to be a dark engine of progress, threatening to run its course indifferent to humanity, its creator.

In conclusion, to be contemporary is to be part of a thousand elusive, ambiguous, and contradictory transactions. It is to be without an ethical compass for our givings and takings.[42] It is to find ourselves in a maze of public, private, societal, familial, and personal obligations.

Always imposing is the task of composing one's conscience. The old man has not died within us. He continues to judge the world along with, and often in direct contradiction to, the voices of Christianity and progressive humanism. The confusions, uncertainties, contradictions, and tensions we suffer cannot be repressed permanently, even though the mass mills of artificial happiness grind continuously. Yet indifference is not possible, for to be human is to be concerned with the ethical—and this has always meant fairness in exchange and gratitude for gifts.

## NOTES

1.  Richard Sennett, *The Fall of Public Man: On the Social Psychology of Capitalism* (New York, 1978); and Christopher Lasch, *The Culture of Narcissism: American Life in an Age of Diminishing Expectations* (New York, 1978), which I reviewed in *MFT Action*, 15, no. 7 (March 1980), 8.

2.  Carlo Cipolla, *The Economic History of World Population* (New York, 1962), 127-28.

3.  Ibid., 131.

4.  In "What is Noble" in *Beyond Good and Evil: Basic Writings of Nietzsche*, ed., Walter Kaufmann (New York, 1968), Nietzsche argues that the good itself was derived from the noble and strong. In contrast to the master's morality, there was the slave morality which, especially under the inspiration of Christianity, made the weak and humble the good, see esp. 427.

5.  The original meaning of the expression "Indian giver" meant to ask a gift for a gift but in the course of the nineteenth century it came to have its popular, derogatory, and now-accepted meaning: someone who takes back something he has already given.

6.  Cited as a prefatory quotation to Laurence Bern's very thoughtful essay, "Gratitude, Nature, and Piety in *King Lear*," *A Journal of Political Philosophy* 3, no. 2 (Autumn 1972), 27.

7.  A short, limited, though provocative essay is Marina Tsvetaeva's "On Gratitude," *Fifty Years of Russian Prose*, 1 (Cambridge, Mass., 1971), 30-33. Of an entirely different nature is Henry Sidgwick's philosophical treatment of the matter in his *The Method of Ethics* (New York, 1966), 259-63. Not to be forgotten is Ralph Waldo Emerson's classic essay "Gifts," in Brooks Atkinson, ed., *The Selected Writings of Ralph Waldo Emerson* (New York, 1940), 402-5.

8.  While overstressing differences between American and Japanese cultures, as would be expected of a work written during the Second World War for military-political reasons, in *The Chrysanthemum and The Sword: Patterns of Japanese Culture*, Ruth Benedict nevertheless excitingly suggests how much of Japanese culture—morality, manners and politics—are formed around the notion of debts incurred and debts to be repaid. She distinguishes between debts, the *on* of the Japanese, in the following fashion: There are debts passively incurred and debts that must be actively reciprocated; debts that are continuous and beyond any specific repayment, like the kind one has to one's emperor or parents and ancestors (*gimu*) and the debts one must repay with exact equivalence (*giri*); and among these latter debts to be repaid exactly, there are those debts one owes to the world (matters of money, contracts, etc.) and those one owes to one's name that involve the intense matters of name, pride, and reputation. Together these debts compose Japanese conscience and are operative at all points in their

personal and public lives. Of special interest in her work are Chapters 5 through 10. (New York, 1946), 98–227.

9. Georg Simmel, "Faithfulness and Gratitude," in Kurt H. Wolff, trans. and ed., *The Sociology of Georg Simmel* (New York, 1964), 379–95. For an argument that treats human morality as derivative from sentiments of approbation and disapprobation, and conceives gratitude and ingratitude to be crucial elements in the formation of approbation and disapprobation, see Edward Westermarck's monumental two-volume *The Origin and Development of the Moral Ideas*, second edition (London, 1917), esp. 2: 153–85; or yet his shorter *Ethical Relativity* (Paterson, N.J., 1960), esp. 86–88, 175–77. Westermarck's sources, especially insofar as he considers feelings and sympathy to form the roots of human values, are found in David Hume and Adam Smith: see, for instance, "Of the Passions," Book 2 of Hume's *A Treatise of Human Nature* (orig. ed. 1739) or his *Inquiry Concerning the Principles of Morals* (1752); and Adam Smith's *The Theory of Moral Sentiments* (1759) or the summary of Smith's views in T. D. Campbell's *Adam Smith's Science of Morals* (Totowa, N.J., 1971), esp. 85–126. For Hume and Smith, see William Curtis Swabey, *Ethical Theory from Hobbes to Kant* (New York, 1961), 178. In a short but philosophically stimulating piece entitled "Of Guilt and Gratitude: Further Reflections on Human Uniqueness," (in *Dialogist* 2 [1970]: 69–84), Roger Wescott argues that gratitude, even more than guilt, is the distinguishing characteristic of the human species.

10. Simmel, "Faithfulness and Gratitude," in *Sociology of Georg Simmel*, 388.

11. Ralph Waldo Emerson, "Gifts," in *The Selected Writings* (New York, 1950), 402.

12. François de La Rochefoucauld, *Maxims*, trans., L. W. Tancock (Baltimore, 1959), 63.

13. Paraphrased line from Westermarck's *The Origin*, 2: 158.

14. In *The Coming Crisis of Western Sociology* (New York, 1970), Alvin Gouldner points out, in his criticism of Talcott Parson's "social system," that for people to have reciprocity with one another there must be a basic equality of interaction of giving and taking, since serious imbalances of power deny social reciprocity, 239–45.

15. According to Philip Bock, even "outstanding obligations . . . contribute substantially to the stability of the social system," for they create a social time of obligation, thus peace and normalcy. Bock also, quoting Gouldner, here says, "We should also not only look for mechanisms which constrain or motivate men to do their duty and to pay off their debts. We should also expect to find mechanisms which induce people to remain socially indebted to each other and which inhibit their complete repayment" *Cultural Anthropology* (New York, 1969), 211. In effect, repayment threatens, if not severs, a social tie. To offer an example of this,

Conrad Arensberg writes in *The Irish Countryman* (Garden City, N.Y., 1968), 157, "To pay off a debt entirely is perforce to dissolve the relationship. It is to destroy the mutuality of expectation. If one's debt is paid off one loses, not only a customer, but a friend, quite literally."

16. Giving can be an expression of guilt; also it can be a form of revenge. In his *Life Against Death: The Psychoanalytic Meaning of History* (New York, 1959), Norman Brown concurs with Nietzsche that all debt is a source of guilt. (The German word *Schuld* means both debt and guilt.) "Giving is self-sacrificial; self-sacrifice is self-punishment—Work is still for most men a punishment and a scourge, says Durkheim—the derivation of work from Adam's sin expresses the psychological truth. In the archaic institution of the gift, what the giver wants to lose is guilt. . . . Money is condensed wealth; condensed wealth is condensed guilt," 267. Then Brown goes on to suggest that the whole sense of obligation to ancestors and culture means the increase of debt-guilt as civilization advances. (For this he is indebted to both Nietzsche and Freud.) This guilt thus creates a society: "Guilt is mitigated by being shared; man entered social organization in order to share guilt. Social organization (including the division of labor) is a structure of shared guilt," 269. As backwards, or inside-out, as Brown's approach is, some interesting coins fall out of man's pockets when he is stood on his head by Brown's artifices.

17. Aside from the testimony to this by the history of manners, interesting lines of exploration into the give and take of human face-to-face interaction are found in Edward Hall's *The Silent Language* (New York, 1959) and *Beyond Culture* (New York, 1977), as well as Erving Goffman's *The Presentation of the Self in Everyday Life* (New York, 1959) and *Relations in Public* (New York, 1971).

18. John S. Mill argued that justice does not extend to what is not considered a moral right: No one has a moral right to claim our generosity or beneficence because we are not morally bound to practice those virtues toward any given individual. Yet not wishing altogether to divide sentiment from reason, justice from morality, Mill (in the tradition of David Hume and Adam Smith) argues that our expectation and our sympathy enter into play. Nothing, he contends, is as painful as seeing a strong expression of ingratitude, or watching a friend abandon a friend in time of need. On this point, morality and utility join in demanding that the good should be met by good, and bad by bad, "On the Connection of Between Justice and Utility," in *Utilitarianism Liberty, Essay on Bentham* (New York, 1962), 306–21. Gouldner, in his article "The Norm of Reciprocity," suggests more or less the same when he says the first laws of society are that people should help those who have helped them, and they should not injure those who have helped them.

19. In *On Guilt and Innocence* (Los Angeles, 1976), Herbert Morris suggests that punishment serves a rite of passage, 31–58. (For the general notion of rite of passage, see Arnold Van Gennep's classic *Rites of Passage*,

translated by Monika Vizedom and Gabrielle Caffee [Chicago, 1960].) In "Primitive Law," A. R. Radcliffe-Brown specifically notes how *ritual* punishment might serve purificatory purposes since wrongdoing creates uncleanliness, *Structure and Function in Primitive Society* (New York, 1965), 214.

20. Some of the works I found useful on torture and punishment, and their relation to overall human considerations of "fairness and justice," were Hans von Hentig's *Punishment: Its Origins, Purpose and Psychology* (London, 1937), James Heath's *Eighteenth Century Penal Theory* (Oxford, 1963); Arthur Koestler's *Reflections on Hanging* (New York, 1957); and Walter Moberly's *The Ethics of Punishment* (Hamden, Conn., 1968). Particularly interesting for medieval Europe are the master historian Marc Bloch's discussions of "the foundations of law," "solidarity of the kindred group," "the tie of kinship," and "relations of vassal and lord" which are found in Chapters 8, 9, 10, and 17 of the first volume of his *Feudal Society* (Chicago, 1961).

21. Henry Sumner Maine, *Ancient Law: Its Connection with the Early History of Society and its Relation to Modern Ideas* (1861; reprint ed., Boston, 1963), 122. To suggest one more example of the sense of collective punishment, Radcliffe-Brown writes: "The Ashanti conception of the law is that all such actions [murder, suicide, incest, assault, stealing, curse upon a chief, treason, cowardice, witchcraft, and other deeds] are offences against the sacred or supernatural powers on which the wellbeing [*sic*] of the whole community depends and that unless these offences are expiated by the punishment of the guilty persons, the whole tribe will suffer," *Structure and Function in Primitive Society*, 219. Of general interest is Bronislaw Malinowski's *Crime and Custom in Savage Society* (New York, 1932).

22. Malinowski, *Crime and Custom*, explores "the idea of giving and taking as pervading tribal life," 38–45, and that of "reciprocity as the basis of social stucture," 46–49.

23. Bronislaw Malinowski, *Argonauts of the Western Pacific*, (1922; reprint ed., New York, 1961).

24. Ibid., 175. Also for primitive exchange see Melvill Herskovits, *Economic Anthropology* (New York, 1940); Marvin Harris, *Culture, Man, and Nature* (New York, 1971), 235–63; Joan Robinson, *Freedom and Necessity* (New York, 1970), 22–35; and Karl Polyani, *The Great Transformation: The Political and Economic Origins of Our Times* (Boston, 1957), 269–73.

25. Marcel Mauss, *The Gift: Forms and Functions of Exchange in Archaic Society*, trans. Ian Cunnison, (1925; reprint ed., New York, 1970).

26. Ibid., 1.

27. In his classic study of the Nuer, E. E. Evans-Pritchard writes: "Another defining characteristic of a tribe is *cut*, blood-wealth paid in compensation for homicide, and Nuer explains the tribal value in terms of it,"

*The Nuer: A Description of the Modes of Livelihood and Political Institutions of a Nilotic People* (New York, 1969), 121.

28. While Raymond Firth does not conclude that sacrifice is purely an attempt at manipulation, he nevertheless suggests several ways in which this is the case in "Offerings and Sacrifice: Problems of Organization," in William Lessa and Evon Vogt, *Reader in Comparative Religion: An Anthropological Approach* (New York, 1958), 324–33. For a few useful examinations of sacrifice, see M. Mauss and H. Hubert, "Essai sur le sacrifice," *Année Sociologique* (1898), 29–139; Sigmund Freud's *Totem and Taboo* (New York, 1918); A. Loisy's *Essai historique sur le sacrifice*, (Paris, 1920); and E. O. James, *Beginnings of Religion* (London, 1958), 83–100, also *Comparative Religion* (New York, 1961), 78–98, 228–49, and his *Sacrifice and Sacrament* (London, 1962); as well as Athur Hocart, *Social Origins* (London, 1954).

29. Joseph Swain, trans., (New York, 1961). For one recent and useful introduction to Durkheim, who was Mauss's uncle and had a deep influence on Malinowski, see Robert Nisbet, *The Sociology of Émile Durkheim* (New York, 1974). For Durkheim's relation to the formation of French sociology, see Claude Levi-Strauss, "French Sociology" in Georges Gurvitch, ed., *Sociology* (New York, 1945), 503–37. For Durkheim's influence on British sociology and anthropology in general and on Malinowski and Radcliffe-Brown, as well as what we know as the British school of functionalist anthropologists in specific, see Malinowski's *Argonauts*; A. R. Radcliffe-Brown's *The Andaman Islanders* (1922; reprint ed., New York 1964); and Adam Kuper's short but useful historical survey of British anthropology, *Anthropology and Anthropologists: British School, 1922–1972* (New York, 1973). One recent attempt to survey functionalism critically is David Goddard's "Anthropology and the Limits of Functionalism," in Robin Blackburn, ed., *Ideology in Social Science* (New York, 1973), 61–75. Perceptive comments on Durkheim, Mauss, and early French sociology are found in Albert Salomon, *In Praise of the Enlightenment* (New York, 1962), 219–53; and Marcel Mauss, *Sociologie et anthropologie* (Paris, 1966).

30. Durkheim, *Elementary Forms*, 388.

31. Almost any standard work on religion probably will prove a mine of ways in which various types of sacrifice serve as forms of exchange. Of great general interest is James Fraser's *Golden Bough* (1890). Of particular interest, to suggest that Catholics are not alone in seeking "to give to get," is "Means for Acquiring Merit: Giving," in Melford Spiro, *Buddhism and Society* (New York, 1970), 103–10.

32. Instructive material on the relation of and the distinction between magic and religion is found in Marcel Mauss, *Sociologie et anthropologie*, 4–137; and Radcliffe-Brown's *Structure and Function in Primitive Society*, 174–75.

33. Firth, "Offerings and Sacrifice," 325.

34. Christoph von Furer-Haimendorf, *Morals and Merit: A Study of Values and Social Control in South Asian Societies* (Chicago, 1967), 267.

35. In "The Worship of the Dead," Fustel de Coulanges wrote: "The belief and the rites which treat the dead as divine beings are the oldest and most persistent of anything which pertain to the Indo-European Race," *Ancient City* (1864; reprint ed., Garden City, N.Y., n.d.), 21–25.

36. For example, Western Indians of North America hung themselves from trees by cords attached to sticks passed through their breasts, and put themselves through yet more awesome ordeals, to make themselves worthy of the great gifts of being priest or hunter. Or to choose another example, European villagers of not too distant past willingly offered themselves, without resistance, to the person who intended to kill them when they concurred that their action was wrong. Yet more extreme examples of self-punishment, the sacrifice of one's children, and even the symbolic killing of gods, suggest that in all things there is never something for nothing; everything has a price.

37. For a description of traditional man's hierarchical view of existence, see Arthur Lovejoy, *The Great Chain of Being* (New York, 1936).

38. This quotation, of which the English translation is mine, is from positivist Hippolite Taine; it stands as preface to Chapter 9, "Give Us This Day," of Eugen Weber's very fine work *Peasants into Frenchmen: The Modernization of Rural France, 1870–1914* (Stanford, Calif., 1976), 130. From a year-long seminar with Professor Weber at UCLA, sponsored by the National Endowment for the Humanities, I came away a convert on this point.

39. On social dislocation Émile Durkheim wrote: "As the market extends, great industry appears. But it results in changing the relations of employers and employees. The great strain upon the nervous system and the contagious influence of great agglomerations increase the needs of the latter. Machines replace men; manufacturing replaces hand work. The work is regimented, separated from his family throughout the day . . . but as these changes have been accomplished with extreme rapidity, the interests in conflict have not yet had time to be equilibrated." *The Division of Labor in Society*, trans. George Simpson (New York, 1964), 370.

40. Karl Polyani, *The Great Transformation* (Boston, 1957), 128.

41. Robert Conquest, *Stalin's Purges of the Thirties* (New York, 1973), 668–69.

42. On the effect of modernization on gratitude and reciprocity, as well as on the notions of honor and respect, instructive is Peter Berger, Brigitte Berger, and Hansfried Kellner, *Homeless Mind: Modernization and Consciousness* (New York, 1973). Particularly instructive is their discussion of an individual's "reciprocity" with a bureaucracy, 41–61; the pluralization of social worlds in which the individual must live, 63–82; and the obsolescence of honor, as a motivation, 83–96.

# 2
# Progress, The Making of a New Conscience

The imagination of the poets placed the Golden Age at the dawn of the human race, amidst the ignorance and rudeness of primitive times. It is rather the Iron Age that should be banished there. The Golden Age of mankind is not behind, but before us; and it lies in the perfection of the social order; our fathers have not seen it, our children will one day reach it: it is for us to prepare their way.

From Saint-Simon and Augustin Thierry, *De la réorganisation de la société européene*, cited in Renato Poggioli, *The Oaten Flute* (Cambridge, Mass., 1975), 29.

As for myself, I would rather believe that if social harmony has a purpose, it is to aid our unfettered progress and to favor the improvement of all by all.

Jules Michelet, *The People* (1846; reprint ed., Urbana, Ill., 1973), 208.

At first, the secularisation of the capitalist world during the 19th century elided the judgment of God into the judgment of History in the name of Progress. Democracy and Science became the agents of such a judgment.

John Berger, *About Looking* (New York, 1980), 54.

This chapter is about the eighteenth-century philosophers of the Enlightenment. The philosophers, the articulate elite of the eighteenth-century West, were the founders of modern secular culture. In their world view they fused together the fundamental premises of Renaissance humanism, the Scientific Revolution, and the early modern ideologies of political freedom and tolerance. At the heart of this world view was the drive to bring all existence under the examination of human reason and all society under the aegis of education and reform. The philosophers' world view was inseparable from all the reforms and revolutions that characterized the West during the last half of the eighteenth century. Then, as now, the philosophers provided us with the language of change, reform, revolution, and progress.

These founders of the new conscience, the man of guilt, shaped the way contemporary man still values his efforts to understand and change the world. Indeed, they are part of us; knowledge of them is knowledge of ourselves.

## CONSCIENCE, SOME DEFINING NOTES

Conscience is not easily defined. Almost by definition it must be understood to be as vast as consciousness and as complex and intricate as the mind itself. No faculty of the mind—intellect, memory, imagination, judgment, and will—nor any passion of the spirit, however subtle, can be understood to be without a relation to conscience. Conscience, in turn, is joined so intimately to a person that it is considered to be inseparable from his personality, temperament, character, and habits. Likewise, conscience is not discussed without reference to the person's society and its traditions, laws, customs, and values. Thus, here, given the dimensions of conscience, we can only set forth a few defining notes.

Conscience must be understood to be conscious. Otherwise it is consigned, along with the entire realm of the ethical, to the kingdom of the subconscious.[1] Right and wrong become mere illusion and the reality of human responsibility—human conventions, mores, morality, ethics, law, and justice—is denied.

Conscience is a matter of deliberation, judgment, and responsibility, all of which imply consciousness. However, this is not to deny that unconscious forces influence, even at times determine, conscience. Nor is this to argue that conscience and consciousness are identical, since clearly all states of consciousness do not present a consideration of the right and wrong. Yet, this does not deny the near inseparable interpenetration of conscience and consciousness, which suggests two questions: How can man be conscious without also being aware that he is a responsible being? How does man ever use his conscience intentionally, or exhort another person to do the same, without calling for a higher consciousness?

This assumption about the connection between consciousness and conscience gives rise to a second assumption: Conscience is shaped by culture. Although culture is not its source, culture defines the forms and content of conscience. Culture—to speak abstractly and as if all cultures were one—defines the boundaries and intensities of man's moral universe by indicating: 1) what are matters of right and wrong; 2) what are the different types of right and wrong; 3) who are the ethical actors; and 4) what are symbols, laws, rewards, and punishments for action, speech, and thought. However, to tie conscience so closely to culture is not to argue for cultural relativism or determinism. There is no intention here to imply that culture per se prohibits universality, that it absolutely fixes and limits any critical self-questioning and its possibilities. In truth, the concept of a single, comprehensive, all-embracing culture, which hermetically seals off one culture from all other cultures, is an abiding historical prejudice of Romantic nationalism (a prejudice that has received support from some social scientists who have confused a "useful" conceptual idea with reality). This concept also is a result of modern industrial national society which increasingly threatens to homogenize all cultures into a single culture. Even among the most supposed primitive cultures, a variety of values and disputes can be found over obligations, rights, and responsibilities. This position raises a paradoxical question: How *many* cultures in fact does any *one* culture contain?

A further assumption implicitly responds to this query: The contemporary West contains many cultures. A multitude of cultures shape our conscience, defining the ethical being from its subtlest impulses about doing what is proper to the most academic discussions of the good itself. These cultures exist not only within us, but they form our whole environment, our institutions, laws, daily rituals, business transactions, and so forth. Consequently our very notions of what is right and wrong, and our expression and application of these notions, are incalculably many. They exist in a variety of ways and in varying relations to one another. Some of our notions of right and wrong are entirely oblivious to one another; others exist in harmony; whereas still others survive under a delicate truce which is maintained adroitly only by a conscious-ness aware of the tacit compromises essential in a multicultural society. Surely we live with a variety of ethical ways, and so in one sense we don't have one conscience, but many.

Aside from mass, commercial, and national cultures and modern ethnic, class, work, sex, and leisure cultures (all of which increas-ingly homogenize themselves and all older cultures into one), there are three essential cultures that form our ethics. Traditional, Chris-tian, and secular progressive culture mark the first formation of the new conscience. Understanding the new conscience—its origins, its attack on the older cultures, as well as its spread from the elite quarters of high European culture to society at large—is essential to understanding ourselves.

This interpretation, which joins history and philosophy, is not intended to be a comprehensive history. Nor, does it propose some new liberating historicist psychiatry, implying humanity needs only to be laid on the couch of time and have its history recited in order to free it of its unwanted past. There are no such therapies. Critical historical self-knowledge involves considerably more and considerably less than that. It is about becoming more consciously human, which is a condition that can neither finally be escaped nor fully accepted.

## CHRISTIANITY, GRATITUDE IN EXTREME, GUILT IN EXCESS

Christianity, in all its forms, has profoundly shaped Western consciousness and conscience across the centuries. Christianity makes our conscience what it is. By altering our very perspective of ourselves, it joins us to progressive history of good and evil. Through Adam and Eve and Christ it connects us to all other humans, those who have been, are, and will be. Christianity in its traditional forms bonds the living and the dead by its teachings about prayer, the Communion of Saints, and the afterlife. Guilt and gratitude have no earthly perimeters.

Above all else, Christianity shapes our conscience by creating within us the sense that God is looking at us. The shimmer of our awareness is excited by the feeling of being watched by an omni-scient being who scrutinizes us to our very depths. We are shame-fully, guiltily, abashedly naked before his all-seeing eye, from which we cannot hide and which knows us as we do not know ourselves. Our conscience itself becomes His piercing glance, His uninterrupted, all-knowing gaze. We are transfigured by His eye; we stand outside ourselves, looking in at ourselves—strangely, alienly, sternly, fantastically, crazily—through the eye of the God we cannot see.

Erich Auerbach understood how the eye of the Judaic-Christian God became our conscience and shaped our sense of self, personality, and meaning. Comparing Homer's Odysseus and the Old Testament's Abraham (who dared to offer his first born son Isaac to God), Auerbach wrote:

> The human beings in the Biblical stories have greater depths of time, fate, and consciousness than do the human beings in Homer; although they are nearly always caught up in an event engaging all their faculties, they are not so entirely immersed in its present that they do not remain continually conscious of what has happened to them earlier and elsewhere; their thoughts and feelings have more layers, are more entangled. Abraham's actions are explained not only by what is happening to him at the moment, nor yet only by his character (as Achilles' actions by his courage and his pride, and Odysseus' by his versatility and foresightedness), but by his previous history; he remembers, he is constantly conscious of, what God has promised him and what God has already accomplished for him—his soul is torn between desperate rebellion and hopeful expectation.[2]

Christianity put another face on the God who is our conscience and redefined the dimensions of our gratitude and guilt. Now a suffering God of love looks at us.

The uniquely perfect gift of the Incarnation and Crucifixion of the Son of God, as nothing else, has defined our sense of gratitude. It constantly puts us before the gift of which we are not worthy: No man could have prepared it; no people, not even all of Israel, merited it. It is the universal gift that astounds and humbles.

A new countenance has been added to the God of the Old Testament who so deeply peered into the hearts of humanity. Infinite love, consumated by going to the cross for all humanity, now looks into us; we are opened like a book. God's eye becomes our very own conscience. We peer at ourselves, forever asking, yet full well knowing, of our unworthiness before that gift. Our gratitude is ever necessary yet never sufficient.

The gift of Christ overwhelms man. Man is altogether without means to repay, even to comprehend, it. How this divine gift contradicts traditional earthly man's giving and taking is voiced by two characters in Nikos Kazantzakis' *Last Temptation of Christ.*

One says:  Do me a favor and don't start up again about God. Where he's concerned there are no boundaries. You walk all your life, this one and the next, trying to reach him, but the blessed fellow has no end. So forget about him and don't mix him up in our affairs. *Listen to me: here we've got to deal with . . . dishonest seven-times-shrewd man.*[3]

Another
says:  We've been getting along just fine without Messiahs; they're nothing but a nuisance. Go on bring me some cheese and I'll give you a panful of fish. *You give me and I give you: that's the Messiah.*[4]

For the faithful, the gift of Christ establishes an insatiable claim upon them. Abraham and Job of the Old Testament become exemplary lives for them as well as all the countless Christian martyrs, saints, and other holy people, who gave up the world and all its trappings to make themselves a fit offering to God. (Here I think of not just well-known saints, as Saint Francis who kissed lepers and called death his brother, but such a far less-known saint as Saint Jane Fremiat de Chantal, the founder of the Order of Visitation. Upon the death of her husband, Saint Jane Fremiat de Chantal branded Christ's name upon her breasts and left home to serve Him, despite the agonizing supplications of her young children that she not leave them orphans but stay home with them.[5])

The Christian ideal, for Catholic and Protestant alike, has always been to offer one's whole life to God in exchange for what he has given. Saint Paul instructed: "In everything give thanks!" The Christian should make every act of his life a sacrifice of repayment to God. The gift consumes the believer. He cannot repay it, but he must try. The believer is instructed not only to attempt to repay it but told that the best way to repay is to commemorate Christ's sacrifice over and over again in his prayer, worship, and sacraments.

Accounting for the most profound divisions in us, Christianity stands in defiance of the most elemental laws of human exchange:

The Christian is counseled to find it more blessed to give instead of receive, to turn the other cheek, to lay down his life for others, to will God's will (rather than his own) be done.[6] Gratitude could not be more demanding.

As few others, Nietzsche, who purposely cast himself as the anti-Christ, understood the hold of Christianity upon us and its specific power to inculcate guilt in a whole civilization.[7] In his *Genealogy of Morals*, Nietzsche identified Christianity as the religion of the guilty, sick conscience. In these terms he described Christianity historically, calling it "that paradoxical and ghastly expedient which brought temporary relief to tortured humanity": "*God's sacrifice of himself for man*. God makes himself the ransom for what could not otherwise be ransomed; God alone has power to absolve us of a debt we can no longer discharge [original sin]; the creditor offers himself as a sacrifice for his debtor *out of sheer love*."[8]

Christianity, Nietzsche asserted, is the religion of the resentful. It serves all who hate the nobility who previously defined culture's good by their strength, will, wealth, and love of life. All suffering, weakness, and misery is used, according to Nietzsche, to throw oneself upon God; all abnegation and all denials of self, nature, and naturalness win one heaven. In contrast, all who yield to their instincts, flesh, and will, are of the Devil, and are to face "the divine Judge and Executioner." With Christianity, Nietzsche argued, Israel triumphed over classical nobility and the weak had their vengeance. Nietzsche asked: "What could equal in debilitating narcotic power the symbol of the 'holy cross,' the ghastly paradox of a crucified god, the unspeakably cruel mystery of God's self-crucifixion for the benefit of mankind?"[9] "Did not Israel attain the ultimate goal of its sublime vengefulness precisely through the bypath of this 'Redeemer,' this ostensible opponent and disintegrator of Israel?"[10] The Romans, "the most noble people," Nietzsche remarked, succeeded to a degree in containing this Jewish-Christian fanaticism through their influence on the Church, but the Reformation restored with a new and greater virulence, this spiritual disease composed of eternal guilt and everlasting punishment—"this most terrible sickness that has wasted man thus far."[11]

For Nietzsche, Christianity hated life. Its sickness showed with its hopes of a life beyond, its bloody phantasmogoria of the sacrificial animal, the redemptive deed, the holy legend and its asceticism. It, too, showed in the new slave who professed equality by virtue of having an everlasting soul. (The French Revolution was, in Nietzsche's opinion, a result of this Christian doctrine of equality.) Nietzsche held Christianity to be responsible for more than the prevalent antilife, "herding-animal morality." Nietzsche judged it to be the teacher of contemporary teachers. From it were derived all the sickly reformers, liberals, democrats, and especially socialists with their fashionable "ethics of pity" and "tragic empathy" for the downtrodden. All this, in Nietzsche's opinion, was a secularized "la nostalgie de la croix," another expression of that terrible Christian guilt.[12]

Even if we concede worth to Nietzsche's critique, what also must be mentioned is that he erringly assumed that the conscience of the majority was established around pure ideals proposed by elites. He overlooked how universally Christians found ways to temper the Christian message, how rituals, sacraments, Bible readings, and other forms of proposing faith served as safe substitutes for personal sacrifice; how churches in general proved to be convenient mediators for one's dealings with God. The Christian message was heard primarily by people who were living in a world whose boundaries were scarcity, envy, violence, resentment, and a constant hunger for anything that would make life less painful. The majority had to struggle bitterly to survive at all. They rang church bells to chase away storms, conjured curses against their enemies, and asked Christian and pagan spirits alike to make their fields, animals, and women fertile. Christianity added to, transformed, and contradicted, but did not eradicate the old man's way of measuring and exchanging gifts which is still in us.

## POSTERITY, A NEW EYE OF CONSCIENCE

Only a new and passionate faith could have contended against Christianity in order to become the controlling moral idea of the West, the commanding vision of its energies and the *new eye of conscience*. This new faith rose out of the vision of humanity's progress, which Diderot defined for himself and that elite group in eighteenth-century Europe and America, when he said, "La posterité pour le philosophe, c'est l'autre monde de l'homme religieux" ("Posterity for the philosopher is what the afterlife is for the religious person").[13]

The most militant of the philosophers and the succeeding generations of their eighteenth- and nineteenth-century followers served the causes of human autonomy, atheism, and revolution. They openly declared war against Christianity. They argued that it supported the retrogressive social, political, and spiritual hierarchies of the old order and taught that humanity was weak, sinful, and in need of supernatural salvation. For the philosophers, the shackles of gratitude, which bound humanity to the old way, had to be broken if humanity was to be liberated. The voices of the most fervent consistently voiced a "liberating atheism": God, who stood as an aristocratic impediment of humanity's resurrection, must be killed so mankind could be born. Their aim was a total transvaluation of human values, a new conscience of and for humanity.

The philosophers became our conscience—at least one very strong voice speaking within us. This is especially the case for Americans whose national culture, in its origins, formation, and embodiment, was the work of the eighteenth-century philosophers. We believe in their ideals of human power, potential, reform, and happiness even when we claim not to. Their beliefs are lent credence not only by our feelings, sensibilities, and values but by our technology, economics, and politics. Our conscience weighs existence as the philosophers taught us. To know them, or more precisely to understand the most essential elements of their world view, is to understand ourselves. It is to carry out a critical historical analysis of our own conscience.

American master historian Carl Becker, who believed the crisis of contemporary conscience was the inability of our inherited eighteenth-century culture to confront twentieth-century experience, cogently set forth the essential articles of the philosophers' world view:

> 1) Man is not natively depraved; 2) the end of life is life itself, the good life on earth instead of the beatific life after death; 3) man is capable, guided solely by light of reason and experience, of perfecting the good life on earth; and 4) the first and essential condition of the good life on earth is the freeing of men's minds from the bonds of ignorance and superstition, and of their bodies from the arbitrary oppression of constituted social authorities.[14]

Becker too saw the belief in posterity as the heart of new faith. Posterity was used, in Becker's words, "to exorcise the double illusion of the Christian paradise and the golden age of antiquity," and "for the *love of God*, they substituted *love of humanity*, for the vicarious atonement, the perfectibility of man through his own efforts; and for the hope of immortality in another world the hope of living in the memory of future generations."[15]

Even when we despair of the philosophers' faith in humanity's progress, as Becker did in the interwar years, we remain a type of fallen-away philosopher. Their vision is in us too strongly to shake. They teach a new conscience; they redefine human rights and responsibilities. They reorder human understanding of nature, God, and the living and the dead.

Inherent to the ethical transformation proposed by the philosophers was a reassessment of what humanity could and should do for itself. Thereafter humanity was the reason of its own guilt and gratitude. In place of the omniscient God peering into the depths of human conscience was a new eye. It was *the eye of humanity, reformed, idealized, perfected.*

## THE PHILOSOPHERS' ASSUMPTIONS

This new eye of conscience was formed out of new premises that contradicted the traditional and Christian cultures. The first of these assumptions was that this world—its human pleasures and pains, expectations, plans, and tragedies—has a meaning in itself. These experiences are not merely illusions, perceptions through the glass darkly or symbols of another world which alone is truly real. Likewise no longer can human affairs be understood to be in the hands of Providence or ancestors, or yet other forces that transcend man's rational control.

The second assumption, a corollary of the first, was that humanity is the agency of its own history. It is for humanity to value and to command its own experience. The third assumption of the new conscience declared humanity as its own proper end; nothing, the self, family, or God, is of greater good. This was not just a reformulation of the instinct that humans know their own kind, nor was it a restatement of the universal religious precepts that all humans are each others' brothers and sisters. Instead this assumption asserted that humanity is its own artificer.

The final assumption involved the most demanding ascetics of this new faith: Each human being is morally responsible for the collective well-being of all humanity. In all we do—citizenship, child-rearing, work, and even thought—we act for all; our very existence

constitutes a will for or against humanity's future. Under the awesome responsibility of this assumption, conscience's horizon is
humanity, real, imagined, and hoped for.

It is this type of inspired conscience that produces humanity's
most fervent servants, from the truly genuine martyrs of peace,
justice, and freedom to the arrogant, distorted, crazed, and self-
annointed prophets of humanity. However, deviations, distortions, and perversions in the service of humanity should not surprise us any more than those that occur in the service of God,
church, nation, party, or other cause. What should interest us instead is the dedication to humanity itself, the belief that men and
women can and should serve each other's good; that the highest
universal duty is owed to humanity. In other words, what merits
explanation is the confidence that underlies the four assumptions
and the progressive humanistic conscience they create.

Briefly, this means noting all the composing elements of European high culture: the Renaissance affirmation of the autonomy of
human politics, arts, and scholarship; the Reformation's decisive
affirmation of individual faith and conscience; the Scientific Revolution's declaration of the autonomy of human reason; and true
and significant movements from the sixteenth century onward on
behalf of tolerance, individual and constitutional freedoms, and
internationalism.[16] In addition, a range of material transformations
occurred in all quarters of European activity and radically enhanced human confidence. Humanity's power over nature increased. All sectors of human activity—navigation, agriculture,
mining, and so on—revealed the progress of a new technology.
Also enhancing the sense of human control was the growth of the
public order. European governments from Spain to Russia radically
accelerated the integration and systematization of all aspects of
their society, as revealed by increasing state intervention into commerce, production, armies, law, and the imposition of taxes. The
public life—the politics, constitutions, law, bureaucracies, institutions, and ideologies—grew radically from the middle of the seventeenth century onward and expanded the sense of human power,
reason, and responsibility. Increasingly the public life became the
new eye of conscience. Thereafter, the state, like God, could claim
an interest in everything.

## THE AUTONOMY OF THIS EARTHLY MAN

Above all else the philosophers, in contradiction to traditional
and Christian culture, would have us know, define, and calculate

our own pleasures and pains. Following their counsel, we would judge our own condition and choose our own means and ends. With them the ethics of utilitarianism and pragmatism was born. According to the philosophers, the universe is a matter of human calculations; no mysterious signs and coordinates are necessary for this math. Like the new physics of Newton, so too should conscience perform its calculations.

Though the philosophers themselves for the most part were not from the middle class, their desire to establish autonomy for all human activities found support from the bourgeoisie.[17] The philosophers' ideal of happiness, for instance, was certainly not the religious contemplative life, nor was it exclusively the vision of man perfected. Rather, in part, it was what made most eighteenth-century urban dwellers content: "Enough good food and drink, comfortable lodging, agreeable sex life, a pleasant family life, and so on, in short, a life in which men have what they want."[18]

Further, the philosophers extended human autonomy by no longer allowing moral supremacy to belong to those who pray and fight. No longer should their "heroic" moral sacrifices to either the gods of heaven or the gods of war be judged to have the ethical right to command society. The philosophers praised those who thought rationally and acted productively. This could not but enhance the status of the third estate, the middle class, whose values of intelligence, work, and profit did not rival the second estate traditions of military honor and the first estate's priestly virtue.

The philosophers' support of man's right to define his own world helped the emerging bourgeoisie.[19] By supporting human autonomy, they indirectly lent their support to a bourgeoisie that justified its charges of interest, which Medieval theologians explicitly condemned as usury, in terms of the doctrine of just profit for risk incurred. This emerging class gave itself a code of ethics, which required ambition, cunning and honesty in its exchanges, and relegated gratitude and traditional reciprocities to the "personal side" of human affairs. Further, the bourgeoisie defined the "human enterprise which allowed a calculable profit" as a calling that merited a high station in society without the slightest risk of forfeiting one's place in heaven. Indeed, with all the powers of the high culture which they commanded, the philosophers consecrated the bourgeoisie's legitimacy. Amintore Fanfani perceived the newborn capitalist to be a man who pursued his economic ends as if they were natural and good. He was no longer morally embarassed by his wealth, or how he acquired, used, or passed it on. He *merited* what he *earned*. He no longer felt the need to give his excess to the church, the city, the poor or other philanthropic cause; nor, unlike his medieval predecessor, did the merchant make his will the occasion for repentance and making amends.[20] In the death-bed depictions we have of him, he dies at his boldest, content, sensing he has done his job well, advising his son to take care of the devils of this world while promising that he will take care of the devils of the next. Death—the consummation of human pain, misery, suffering, and helplessness, more than anything else the proof of human limits—no longer led him or the philosophers to renounce the autonomy of human ways.[21]

The philosophers and bourgeoisie can be understood to be co-conspirators in creating the new eye of modern conscience. What the latter taught in action, the former legitimated in culture. Elinor Barber describes this well:

> As social values in other areas of life became more and more secular, as politics, art, and learning, for example, became secularized, and as, furthermore, the commercial and industrial bourgeoisie became an ever larger minority of the population, so it became more difficult for this bourgeois class not to assert, to some extent, the this-worldly and rational assumptions underlying its work and its life. A more general secular morality was now conceivable, and for the bourgeoisie, which had no place in traditional religious and aristocratic conception of man and society, it provided a meaningful definition of its human condition.[22]

## A COSMIC HOUSECLEANING

So humanity could regulate its own affairs autonomously, the philosophers wielded a giant broom. They started the great clean-up that leaves no part of the old way and no heavenly faith in its place. They attacked all transactions with the dead, the forces of nature, the irrational, and the supernatural. Their cosmic housecleaning, if ever completed, would leave no voices of "the old man" or transcendence in our conscience. Existence would be measured by humanity, its reason and ends.[23]

The philosophers undertook to dethrone the personal God, the linchpin of the Western supernatural world. Christ, Mary, the angels, saints, and the dead—all with whom Christians bartered, bargained, and supplicated—were understood to stand in the way of rational, calculable, predictable existence. Wanting a rational, simplified, and to a degree homogeneous universe, in which man did his own giving and taking, they sought to exorcise all that was dark, irrational, uncontrollable, and incomprehensible. The peasants and their ways, Christian mysteries, magic, sorcery, witchcraft, death, sex, and violence were all conceived to be enemies and were to be done away with by illumination, reform, and improvement. The world must be made open, rational, tame, clean.

Illustrative of the attempt to empty human conscience of the claims of the supernatural was Thomas Paine, an American who defended the French Revolution. Paine declared that the spiritual essence of the old order demands that man bow down before "a supernatural tyrant of priestly imagination" who *punished the innocent for the guilty*, who lighted the fire of everlasting torment for the mass of mankind."[24] In a similar vein, David Hume judged Providence to be an anthropomorphic concept and monotheism to be an attempt to flatter God. He declared the Old Testament's representation of the Almighty as avenging the sins of the guilty upon the innocent to be "indecent if not blasphemous."[25] Baron Von Holbach, one of the most militantly antireligious philosophers, attacked sacrifice as the evil essence of all priestly religion:

> We find, in all religions of the earth, a *God of armies*, a *jealous God*, an *avenging God*, a *destroying God*, a *God*, who is pleased with carnage, and whom his worshippers, as a duty, serve to his taste. Lambs, bulls, children, men, heretics, infidels, kings, whole nations are sacrificed to him.[26]

In essence, the philosophers wanted autonomy for humanity. It was that fundamental desire, so elemental in our contemporary conscience, that set them against the senseless pain and suffering of this world. It explains their revulsion to war, violence, ignorance, prejudice, and superstition and, perhaps above all else, to sacrifice, which assumes the most important human commerce is with forces that cannot be entirely understood or controlled. For them humanity could have its own pride only when it defined its own exchanges; if religion was to have a purpose at all it would be in the service of a fraternal, tolerant, and rational Deism. Voltaire, who perhaps more than any other expressed the range of the enlightened philosophers' interests, considered everything that implied transaction with the supernatural to be superstitions—that is Providence, the Incarnation, Resurrection, miracles, eternal life and so on.[27] He told his readers "in a staggering array of metaphors, Judaic-Christian religion is a virulent infection, a terrifying madness, *a bloodthirsty monster*," and he proposed to reduce religion to a mere matter of public thanksgiving in correspondence with Boswell: "Let us meet four times a year in a grand temple with music, and thank God for all his gifts. There is one sun. There is one God. Let us have one religion. Then all mankind will be brethren."[28]

With the Judaic-Christian God and all He sustained banished, the ethical universe was reordered. *The moral atom of this new universe was the individual.* No philosopher expressed this as strongly as Immanuel Kant. His epistemology put the rationality of the individual at the center of human knowledge, and his ethics placed the autonomous individual of good will at the center of value.

No philosopher went as far as Jeremy Bentham in seeking to join rational, autonomous individuals in a community of shared interests. In his utilitarianism he divided life into two sets of experiences, those that bring pleasure and those that bring pain. He counseled radically: Let every man be the king of his own happiness. Only when "these monarchs" clash, and mutual need calls for legislation, should one apply the highest principle of utility: "The greatest good, for the greatest number." In reducing the essence of Bentham's utilitarianism to two cardinal principles, Élie Halévy grasped its ethical significance.

> First postulate: pleasure and pain are susceptible of becoming objects of a calculus, and a rational and mathematical science of pleasure is possible. This is what we will call the rationalistic postulate of the Utilitarian doctrine. Second postulate: all the individuals who together make up society have an approximately equal capacity for happiness. This is what we will call the individualistic postulate of the Utilitarian doctrine. The value of Bentham's system is the value of these two postulates.[29]

However, something more inspiring than utilitarianism was needed to inspire men and women to serve humanity, the new collective cause. Something more than a recognition of mutual convenience was required if they were to conceive of humanity as more than a valueless aggregate of individual parts and take up the cause of humanity as a good worthy of the highest sacrifice. Utilitarianism offered a functional, though not easily applied, measure of value for transactions in a democratic society, but it did not offer an inspiring vista.

Some of the philosophers, of course, found their inspiration in humanity as a concept because it served their entrance into public life. In humanity's name they could counsel kings and parliaments, they could join their thoughts and aspirations to the power of their era. Behind the desire to be in the public life itself, an ideal supported by the classical and Renaissance humanisms, there was the desire for esteem. To shine in the eyes of others, to have them look upon you and say you are good, is a compelling goal. Insightfully, Hannah Arendt wrote of the architects of the American Revolution: "what moved them was *the passion for distinction,*' which John Adams held to be *'more essential and remarkable'* than any other human faculty."[30]

But the quest for esteem, the search for reputation in the realm of a fickle public and degrading power, is not sufficient to support a faith in humanity. The cohesion of humanity must be stronger than the search for public recognition, for that can be but an elite faith of the few.[31]

## SYMPATHY, A NEW HEART OF MANKIND

The philosophers' world view has always depended on more than reason. Passion has always been associated with the believers, servants, and martyrs of humanity's causes. In part, the passion derives from the sense of belonging to the forces of change. For the philosopher of the Enlightenment, to serve this faith of humanity, as Franklin and Jefferson did every bit as much as Voltaire and Diderot, was to make himself part of an international elite, a *cosmopolitan respublica literatorum.* His badge was *Sapere aude!* Dare to Know!, even if this led him into direct confrontation with public authorities, if it meant risking his immortal soul. Knowledge was noble and perilous business.[32]

Also exhilarating was the sense that in making this change he was joining himself to the family of da Vinci, Galileo, Bacon, and others, and at the same time indissolubly associating himself with all the reforms of his own era. It was uplifting and contagious for him to believe, as proven by the elites who made the American and French Revolutions, that he was instrumental in causing what Ernst Cassirer described as "the liberation of man from his own self-caused minority." The enlightened man ushered in a new age when men and women could live with greater happiness and dignity since they were guided by human reason instead of being regulated by prescription: "the assumption that attitudes, privileges, and customs had social legitimacy, if not indeed divine sanctions, by the mere fact of having existed for a long time."[33]

In spite of this passion one problem still had to be met in defining the new humanity. Why should we care for one another? How was the individual, if not for reason of God's creation or Christ's love, or some residual animal instinct, to be ethically concerned about humanity at large? Why should anyone believe it to be his obligation to sacrifice himself not just for family and friend, but also for abstract humanity which, by definition, includes not only all strangers but also all those human beings who are mean, cruel, lecherous, and detestable?

The philosophers found their first answer in sympathy, the spirit that allows us to go out of ourselves into another. It is sympathy (syn pathos or like feelings) that permits us to share feelings, thoughts, aspirations, and situations with others, and they with us, thereby creating a community of affection, interest, and responsibility. They praised sympathy, as well as philanthropy and altruism, as natural human virtues.

David Hume wrote: "No *quality of human nature* is more remarkable both in itself and its human consequences, than that propensity we have to *sympathize with others,* and to receive by communication of their inclinations and sentiments, however different from, or even contrary to our own."[34] Sympathy is at work when we take pride in a child's accomplishments, anger at the story of an outrage done to a stranger, or the way in which we move our lips in unison with the stuttering speech of another. Sympathy formed for Hume a middle territory between the individual and the group. Sympathy, anticipating its service to democracy in our world, does not accept social rank and status as impenetrable boundaries. In his *Theory of Moral Sentiment* (1759) Adam Smith, inspired by Hume, used sympathy not only as the sense of commiseration, but the basis upon which the observer and the observed have a real connection. "We sympathize even with the dead," he remarked. "We are so strongly joined inside to others there are very strict limits to the extent to which the man within can break free from the clamour without."[35] Anticipating contemporary social psychology, as well as inferring what is a central premise of this work, Smith went so far as to conceive of our conscience as a repository of social opinions and ideals that surround us.

Sympathy as well as philanthropy increasingly won an important place in the eighteenth-century high culture, particularly in the nascent literature of reform. The authentication of feeling itself also was witnessed by the growth of Quietism, Methodism, and other religions, as well as a whole cult of sentiment whose concern for feelings, especially those of the solitary protagonists, gave birth to the sensibility out of which the modern novel was born.[36] Also revealing the increase of empathy was an increasing appreciation of non-Western ways, which is still so alive in our conscience. German philosopher Herder's formulation that all peoples were equal in the sight of Providence was surely one of the period's most profound testimonies to an increased interest in non-Western cultures.

The high culture of the eighteenth century, under the impetus of emerging Romanticism, increasingly gave intrinsic value to feelings in themselves and associated them with the person of good conscience. Feelings, heart, and conscience became synonyms in certain contexts.[37] Active sympathy for the suffering of others increasingly was considered to be an essential attribute of the good man. Concern for the well-being of others and commitment to humanity in general became for an ever-growing number of the elite a prerequisite for being moral; the heart replaced the sword as the commanding virtue of the West.

In contrast to Christian charity—whose long history of personal and institutional good works cannot be ignored—the spirit of this new philanthropy included an increased sensitivity to a range of human feelings, problems, and dilemmas. In revolutionary fashion it no longer accepted the inevitability of human suffering; it fought both against injustice and for the realization of all human potential. Reform spread wide and deep. The new secular charity meant efforts to reform education, law, and punishment, and to fight for causes that served the slaves and serfs, the poor, sick, and orphaned, the insane and criminals.[38] A heart was being added to our consciences. Now men and women should look on each other as brothers and sisters. No walls should be between them.

No one philosopher expressed this new heart, this new active sympathy, as profoundly as Cesare Beccaria. If one passion motivated him, it was the desire to reform the law: to save innocent victims from the cruelty of its punishments; to demolish its accumulated errors of centuries; to end once and for all the ill-directed course of the law which "has continually produced a long and authorized example of the most cold-blooded barbarity."[39] Reflecting a new conscience, which makes another's suffering one's own, Beccaria attacked the cruel conditions that "confront a man with the terrible alternative of either sinning against God or concurring in his own ruin,"[40] as well as the pitiless torture that "leads the sensitive innocent man to confess himself guilty when he believes by so doing, he can put an end to his torment."[41] The cruelest of all, he felt, was capital punishment. Sounding so much like one of our humanitarian contemporaries, Beccaria dedicated his life to the amelioration of suffering: "If then, I can show that death is neither useful nor necessary I shall have gained the cause of humanity."[42] Further, he wrote: "If, by defending the rights of man and of unconquerable truth, I should help to save from the spasm and agonies of death some wretched victim of tyranny . . . *the thanks and tears of one innocent mortal in his transports of joy would console me for the contempt of all mankind.*"[43]

Beccaria's thoughts revealed the growing interconnection between sympathy and reform, which first characterized the prevailing sensibility of a significant section of the ruling elite during the closing decades of the eighteenth century. As people increasingly saw themselves capable of realizing the earthly good, a sense of responsibility for it developed. Since then, Beccaria's concern to care about humanity and to work to improve it has become the hallmark of our modern progressive conscience.[44] Undeniably the philosophers' vision of a perfect humanity created the *eye of conscience* that is so prevalent today.


## REFORM, REVOLUTION, AND RESURRECTION

The French Revolution swept away the old feudal, seigniorial order. No longer did the bonds of aristocracy and church hold. The old man—in the form of king, lord, bishop, and priest—was beheaded; *the era of new humanity had begun.* A new order of rights and responsibilities was announced. A new conscience would seek embodiment.

The French Revolution was a great stage. Upon it men and women, first the bourgeoisie and then the *sans culottes*, declared themselves to be disciples of the philosophers. They set themselves before the eyes of the world. They named posterity as their heir.

The revolution irretractably posed the question of humanity's progress. Progress was no longer merely an interesting hypothesis to be debated in the confines of the salons of France or the more democratic coffee houses of the English-speaking world. There was no longer any doubt about humanity directing itself; at issue was the question of what it would make itself. No one professed this new faith as strongly as the philosopher Condorcet. While actually proscribed and hunted, and then incarcerated and probably assassinated, by the new leaders of the Revolution, he continued to praise the Revolution. His consolation, unlike past philosophers, was not the life he had lived or the God he believed in, but the future of humanity he served. "How consoling," he wrote,

> for the philosopher who laments the errors, the crimes, the injustices which still pollute the earth and of which he is often the victim is this view of human race, emancipated from its shackles, released from the empire of fate and from that of the enemies of progress, advancing with a firm and sure step along the path of truth, virtue and happiness! *It is the contemplation of this prospect that rewards him for all his efforts to assist the progress of reason and the defense of liberty. . . .*[45]

It was this vision of progress, so well expressed by Condorcet, that formed the commanding vision of progressive conscience during the first decades of the nineteenth century. Since then, in one form or another, it has come to rule all who have wished to speak positively of a humanity caught in the unceasing change unleashed by the French Revolution and the Industrial Revolution.

These two revolutions and their convergence made the modern world. They made social change seem real, and eternity seem illusionary. They convinced everyone that humanity was being driven irresistibly onward upon a path of tremendous transformation.

Progress justified change and inspired revolutions. The new industrial capitalists praised progress as their own, not hesitating to claim the future as theirs. Andrew Ure, a Benthamite promoter of the factory system, spoke for many of his peers and the following generation of industrialists when he said "Providence has assigned man the glorious function of immensely improving on the products of nature by skillful initiative."[46]

Young students, artists, radicals, and intellectuals who were among the followers of the philosophers gave their souls to humanity's progress. Visions of it moved to the center of their conscience. They embraced humanity with a cosmic sympathy, which Romanticism gave existence and German idealism philosophical form. They promoted an historical theodicy which suggested that humanity is self-revealing in history. They were humanity's natural prophets. They believed humanity's future to be their responsibility.

This was, and is, a religious faith. One comes to it by conversion. For example, the young John Stuart Mill, who had been nurtured since childhood on Enlightenment thought, described a conversion archetypical of all liberals, socialists, and revolutionists who take humanity to be their cause: "From the winter of 1821, when I first read Bentham, and especially from the commencement of the *Westminster Review*, I had what might truly be called an object in life: to be a reformer of the world. My conception of my own happiness was entirely identified with this object."[47]

Romanticism, of which we are all the heir, shaped our conscience.[48] It swelled the human heart. It expanded sympathy and made it more intense. The human heart, becoming Christ-like, must open itself to all suffering humanity; especially to those caught in the grip of expanding industrial society, all those who became the object of contemporary social work, that is, the poor, criminal, alcoholic, the abused child, and still others. They were reasons not only to attack exploiters—the mill and mine owners, church, aristocracy, and government—and to form new parties, but also to begin to work toward the redemption of the whole.

This spirit led reformers to wish to redress every wrong, to cure every defect, to end pain itself. Guilt now lay in not opening oneself entirely to humanity, not to join Victor Hugo in his Christlike summons: "Come on to me all of you who tremble and suffer."[49] The new conscience directed man to treat humanity as his family. In the words of Lamartine, "You will be each other's children, fathers, and mothers."[50] The man of the new conscience, if the poet Vigny is to be heeded, will not display his gratitude in ceremony, in thankful commemoration; he will show it by "his time and life transformed in labor"; from him will come "the heritage and the nation."[51]

The intellectuals who served the cause of political reform and revolution spoke in the most universal terms. As the philosophers reduced the meaningful past to those eras that had inspired a humane civilization (Athens, the Roman Republic, the Italian Renaissance, and France of Louis XIV), so these political intellectuals did not hesitate to reduce the future to the emergence of a new order of humanity. They did not hesitate to suggest that the whole past, all its follies, its accomplishments, its inheritance of debt and sin, could be overcome. Humanity for them was not fixed. It contained boundless possibilities of reason, imagination, and will; conscience, accordingly, was to serve these possibilities. Conscience was torn from the past and thrown into the future. The only gratitude they recognized as being legitimate was that which could be repaid by service to the future. The only guilt worthy of having was that which pushed them to make humanity all that it could be.

These new idealizations of nationalists, democrats, and socialists substituted the *corpus mysticum humanitatis* for the *corpus mysticum Christi*.[52] In all things man was joined and obligated to humanity, not just by nature but by historical conditions and possibilities.

These new idealizations of humanity were conceived in terms of nations. Walt Whitman found humanity in American democracy. Adam Mickiewicz found it in suffering Poland. Jules Michelet spoke of the French people as the hero of universal history and he identified their revolution as the second coming of Christ. Italian patriot and perpetual revolutionist-in-exile Giuseppe Mazzini defined nationality as the role assigned by God to each people in the work of humanity. "The nation," Mazzini wrote, "was a confraternity, sharing the same destiny, fulfilling a definite mission, welded into one by intense sentiments of love, devotion and pride. . . . *The life of the people was a life of service, and its highest manifestation was the strenuous fulfillment of duty and self-sacrifice.*"[53] Here nation and conscience were joined.

Saint-Simon, founder of modern sociology, sought to look beyond nations to the formation of a whole new civilization. He brought, to quote Ernest Becker, "the whole Enlightenment to bear on the problems of industrial society after the collapse of the feudal-theological synthesis, and suggested a new rational, thorough-going social reconstruction: a secular community under the supreme guidance of a Science of Man in society."[54] Later, to secure social solidarity, he proposed a "New Christianity" which would provide "a new morality allowing the development of human passions and pursuit of well-being; a religion without any miracles, without any supernatural belief, but which, like Catholicism, would have its own morality and creed which would comprise the supreme requirement of social life: the fastest possible improvement of the lot of the poorest class."[55]

We can choose a few more examples from this period in which the modern progressive conscience took its full form. Georg Wilhelm Hegel built his vision of humanity around the dialectic advance of the human spirit across time. At the end of the historical process, according to Hegel, the human spirit returns to itself. Having passed through and subsumed all existence by its embodiment, the spirit finally returns to itself, conscious, full, and free. Hegel's final man is nothing other than God. Ludwig Feuerbach, like Karl Marx, further radicalized the humanistic ethical impulses in the Hegelian philosophy. In *The Essence of Christianity*, Feuerbach argued that man, when in his minority, attributed to God the powers of being all-knowing, all-just, all-powerful, and all-loving; now, ready to begin his own majority, man must reclaim all these powers from God. Carrying his logic to the heart of Christianity itself, Feuerbach argued that humanity must renounce God to love man:

> Love conquers God. . . . For though there is also a self-interested love among men, still the true human love, which is alone worthy of this name, is that which impels the sacrifice of self to another. Who then is our Saviour and Redeemer? God or Love? Love; for God as God has not saved us, but Love, which transcends the difference between the divine and human personality. *As God has renounced himself out of love, so we, out of love, should renounce God; for if we do not sacrifice God to love, we sacrifice love to God.*[56]

## WE ARE THE PHILOSOPHERS' DREAMS

With these thinkers—Feuerbach, Hegel, Saint-Simon, and others —the philosophers' vision reached its fullness. Faith in humanity replaced faith in God. *The human heart replaced the heart of Christ.* Humanity became the object of its own guilt and gratitude. It served and redeemed itself in time.

These were young, strong, passionate hopes. They were predicated on the total transformation of humanity. The Enlightenment gave large visions, Romanticism provided great passions, the

French Revolution and the Industrial Revolution each in its own way forced dramatic changes and removed all doubt that humanity was its own artificer. The vision of humanity saving itself burst forth repeatedly in the period from 1815 to 1848; and in 1848 it was to be seen in all those glorious revolutions which, even when serving nation and class, remain humanity's most generalized attempt to acquire freedom, equality, and fraternity.[57] These revolutions, which reached from Paris to Palermo, from Frankfurt to Prague, shook the entire old order of the continent, until they were crushed, first in France by reaction, then throughout Eastern Europe by Russian troops, and last in Venice by the armies of a restored Austria. These revolutions, which magnificently and awesomely, yet contradictorily and tragically, displayed the whole horizon of revolutionary forces (from constitutional liberalism and socialism to an array of nationalisms) voiced Europe's highest and most progressive ideas. They expressed a fitting testimony to all those who dreamed the philosophers' dreams, suffered the social romantics' heart, and dared to embody the highest promises of the French and the Industrial Revolutions. They were the work of a new conscience.

The revolutions of 1848 failed in the world of power. Perhaps the dreams they sought to convey were too big for the human heart. After all, it could be asked, how can any individual ever love humanity as he loves himself and those close to him? Is humanity perfected in the collective ideal or by the particular individual? Further, it might be asked, is not the very ideal of perfected humanity dangerous for the human spirit? Might not the individual of such high ideal, when confronted by real humanity, become filled with disgust, turn misanthropic, even give himself over to feeling profoundly superior and able to do what he wants to fellow human beings? Camus in this century and Dostoyevsky in the nineteenth century considered the question of those who preach mass murder in the abstract name of humanity's perfection. Whitman, too, was prophetic when he praised the most general conscience: "The climax of this loftiest range of civilization, rising above all gorgeous shows and results of wealth, intellect, power, and art, as such—above even theology and religious fervor—is to be its development, from the eternal bases, and the fit expression of absolute Conscience, moral soundness, Justice." Yet he cautioned: "Conscience, too isolated from all else, and from emotional nature, may but attain the beauty and purity of glacial, snowy ice."[58]

Perhaps these dreams of the philosophers, if not too big for the human heart, were too sublime for human history, for history is the territory of hungry, selfish, fearful man. It is the place where men and women play their hand at sex, love, and power. It is the kingdom where pain, suffering, and death touch all. How could any dreams harness such powers, or slay such enemies?

There are additional reasons not only why the philosophers' dreams, indeed our highest progressive hopes, failed to be embodied in fact, but why we, in our time, should strive to put them out of our spirit. The world view of the philosophers and their followers, that elite high culture, was shot through with ambiguities, ambivalences, tensions, contradictions, and questions such as: What is the relation between the private and public? Is humanity ultimately material or spiritual, plural or singular, reality or ideal? How are differing views of humanity to be reconciled? On what conditions could, indeed should, one part of humanity fight another part of humanity? With such questions as these unanswered, to accept the philosophers' vision would seem tantamount to fostering chaos.

A whole range of doubts shadow their optimism about history. Their optimistic theodicy has been washed away like a straw in the stream of twentieth-century events. Coupled with the inability to predict history is an additional fact that darkens their beacon, namely posterity. There is no guarantee that humanity will essentially change at all. People indeed may remain as they usually are: more selfish than generous, more pawns than lords of their institutions, and more concerned with the immediate problems of feeling, affection, and livelihood than with the overall causes of mankind. In addition, if there is significant change there is no longer assurance that it will be for the better. If change is brief and quick, might it not be the apocalypse of nuclear war? If it is steady and deepening, might it not be that terrible cultural homogenization described by Roderick Seidenberg?

> The convergent trends of life under the dominance of intelligence will inevitably accelerate the coming of universal organization; and the future condition of man, as we have seen, gives evidence of ever greater stability and fixity, approaching in an asymptotic sense an ultimate state of final crystallization. Nor can we doubt, under this equation of change, that man will in time direct his psychology in extrovert harmony with the established drift of life, eliminating ever more ruthlessly the friction of divergent personalities and tangential

philosophies under the plea of social efficiency and social health. Thus, the meshes of the social sieve are being constantly tightened, so to speak; and the acceleration toward an ever more highly organized condition of man's affairs must in itself become the dominant directive force of society. Under these circumstances the meaning of the individual, and the moral, ethical, and religious relationships arising out of the conception of the person as the fountainhead of spiritual values, will gradually lose definition and become dissipated under the impact of a purely collectivist dispensation. But even more basic, perhaps, in the final long-range perspective of this aspect of man's future estate, is the fact that human consciousness itself will slowly relax its tension and become dissipated.[59]

Further, the philosophers' vision has one especially vulnerable point. It seeks to hold to a spiritual position with what is ultimately a temporal faith. This means it has to try to maintain itself against pain, death, and suffering, all of which cry out for supernatural explanation. It must maintain itself against the immanent mortality it affirms. Progressive humanism has to defend itself against the relativism, utilitarianism, and cynicism that invariably arise when the transcendent is denied. Sorokin insightfully described this problem of immanent ethics when he wrote: "Under such conditions no logic, no philosophy, and no science can invoke any transcendental value to mitigate the struggle and to distinguish the right moral relativism from the wrong, the right means for the pursuit of happiness from the wrong, or to distinguish moral obligation from selfish arbitrariness, and right from might."[60] Even if Sorokin's predictions of an inevitable atomization and self-annihilation, the end of all temporal value systems ("sensate cultures") are not true, humanity's happiness does seem a vague idea, of no certain power or authority, to command the human heart in the arena of history. Its armies, whatever they are, hardly seem invincible to omnipresent forces of fraud, deceit, laziness, power, sensualism, and fanaticism.

Finally, the philosophers' faith, if it is to grow and influence the majority of men and women, must be able to be disseminated from an essentially elite literate culture to the masses at large. How is this possible? What means are pure enough to pass it on, or is it essential to use rude conditioning and indoctrination? Also, how will bitterness, hatred, and defeat be evaded, when invariably (as occurred in 1848) the new vision's search for embodiment will summon against it all the powers of older authority? Also, are there not even more dangerous forces, such as class and nation, that will corrupt the vision to their own ends of power, subjecting the idea of humanity to their own demons? These questions, which all revolve around the matter of how this new vision could be transmitted, are the subject of the next chapter.

Perhaps we should let the philosophers' vision have no place in our conscience; dismiss it as a matter of historical interest, an impulse that moved the minds, reason, and hearts of past generations. Perhaps we should say simply that we are too old for those dreams.

Yet we cannot do this. The philosophers' vision makes the world around us. The institutions that shape our world, even the most hateful and tyrannical, speak the language of humanity's progress. They are conceived and justified as if humanity is rational, as if its improvement and reform are possible. Also the philosophers' dreams are within us. We no longer easily forsake the promise of earthly happiness for ourselves or others. Our fear of death and our practice of medicine testify to that. We do not suffer the inevitability of pain, the flawed, and the defective for the sake of past authority and fate or even the will of God.

So within our conscience the philosophers argue their case, always contesting, often besting, the old man and the Christian in us. And as remote as the ideal of humanity at times seems, we somehow sense that we are one with all humans in these perilous times. Consequently our sympathy for them must be full, our guilt and gratitude in their service, and we cannot deny easily the sacrifice they require. Posterity, humanity's progress, is an imperative way of speaking about our tie to all people of this singular earth. It is the philosophers' words, visions, and cultures that we use to give purpose to all the change we have brought about and to express our responsibility for it.

Thus, in some degree, the philosophers are our conscience—and we are their dreams.

## NOTES

1. For a perceptive discussion of the relationship of conscience and consciousness see "Conscience and Consciousness: Dualism or Unity?" in Edward Engelberg, *The Unknown Distance From Consciousness to Conscience* (Cambridge, Mass., 1972), 8–39.

2. Erich Auerbach, *Mimesis: The Representation of Reality in Western Literature* (Garden City, N.Y., 1957), 9–10.

3. Nikos Kazantzakis, *The Last Temptation of Christ*, trans. P. A. Bien (New York, 1961 [Bantam ed.]), 126. Emphasis is mine.

4. Ibid., 106–7. Emphasis is mine.

5. This description of the Founder of the Order of Visitation is offered in the August 21 feast celebration of her, *St. Andrews Daily Missal* (St. Paul, Minn., 1946), 1408.

6. The teachings of Christ, in great part, can be understood as a conscious defiance of what men take to be the norms of earthly giving and taking. On this point verse after verse comes to mind, but none come as forcefully as those from the Sermon on the Mount: "Blessed are you poor, for yours is the kingdom of God. . . . Woe to you who are rich. . . . To him who strikes you on the cheek, offer the other also; and from him who takes away your cloak do not withhold your coat as well. Give to everyone who begs from you; and of him who takes away your goods to not ask them again. And as you wish that men would do to you, do so to them. If you love those who love you what credit is it to you? For even sinners love those who love them. And if you do good to those who do good to you, what credit is that to you? For even sinners do the same. . . . But love your enemies, and do good, and lend, expecting nothing in return; and your reward will be great, and you will be sons of the Most High; for he is kind to the most ungrateful and the selfish. Be merciful, even as your Father is merciful," *Luke* 6:22–30.

7. For a critical introductory discussion of Nietzsche's ideas of the genesis of conscience see Chapter 4 of my *Ethics, Living or Dead?* (Tuscaloosa, Ala. and Marshall, Minn., 1982), 53–70.

8. Friedrich Nietzsche, *The Genealogy of Morals*, trans. Francis Golffing (New York, 1956), 225. Emphasis is mine.

9. Ibid., 169.

10. Ibid.; Walter Kaufmann, ed., *Basic Writings of Nietzsche* (New York, 1968), 471.

11. Nietzsche, *Geneology of Morals*, 226.

12. Kaufmann, ed., *Basic Writings of Nietzsche*, 200.

13. This quotation of Diderot is used prefatorily to Chapter 4 of Carl Becker's *Heavenly City of the Eighteenth-Century Philosophers* (New Haven, Conn., 1932).

14. Ibid., 102–3.

15. Ibid., 130. Emphasis is mine.

16. Of the vast literature written on man's movement to self-mastery, singularly worth mentioning is Erich Kahler's *Man the Measure* (New York, 1961). Revealing the influences of Hegelian idealism, Kahler there seeks to trace the stages by which man differentiates himself from God, nature, and society and has, despite this era's darkness, "come of age."

Cassirer's works on modern thought in general, and his *The Philosophy of the Enlightenment* (Boston, 1955), in particular, bear the stamp of Kant and are written from the perspective of man's movement to autonomy in knowledge and ethics. A provocative, though not easily readable, inquiry into the problematic character of man as definer of reality is Michel Foucault's *The Order of Things: An Archaeology of the Human Sciences* (New York, 1970).

17. Aside from the near interminable, but yet unconcluded, debate surrounding Max Weber's provocative intellectual interpretation of capitalism, *The Protestant Ethic and the Spirit of Capitalism* (1904–1905, reprint ed., New York, 1950), more recent insights into the material origins of capitalism and the bourgeoisie can be found in Carlo Cipolla, *Before the Industrial Revolution: European Society and Economy, 1000–1700* (New York, 1976); Fernand Braudel, *The Mediterranean and the Mediterranean World in the Age of Philip II* (New York, 1973), and his *Capitalism and Material Life, 1400–1800* (New York, 1973); and Immanuel Wallerstein, *The Modern World System Capitalist Agriculture, The Origins of the European World: Economy in the Sixteenth Century* (New York, 1976).

18. Crane Brinton, *The Portable Age of Reason* (New York, 1956), 20.

19. Aside from classic writings of Marx, Weber, and Twaney, works additionally useful to understand how the bourgeois concept not only involves matters of class and class conflict but modes of Western and world self-understanding and judgment are: Bernard Groethuysen, *Les origines de l'esprit bourgeois en France*, vol. 1 (Paris, 1927); Werner Sombart, *The Quintessence of Capitalism*, M. Epstein, trans. (London, 1915); Nicholas Berdyaev, *Bourgeois Mind* (New York, 1934); as well as my *Mounier and Maritain: A French Catholic Understanding of the Modern World* (University, Ala., 1975).

20. Amintore Fanfani, *Catholicism, Protestantism, and Capitalism* (New York, 1935).

21. For these descriptions see Sombart, *Quintessence of Capitalism*, ed. M. Epstein (1915; reprint ed., New York, 1967), 103–29. For a general examination of death and dying in this period, see Philippe Ariès, *Western Attitudes toward Death from the Middle Ages to Present* (Baltimore, 1975).

22. Elinor Barber, *The Bourgeoisie in the Eighteenth Century* (Princeton, N.J., 1955), 36.

23. One book that is useful to analyze why the emphasis of the supernatural declined in eighteenth century conscience is D. P. Walker's *The Decline of Hell: Seventeenth Century Discussions of Eternal Torment* (Chicago, 1964).

24. Cited in Leslie Stephen, *History of English Thought in the Eighteenth Century*, 2 vols. (1876; reprint ed., London, 1962) I: 393. Emphasis is mine.

25. This summary of Hume's *Natural History of Religion* (1757) was found in Norman Hampson, *The Enlightenment* (Baltimore, 1968), 121-22.

26. This excerpt from Holbach's *Priestly Religion* is cited in Frank Manuel, ed., *The Enlightenment* (Englewood Cliffs, N.J., 1965), 59.

27. In order to survey Voltaire's systematic attack upon Christianity and the supernatural, see his *Dictionnaire philosophique* (1976).

28. Cited in Peter Gay, *Voltaire's Politics* (New York, 1965), 270-71.

29. Élie Halévy, *The Growth of Philosophic Radicalism* (Boston, 1955), 492.

30. Cited in Hannah Arendt, *On Revolution* (New York, 1965), 115.

31. Representative of the new social history is Robert Darnton's fine critical historiographical essay on the Enlightenment: "In Search of the Enlightenment, Recent Attempts to Create a Social History of Ideas," in *Journal of Modern History*, vol. 43 (March 1971), 113-32. Darnton is particularly critical of the literature that seeks to compress the essence of a whole era into the ideas of a few thinkers, "making the history of the Enlightenment a lofty affair."

32. A well done essay dedicated to the modernity of the motto *Sapere Aude* is Carlo Ginzberg's "High and Low: The Theme of Forbidden Knowledge in the Sixteenth and Seventeenth Century," in *Past and Present*, no. 76 (November 1976), 28-41.

33. All Cassirer's works bearing the stamp of Kant trace the progressive development of modern thought from the perspective of man's movement to autonomy in knowledge and ethics.

34. David Hume, *A Treatise of Human Nature* (Baltimore, 1969), 367. Emphasis is mine.

35. Cited in J. D. Campbell, *Adam Smith's Science of Morals* (Totowa, N.J., 1971), 156.

36. Aside from the works by Stephens and Halévy already cited here, useful for a general introduction to eighteenth-century ethics and its use of sympathy and brotherly love are: John Randall, "The Romantic Protest Against Reason," in his *The Making of the Modern World* (New York, 1976), 389-426; Crane Brinton, *A History of Western Morals* (New York, 1959); Abraham Edel, "Right and Good," in his *Dictionary of the History of Ideas* (New York, 1973), 173-86. The new and more earthly character of philanthropy affecting believers and nonbelievers alike interested itself in the abolition of slavery, the education of children, penal reform, and the improvement of social law. For a few works suggestive of this new spirit, see John Neff's discussion of "The Infusion of Charity into Modern Reality" in his *The Cultural Foundations of Industrial Society* (New York, 1960), 91-106; David Brian Davis, *The Problem of Slavery in the Age of Revolution*, 2 vols. (Ithaca, N.Y., 1975); E. P. Thompson, *The Making of the English Working Class* (New York, 1966), esp. 26-54; David Rothman,

"Charity and Correction in Eighteenth Century," in his *The Discovery of the Asylum* (Boston, 1971), 31–56; Michel Foucault, *Madness and Civilization: A History of Insanity in the Age of Reason* (New York, 1973); J. H. Plumb, "The New World of Children in Eighteenth Century England," in *Past and Present*, no. 67 (May 1975), 64–95; Marlene LeGates, "The Cult of Womanhood in Eighteenth Century Thought," in *Eighteenth Century Studies*, vol. 10 (1976), 21–39; and Norman Fiering, "Irresistible Compassion: An Aspect of Eighteenth Century Sympathy and Humanitarianism," in *Journal of the History of Ideas* (April–June 1976), 196–218.

37. Louis Brevold, *The Natural History of Sensibility* (Detroit, Mich., 1962); Robert Mauzi, *L'idée du bonheur dans la litterature et la pensée au XVIIIᵉ siècle* (Paris, 1961); Henri Peyre, *Literature and Sincerity* (New Haven, Conn., 1963).

38. The tombstone of Scottish Enlightenment thinker Adam Ferguson, buried at St. Regulus in St. Andrews, singularly expresses the age's ideal of the good life:

> Professor of Moral Philosophy in the
>     University of Edinburgh
> He was born at Logierait in the County
>     of Perth on the 20th of June 1723
> And Died in this city of Saint Andrews
>     on the 22nd Day of February, 1816,
> Unseduced by the temptations of Pleasure,
>     Power, or Ambition,
> He employed his interval betwixt his
>     childhood and his grave with
> Unostentatious and Steady Perseverance
>     in acquiring and Diffusing knowledge.
> And in the practice of public and
>     domestic virtue to his venerated memory
> This monument is erected by his
>     children.
> That they may record his piety to God
>     and Benevolence to man, and
>     commemorate the
> Eloquence and energy with which he
>     inculcated the precepts of
>     morality
> And prepared the youthful mind for
>     virtuous actions
> But a more imperishable memorial to his
>     genius exists in his philosophical
>     and historical works,

Where classic elegance, strength of
   reasoning and clearness of detail,
Secured the applause of the age in which
   he lived
And will continue to deserve the
   gratitude and command the administration
   of posterity.

39. Cesare Beccaria, *On Crimes and Punishment* (1764; reprint ed., New York, 1965), 9.

40. Ibid., 29.

41. Beccaria, *On Crimes and Punishment*, 32.

42. Ibid., 45.

43. Ibid., 10. Emphasis is mine.

44. An excellent survey of the interrelation between idealism and reform is Franco Venturi's *Utopia and Reform in the Enlightenment* (Cambridge, 1971), 135–36. Also insightful on the growth and reform in this period is James Leith's *The Idea of Art as Propaganda in France 1750–1799* (Toronto, 1965).

45. This piece from Condorcet's *Sketch* is found in Peter Gay, ed., *The Enlightenment: A Comprehensive Anthology* (New York, 1973), 810. Emphasis is mine.

46. Cited in Charles Morazé, *The Triumph of the Middle Masses* (New York, 1968), 194.

47. *Autobiography* (1873; reprint ed., New York, 1961), 83.

48. Aside from the primary writings of Rousseau, Diderot, Goethe, and other representatives of European romanticism, see for an introduction and the controversy surrounding the new value given feelings in human ethics: Irving Babbitt, *Rousseau and Romanticism* (Boston, 1919); Ernst Cassirer, *The Question of Jean Jacques Rousseau* (Bloomington, Ind., 1967); Jacques Maritain, *The Three Reformers: Luther, Descartes, Rousseau* (New York, 1929); and Arnold Hauser, *Rococo, Classicism, Romanticism*, Social History of Art vol. 3 (New York, 1958).

49. Cited in David Evans, *Social Romanticism in France: 1830–1848* (New York, 1966), 37.

50. Cited ibid., 84.

51. Cited ibid., 87.

52. This phrase is used by Eric Voeglin in *From Enlightenment to Revolution* (Durham, N.C., 1975), 10.

53. J. L. Talmon, *Romanticism and Revolt: Europe 1815–1848* (New York, 1967), 116–17. Emphasis is mine.

54. Cited in Ernest Becker, *Structure of Evil* (New York, 1968), 43.

55. Jacques Droz, *Europe Between Revolutions: 1815–1840* (New York, 1967), 70. In his *Prophets of Paris* (New York, 1962), Frank Manuel

remarked: "Comte abandoned the idea and name of God for a love of humanity so general that it led to a total absorption in the Great Being," 309. Manuel concluded that Comte as well as Turgot, Condorcet, Saint-Simon, and Fourier failed "to contemplate the inherently tragic aspects of life itself, beyond the consolation of philosophy and history, that reduced humanity to their philanthropy," 315.

56. Ludwig Feuerbach, *The Essence of Christianity*, trans. George Eliot (New York, 1957), 53. Emphasis is mine.

57. For an insightful and concise treatment of the 1848 Revolutions, see "The Springtime of Peoples" in E. J. Hobsbawn, *The Age of Capital; 1848-1875* (New York, 1975), 9-26.

58. Walt Whitman, *Democratic Vistas*, in *Walt Whitman: Complete Poetry and Selected Prose and Letters*, ed. Emory Holloway (1938; reprint ed., London, 1964), 710-11.

59. Roderick Seidenberg, *Post-Historic Man* (Boston, 1957), 187-88.

60. Pitirim A. Sorokin, *The Crisis of our Age* (New York, 1957), 159-60.

# 3

# The Transmission of the New Conscience from the Philosophers' Ideal to Mass National Sacrifice

Possibly patriotism in this respect was chiefly what Clutton-Brock, the English humanitarian, called "pooled self-esteem." Perhaps as the vitriolic American economist Thorstein Veblen defined it, patriotism was only a "sense of partisan solidarity in respect of prestige." But in the Western culture of the nineteenth and twentieth centuries it afforded for many men a community of feeling in which they could find hope for greater security and happiness. In America the young Daniel Webster affirmed that patriotism produced "an elevation of soul" which lifted men "above the rank of ordinary men. Above fear, above danger [the true patriot] feels that the last end which can happen to any man never comes too soon if he falls in defense of the laws and liberties of his country." If men died, then, in the name of the country, they might feel in the words of Maurice Barrès, "a magnificent sweetness." They might, if the Belgian Cardinal Mercier of World War I were to be believed, by virtue of such an act of perfect love, "wipe out a whole life of sin." Indeed with Kipling's Englishman they might ask: "Who dies, if the country lives?"

Boyd Shafer, *Nationalism, Myth and Reality* (New York, 1955), 180–81.

"When the fatherland is in danger," Danton proclaimed on September 2, 1792, "no one can refuse his service without being declared infamous and a traitor to the fatherland. Pronounce the death penalty

for every citizen who refuses to march, or who directly or indirectly
opposes the measures taken for public safety."
  Hans Kohn, *Nationalism: Its Meaning and History* (New York,
1955), 28.

  L'insurrection est le plus sacré des devoirs.
  *The Section des Sans-Culottes* of the Revolutionary Government,
Sept. 2, 1793, cited in George Rudé, *Ideology and Popular Protest*
(New York, 1980), 114.

  But in general most working-people are non-political and non-meta-
physical in their outlook. The important things in life, so far as they
can see, are other things. They may appear to have views on general
matters—on religion, politics, and so on—but these views usually
prove to be a bundle of largely unexamined and orally-transmitted
tags, enshrining generalizations, prejudices, and half-truths, and
elevated by epigrammatic phrasing into the status of maxims:
  "They're all talk—they've never done a day's work in their lives."
  "Of course, all politics are crooked."
  "Progress always goes on."
  Richard Hoggart, "The Real World of People," *The Uses of
Literacy* (London, 1967), 86–87.

The philosophers and their followers intended the ideal of a self-
fulfilling humanity to become the commanding conscience of the
world. This intention has not yet been realized.

Aside from the tendencies of human nature, reasons for the
ideal's failure to become well-established in the human spirit can be
found in the nature of its transmission, which carried it from the
elite, literate culture of the eighteenth-century philosophers to the
national and popular cultures of the twentieth century. The ideal
had no pure carriers, conductors, or transmitters. Instead, it was
disseminated by all the material forces, sensibilities, and ideologies,
as well as by the events, reforms, and revolutions that made
modern society what it is.

The philosophers' dream was not brought to humanity on the
wings of a descending dove, but was transmitted by vast, universal
forces. These agencies of its transmission included industry, technology, the growing world market, and the new sovereign national
societies with their armies, police, law, schools, public health officials, and growing bureaucracies. The new ideal and the new conscience it formed were, for the majority of mankind, inseparable

from that profound transition from traditional society to modern industrial society.

## CLASS AND NATION,
## TEACHERS OF THE NEW CONSCIENCE

The two most important agencies that carried traditional man into the modern world and gave him a new conscience were class and the nation-state. These two agencies simultaneously, though not always complimentarily and rarely uniformly, constituted for traditional man a new environment, a new consciousness and a new conscience. They were the primary vehicles that carried traditional man from the old world of isolated, rural settlements into modern mass industrial society. They provided him with a sense of the public life and supplied him with rights and obligations in it. In effect, class and nation forced man to redefine himself, and our new conscience came out of the crucible of that redefinition.

Class consciousness in a general sense is the awareness that there are those above us and those below us. This awareness is radically intensified in modern, urban industrial society. All modernizing and centralizing societies give people public identities. These identities always carry, and at times even develop, focus, and intensify class consciousness. By virtue of this identification, and the class consciousness it engenders, conscience in modern society is preoccupied with the matters of employer and employee, owner and worker relations, and answers to the questions: Which class gives and which receives? Which class sacrifices and which benefits? These ethical questions, which by necessity utilize broad social and public definitions of self and society, come into play both in our limited exchanges with public institutions and in our grandest considerations of humanity. The answers we give to these questions, in turn, shape our guilts and gratitudes and define our senses of equity, fair exchange, and justice.

In like manner, we give the nation-state no special technical definition. We do argue, however, that in the last half of the nineteenth century, the nation-state—the most powerful form of human organization ever developed—began to integrate territories, commerce, peoples, cultures, and legal systems into homogeneous societies. During World War I, the homogenization of the spiritual

lives and material forces of national societies reached unprecedented levels as the entire resources of societies were mobilized to
fight a total war. In the interwar years, especially the 1930s, nation-
states made unlimited bids in the form of autarchies and total-
itarianisms to control all aspects of human existence by seeking to
nationalize conscience. At each of these stages of their development, an ever-increasing role played by the nation-states in defining and valuing human life can be perceived.

In one sense class and nation have done the work of spreading
the philosophers' view. Class and nation teach the primacy of the
public order. They increase awareness of human transactions.
They affirm that the human condition essentially can, and should,
be known and improved. Class and nation instruct traditional man
that he is tied to humanity by the fact of mutual influence; that improving the human condition is not only a possibility but a duty.
Mutually they serve the philosophers' ideal and the creation of the
new conscience by subordinating the ethical claims of the past,
whether familial, social, political or theological, to those of the
future. The fundamental transformation they universally effect is
the passage from "folkways" (instinctive or unconscious ways of
satisfying human needs) to "stateways" (the contractual relations
mediated by state institutions).[1] The essential change for conscience
was the passage from a mentality ruled by unconscious traditionalism to that dominated by the spirit of conscious innovation.

In another sense, however, class consciousness and national consciousness are antithetical to the philosophers' dreams and distort
them. Class consciousness divides, instead of joins, humanity.
Gratitude, it counsels, should not cross class lines; guilt is appropriate only when it is felt for one's own kind. Sympathy and
goodwill are owed only to one portion of humanity, whereas the
remainder of mankind is denied all value and, therefore, human
standing. National consciousness also divides humanity. To the
continued horror of the philosophers' followers, humanity has been
sacrificed countless times in this century to bloodthirsty nation-
alistic causes. Nationalism, when fervid, always claims that right is
on its side; conscience loses its equanimity, and justice is thereby
banished.

Indeed, class and national ideologies have distorted the philosophers' ideal and have attacked it with forces darker and crueler
than the philosophers had ever even imagined. This discussion,

however, is not per se to show the defeat of the philosophers' idea, but instead to conduct an ethical analysis of our own conscience and our responsibility to humanity.

## HOW THE OLD MAN HEARD
## THE PHILOSOPHERS' WORDS

Before an examination can be made of class and nation-state as transmitters of the new conscience, the elemental grounds upon which the old man encountered the philosophers' ideal must be identified. The grounds upon which they met were the promise and expectation of happiness. Increasingly, the majority, not just by imitation of its superior classes but also by firsthand experience, came to believe in human happiness, that horizon of human experience reaching from the satisfaction of our most basic needs to the fulfillment of our highest potential. In ever greater numbers and at accelerating rates, the majority accepted earthly happiness as a primary good. With that acceptance came, at least to a degree, a belief in the philosophers' ideal of human progress through human reason, technology, reform, and altruism. As a result, the conscience of the majority was changed.

The promise of happiness, therefore, was one of the conduits through which the old man and the old woman were led out of the traditional world into the modern world. As could only be expected, however, they followed their feet, not their heads. The abstract ideal of universal earthly happiness was incomprehensible to the vast majority of Europe's population, to the 90 percent of the 180 million who, in 1800, still resided in the countryside.[2] They bore a far closer resemblance to their ancestors than they did to their own grandchildren who, in the course of the next few generations, would undergo that great transformation of European society initiated by the Industrial Revolution in England.

To speak of a new world of happiness to that vast majority who comprised traditional, rural Europe was to propose something more bizarre than fairy tales. It was strange enough when they heard ministers speak of the existence of a kingdom of love, justice, peace, and, above all else, no pain. But to be told that all this would be realized on this earth—for and by humanity alone— defies everything they knew, the millenia-long experience of their blood and bones.

Across two centuries the belief that humanity could make its
own happiness captured the imagination and conscience of almost
every Westerner and, by now, has penetrated the spirit of the vast
majority of the peoples of this world. This belief, voiced and unvoiced, came as an inherent part of the forces, institutions, events,
and technologies that so totally transformed the traditional order.
The words progress and happiness, which increasingly became syn-
onymous, appeared in the villages in the form of money, traveling
merchants, written contracts, and new products. The public
school, the military draft, the ubiquitous bureaucrat, the spreading
nets of enmeshing party-patronage politics, as well as news from
children, relatives, and fellow villagers who were doing better
somewhere else were all a part of the new ideal. The words of progress began to be heard everywhere in the countryside. It was as if
they were written on the winds. The countryside, out of both
choice and necessity, was changed as it had not been in the previous five millenia. The European peasant and his way of life were
being transformed forever by the Western cities and industries, and
their new engines of human creation and action. He was experiencing the revolution of modernization which, according to Cyril
Black, brought change "of a scope and intensity that mankind in its
entire history had experienced on only two previous occasions [its
clear emergence a million years ago and its transformation from
primitive to civilized societies, culminating seven thousand years
ago]—and its significance cannot be appreciated except in the context of the entire course of world history."[3]

Modernization's successful penetration of the countryside cannot
be explained simply by pointing to the ruthlessness of the forces
that invaded it. The new way and its conscience triumphed not
because of what it took, but because of what it gave. It answered
the oldest prayer: *"Libera nos a peste, fame, e bello"* ("Deliver us
from plague, hunger, and war").[4] As hunger, famine, and, it
seemed, war were done away with, converts to the new way multiplied. They counted for the first time on having their daily bread,
and they voted for the god who fed them. In effect, the majority
chose the new way because of the happiness it gave, or at least the
promise of it, for their children.

Traditional man and woman chose the future for its possibilities.
In order to escape the toil, filth, coarseness, and tedium of the old
way, they undertook great perilous migrations. They left the old

and chose the new. They gambled life and even family against happiness, regardless of whether it meant no more than a chance for enough to eat, a chance to work, and a modicum of respect.

The transition came easily for none. To venture from countryside to city, from being a peasant to being a member of the bourgeoisie, and to becoming literate, was an awesome journey for the majority.[5] The transformation involved much pain; and they experienced a lot of guilt and shame as they left the old way for the new way. No one could complete this process in one generation. Inside, there were instinctual remnants and moral residues of the old community: old ways of giving and taking, of being thankful. It took several generations for *the transformation of traditional man into modern man* who, in Mircea Eliade's words, *"is a being who proclaims himself a historical being, constituted by the whole history of humanity . . . [and] sees in the history that precedes him a purely human work and more, especially believes that he has the power to continue and perfect it indefinitely."*[6] Above all else, the promise, the belief, the search, the realization, and the expectation of happiness transformed traditional man into modern man.

## HAPPINESS, A CONTRADICTION TO "THE SUFFERING THEORY OF VALUE"

The idea of progress contradicted the fundamental assumption of traditional humanity that good is limited. For traditional humanity, the good was understood to have two essential sources: that which is given and that which is won.

The sources of the good which is given are essentially fourfold. The good given by God includes nature, a person's talents, conditions of birth, and the specific gifts He grants in the form of miracles, large or small. Next is the good that is given by the person of a higher station—the more powerful, rich, knowledgeable, and venerable. Then there is the good of the tangible and intangible gifts that are exchanged by equals. Finally there is the good that comes to one by luck—windfall, fortune, accident, or some other source that is beyond our control. All these gifts, given humanity's precarious position, occasioned gratitude, which is our acknowledgment that what is given is good.

The second source of the good is that which is fought, struggled, and suffered for and won. This notion of good suggests that life, in one form or another, involves the sufferance of pain to bring forth the good.[7] To undergo pain, whether physical or spiritual, is inseparably part of all human abnegation, discipline, and work, as it is the condition of having such virtues as patience, courage, faith, and hope. To put this in a formula, there is no man-made good without suffering. It is this sense that underlies the value traditional man gave to sacrifice.

Traditional man believed that all he possessed that was good was a result of his and his family's labor. The house, the animals, the land, the crops, the church, and the order and security of his family were all won by his, his wife's, their ancestors', and fellow villagers' work. No higher insult could be paid to someone in the old order than to call him lazy, shiftless, or a good-for-nothing, a do-nothing, a *fainéant*: such a person creates no good. What was not given by nature, a lord, or God, the people of the old order knew, was wrought by suffering, by undergoing pain. Man and woman were born, lived, and died with suffering. There can be little surprise that character was measured in the old order by the individual's capacity for suffering. Truth was sought in trial by the infliction of pain, punishment was sought with pain to equal the pain of the crime, and sacrifice, or concentrated pain, was used to make exchanges with higher forces. Nor could there be any surprise that the gift of suffering, especially innocent suffering, was the greatest gift anyone could receive. There could be no doubt, then as now, that all that is human—life, sex, wealth, and so on—has a cost in pain and suffering.

Traditional humanity, therefore, had radically opposite notions of the sources of good. It was either given, entirely free, or it was never free, it always had to be won and had a price in human suffering. This dichotomous view however did not deny traditional humanity's agreement on one essential assumption regarding the good. Regardless of its source, the good was limited.

Nevertheless, traditional humanity did not surrender itself to the proposition that man must accept his lot as it is. At all times in human affairs there is likely to be, to use the words of Barrington Moore, "An undercurrent of grumbling and opposition." The human situation always elicits such accusations as "too little," "too much," "not enough," "the rich should share more." Or "the do-nothing loafers should be set to work, or allowed to starve," "the hoarders should have their goods expropriated," "those who have power should care more about justice and equity."[8] These elemental charges filled early modern history with banditry, spontaneous food riots, and peasant uprisings.[9]

Traditional humanity operated on what can be called a basic moral economy.[10] Its conscience carried a basic human demand for reciprocity, fair exchange, and equity, as well as the right to survive and to be respected. On occasion this essential moral core led the people to express themselves in rebellion.[11] The rebellions, in contrast to modern revolts, were not guided by reasoned criticism, commanding ideologies, or a coordinated sense of strategy. They were like fire in an open field on a windy day. Their rebellions, always voicing the cry of injustice, dealt with elemental matters like an increase in the cost of bread, the loss of the right to forage, or the abridgment of traditional rights and reciprocities upon which survival depended. E. P. Thompson caught the ethical spirit of the preindustrial revolts when he characterized them as "rebellious, but rebellious in defence of custom."[12] Their conscience insisted on the rights of old; the good lay in the restoration of their old ways. Even on occasions when the primitive rebellions grew in size far beyond the small groups moved by moral outrage and the demand for immediate relief, they were not caught up, as modern revolts and revolutions are, with such abstract contemporary notions of justice and new order.

As Ignazio Silone so wonderfully suggested in his *Fontamara* regarding the embattled peasants of southern Italy, it was easier for these traditional rural people, even amidst revolt itself, to recite fatalisms thousands of years old than to believe in revolutionary theories about a new order of human happiness.[13] The peasants throughout the world believed that they were like the animals; they would remain the same throughout time. Their most certain "proof" of this was the belief that it is man who creates the changing city, but it is God who created the unchanging countryside.

Traditional humanity could not think of happiness as man-made and progressive. Its mentality could not grasp this. The world had to be altered in its essential conditions and assumptions to transform that mentality and conceive the new idea of good. It would take the combined realities of the French and Industrial Revolutions to effect a change of that magnitude. In turn, it is these two revolutions that created the modern class and national consciousness and determined our modern conscience.

## CLASS, A NEW MEASURE OF
## SUFFERING AND HAPPINESS

The French Revolution and the Industrial Revolution created the changing, forward-looking public life and, as could only be expected, increased the real and conscious divisions in society. They formed modern society which, in the words of Raymond Aron, is paradoxically "egalitarian in aspiration and hierarchical in organization."[14]

The very origins of the French Revolution are found in the process of how each class in France became conscious of itself. The *Cahiers de doléances*, in which all groups of France set forth their grievances, formed a laundry list of national resentments and affirmed new claims upon society at large.[15] The actual unfolding of the revolution itself created a national public life. It established a law before which all were equal. It abolished feudalism, disestablished the church, and limited, and later destroyed, the monarchy. The national public life, as articulated by the Declaration of the Rights of Man and the early constitutions, postulated a general good and a government and law to which all citizens could look for redress of wrongs, fairness, and the defense of their rights.

In a very real sense the French Revolution declared a new conscience for humanity. The revolution "righted the wrong" denounced by the bourgeoisie. It swept away the First and Second Estates and dismantled the entire feudal, paternal order of the *ancien régime*.[16] The revolution, as Georges Lefebvre indicated, dealt a strong blow against the traditional patriarch and his near absolute power over wife, child, and property. At age twenty-one children were "liberated" and could take control of property. A husband could no longer imprison his wife by *lettres de cachet*, and she now, like her husband, could pursue divorce. "Natural children" were now rehabilitated, and considered legally to belong to the family. If this was not enough to undermine the father's power, he was now required to share his disciplinary authority with a family court.[17] The old man, at the center of the old moral order of gratitude, was no longer, so to speak, king of his own castle.

By terminating all feudal rights, expropriating church land, nationalizing the clergy, and executing the king, revolutionary France destroyed the symbols of the old order of conscience. The old man surely was not dead, but had been weakened considerably. He had been made more vulnerable to the disaffection, resentment, and aggression of those below him. To be old no longer assured respect; indeed, it increasingly occasioned abuse.

In fact, the combination of revolutionary enthusiasm and Romantic sensibilities put a premium on youth, change, and rebellion. For the first time in European history, the *good leaned to the side of the young*.[18] Youth's innocence and potential became the good of the new conscience.

Upon the new revolutionary tablet was inscribed "Liberty, Equality, and Fraternity." *Citizenship in the nation was a new imminent and secular way of being part of the world, part of an all-encompassing social-moral order.* Hereafter men, and to a degree women and children, were to know their rights and obligations, make their demands for justice, equity, and respect and feel guilt and gratitude with regard to the public order. The public good became the first order of existence; the state became the eye of conscience.[19] God, the dead, and their spiritual allies were banished to the cemeteries. Hereafter they were to be revived only on occasion by patriots for service to the nation.

In one sense the revolution was a class matter. It was a bourgeois revolution. The bourgeoisie's definition of the good—that man was worth his activity, work, and self-made wealth, not his inheritance and title—won the revolution. An ethics, which the bourgeoisie spawned over several centuries, triumphed with the revolution.[20]

Such great critics of bourgeois capitalism as Amintore Fanfani, Wiener Sombart, and Max Weber agreed that early modern history witnessed an expanding bourgeoisie carrying out its business transactions despite traditional and moral prohibitions against them.[21] The bourgeoisie's economic successes as a class, though, were not matched by cultural legitimacy and political power. In what proved to be the decisive case of middle eighteenth-century France's *ancien régime*—where patriarchalism, the system of father over family, priest over parish, lord over lord, king over kingdom, still prevailed[22]—a tragic impasse existed between the centralizing government, aristocratic reaction, and the bourgeoisie in ascent.[23] Emmanuel Joseph Sièyes in his famous pamphlet "What is the Third Estate?" argued for the bourgeoisie. He claimed that the Third Estate, not the clergy or aristocracy, was the source of France's wealth, for it comprised the nation's energy, work, and intelligence. He judged the political exclusion of the Third Estate to

be a "social crime." "What is the Third Estate?" he asked. He
answered: "Everything, but an everything shackled and
oppressed." "What would it be without the privileged order," that
indolent and exploitative aristocracy? "Everything, but an
everything free and flourishing."[24]

The French Revolution itself can be said to have embodied
Sièyes's ethical conclusions: "The Third Estate embraces then all
that which belongs to the nation; and all that which is not the Third
Estate, cannot be regarded as being of the nation." The Third Estate
"is the whole."[25] There is no doubt that some of Paris's small shop
owners, guild members, and others who comprised the Third Estate
entered forcefully into the revolution with their demands, some of
the *sans-culottes* even declared "insurrection to be the most sacred
of duties."[26] The great majority of the Third Estate in France and
elsewhere in Europe, however, were still short of power, wealth,
and education to make the revolution's universal claims their own.
The majority of those who lived in isolated rural villages and small
provincial towns continued to exist in the shadows of scarcity, inferiority, and tradition. They lived more by the old man's mentality than by a spirit stimulated by expectation of the new.[27]

For the great majority the claims of the French Revolution only
came alive when the Industrial Revolution gave them more cohesion by making them into a class and giving them a new consciousness.[28] The Industrial Revolution promised a new order of
human giving and taking.[29] It challenged the fundamental idea of
the limited good.[30] It denied the ancient assumption of the inevitability of scarcity—which had been formulated as recently as
1798 by Malthus, who proposed that the population eventually
always outstrips the food supply. The Industrial Revolution,
directly and indirectly, accelerated the colonization of the countryside by economic and political forces. Consequently, the tendency
was for farms to grow larger, for depressed economic regions to
lose further ground to economically developing regions, and this,
coupled with the overall increase of population, made migration
out of the countryside, as unwanted and painful as it was, a matter
not of choice but of necessity. In effect, the Industrial Revolution
caused many the loss of their home, and everything associated with
it.

The dark side of the Industrial Revolution also showed in the
new urban environments, which though often far less miserable

than the stark villages of the countryside the immigrants had left, were bleak, brutal, and degrading. They resisted attempts to maintain the old village culture. They provided the majority with neither steady work nor certain wages. They confronted the new arrivals with overcrowding, unsanitary conditions, alcoholism, prostitution, and so much else that threatened community. It was not uncommon to be cheated out of one's wages, to have one's rent arbitrarily raised, bread adulterated, wine watered, and to be fleeced in countless other ways, and then to have one's complaints ignored or met by a show of police disapproval. Above all else, these new urban dwellers for the first time had to learn to judge an abstract world. Here they were indissolubly tied to strangers whose power, interests, culture, and behavior they didn't understand. They had to learn to live in and to give an order to a new world divided between owner and worker, those who bought labor and those who sold it.

In the new urban environment these powerless immigrants had to recalculate their exchanges and reciprocities as well as alter the fundamental premises of their conscience. These adjustments were required in order to survive and to give meaning to one's new life.

Some semblance of class consciousness dawned almost universally on these urban dwellers as they found themselves in the new, man-made environment in which they were without full political rights and were denied the respect to which they believed all humans were entitled. This class consciousness, of course, developed into the unions of the urban workers.[31] Unions became, so to speak, the churches of this new class consciousness; and a bloody strike, to extend the analogy, was their consecrating sacrament.

In the city, the majority's demand for rights and justice became more abstract. The more personal ties of gratitude and loyalty, though far from diminished, were left to play their primary role in the private world. The public life entailed increasingly calculated transactions involving labor, wages, and profits, business and politics. No amount of personalization by emotional tie, no use of the village understanding of human transactions—though this was forever applied—sufficed to provide conscience with an understanding and a judgment of this new environment. As one's class and status, as well as one's rights, potential, and expectations increasingly were associated with society at large, so too did conscience have to extend itself to the most general considerations about society. This helps us understand why, at least in some general sense, to be modern is to be a social philosopher.

An examination of Marxism is an ideal way to conclude our discussion of class as a transmitter of the new conscience.[32] On the one hand, Marxism's commitment to the philosophers' ideals is absolute. It declares that humanity is its own end. It contends that the entire sphere of the transcendent will become merely a matter of spiritual archaeology when humanity reaches its maturity. On the other hand, Marxism makes all reality absolutely dependent upon class consciousness, class struggle, and class victory.

Although the industrial capitalists as a class have won humanity's battle over scarcity, Marxism defines the proletariat as the embodied good. The proletariat is judged to be the culmination of the good which resides in pure suffering innocence and the hero whose struggle, unlike that of any other social group, will serve not narrow class interests but universal human liberation. The proletariat's struggle is humanity's struggle.

Describing the most elemental demand for fair exchange, the historical-ethical logic of Marxism is that everything has been taken from the proletariat. The proletariat has been emptied of the past; every part of his mentality, tradition, and conscience has been drained. In the Marxian view, he has been left a commodity. Marx described this ethically outrageous condition in his *Wage-Labour and Capital* (1849):

> Labour is the worker's own life-activity. . . . And this life-activity he sells to another person in order to secure the necessary *means of subsistence*. Thus his life-activity is for him only a means to enable him to exist. He works in order to live. He does not ever reckon labour as part of his life, it is rather a *sacrifice of his life*.[33]

Suffering the greatest evils of the capitalist system, the proletariat revolts for all people. Above all others, the proletariat does not need to feel gratitude to any part of the past; his revolution is entirely justified. His justice is humanity's: Once and for all he rights the wrongs of the past. At the same time he liberates industrialism, that new mode of producing wealth which, for the first time in history, has assured human control over nature. In Marx's words, "The proletariat is the complete loss of humanity and thus can only recover itself by a complete redemption of humanity."[34]

The ethical power of Marxism as a philosophy of human transaction and justice in modern society is beyond question. According to Ziyad Husami, a student of Marxism, "Marx's evaluation of capitalist distributive arrangements is overwhelmingly *moral*, not legal."[35] Since the last third of the nineteenth century, Marxism has flourished throughout the developed and the underdeveloped world, inspiring individual intellectuals, forming schools of thinkers, and providing revolutionists and new governments alike with claims to scientific and moral legitimacy. Yet Marxism is not a popular doctrine; instead, it belongs to the secular intellectual's culture. Marxism's redemptive vision of humanity belongs far more to intellectuals who are trained to live by abstractions, than to the majority whose mentality is shaped by more immediate realities.

The Marxian definition of the good as labor, its value and its vindication, will never win the conscience of the majority. For the majority, the good is simply not a political or an historical matter. The good the people have, especially that gained by suffering, is too personal to be subordinated to and compensated by a secular vision of human experience. In simplest terms, the future of all humanity is never in itself equal to comforting any one individual.

Marxism overlooks the power of culture to shape class consciousness and conscience. It particularly ignores the abiding tendency of the inferior class to imitate the superior class. Across the sixteenth, seventeenth, and eighteenth centuries, the bourgeoisie imitated the aristocracy, and throughout the nineteenth century the laborers followed the example of the middle class. According to Marxism, class would entirely dominate culture; and nothing could decisively bridge the division between classes. Traditional and Christian cultures would vanish. The public world, its issues, struggles, and justice, would not only determine the private world but entirely engross it. The workers would choose not only class identity but they would eventually sacrifice their lives for it. Once the revolution has occurred, in Marxian prophecy, the division of labor, the unequal distribution of goods, and the contest over authority would vanish and a stateless community, in which men and women realized themselves in all their potential, would emerge.

None of this has come to pass, for as important as class has proven to be in introducing men and women into the modern world, national society has proven to be still more important. In the West, national society has been unquestionably the most powerful instrument in joining the great majority of men and women to the public order. It has become the fundamental, collective, moral identity of our times. Men and women not only look to the nation-state for justice, but they identify with it, as if it had a personality worthy of gift, loyalty, and sacrifice. Great numbers accept its primary claim to our guilt and gratitude.

National society shaped the conscience of the majority around the reality of the progressive secular world. All national societies promoted the promise of earthly happiness, which may be the ultimate foundation of all democratic nation-states and their "moral currency."

## THE NATION STATE, FIRST GIVER AND TAKER

In prerevolutionary Europe no single country was capable of controlling the energies and the loyalties of the majority. The nation was not yet a moral entity. Nowhere was there a constitution that made everyone an equal under the law, a unifying culture that gave people a shared language, a set of traditions, and common aspirations. In addition, nowhere in Europe, not even in England, was there a clearly articulated national idea of an homogeneous people, whose traditions, interests, and destiny made them members of a single community. Only with the French and Industrial Revolutions and the Napoleonic wars was the national idea formed.

It is ironic that when Marx was formulating his theory that denied the primary power of the state in human affairs, statesmen like Napoleon III, Cavour, and Bismarck showed by example the awesome power of the state. The state, they demonstrated, was not simply a reflector of class, as Marxism would have it, but an instrument of historical creation.

In this period from 1850 to 1870, Western states entered full-scale into the process of nation building.[36] Such diverse but monumental events as the unifications of Italy and Germany and the American Civil War gave evidence that a centralized national society became a condition of survival. It also became apparent in this period that centralization, equality, and democracy were interrelated. Slavery was no longer tolerable in America. Serfdom was no longer acceptable in Europe. Extended suffrage, increasing public education, and the expanding market place invited the majority into national life. The people of Europe were being given a public identity.

By the end of the nineteenth century, a great revolution was underway. Nationalism had become the ethical idiom of competing states.[37] It was no longer a universal language of humanitarianism, as it had been for Mazzini and his generation. Nationalism served imperial purposes abroad. No claim was allowed to stand against the dynamism of the Western industrial societies and their ruthless pursuit of the future. At home, nationalism was pressed into the service of justifying national consolidation. Never before, as Russia and the United States so dramatically illustrated, did states so fully enter into the revolutionary process of integrating the countryside into society.[38] The revolution arrived in the countryside in the form of the school teacher who taught patriotism along with reading, writing, and arithmetic. The military draft was a further element of the new nationalism, which introduced peasants into a world far different from that which they had known in their native villages. The revolution came with every mile of track laid in the country-side. The railroad formed the grid of a new existence. Along the tracks came the city's goods and ways. As never before, cash and the written law measured transactions; gifts, personal sacrifices, exchange, and bartering—the sinew of human relations—received a monetary and a legal equivalent. The tracks, however, did not simply carry the city ways to the countryside. They were also the route out for the peasants' products, sons without land, daughters without a dowry, or families in seach of a better life.

The children of the old man universally were being made into citizens. What D'Azeglio had planned for Italy upon its unification, "We have made Italy, we now must make Italians," was being realized. In France, peasants were being made into Frenchmen; in Germany, peasants were being made into Germans. Throughout Europe national identities were being formed and consciences were being nationalized.[39]

However, in the decades immediately preceding World War I, nationalism didn't command exclusively. In larger industrial cities, which had multiplied five and ten times in less than fifty years from great rural immigration, demands for justice were intensified and politicized as varied classes of society were thrown into contact with one another. Resentment, envy, anger, open class antagonisms, as well as senses of superiority, pity, and fear sprang up as "fellow citizens" encountered one another for the first time. The bourgeoisie thought of their superior place as morally earned and merited. The workers, whose interests could include high spiritual goals like freedom and brotherhood and material benefits like good wages, insurance, shorter hours, and workmen's compensation made respect their first ethical demand. They wanted it to be understood that the inferiority of their material condition was in no sense preordained or in any way proof of their moral inferiority. Inevitably, the workers' sense of what their labors, sacrifices, aspirations, and citizenship entitled them collided with the ruling classes' presumed righteous authority.[40]

The struggle between the worker and the bourgeoisie threatened to be the rock upon which national society would split. As national societies from Spain to Russia and Italy to Norway entered upon the path of economic development, the governments could not escape intervening in the struggles of labor and capital. Almost without exception they took the side of property. Yet, at the same time, governments increasingly tended to expand national suffrage and social benefits to win the support and the gratitude of the many.

By the eve of the First World War, the national ideal had won out in the West. For worker, peasant, teacher, and businessman alike, the nation had become the commanding identity of the public life. Internationalism was in retreat.[41] Protectionism dominated world economics. An arms race was in full swing. Intensifying military alliances and a succession of diplomatic incidents from 1900 onward gave an air of inevitability to the Great War.

Against these forces, the advocates of internationalism were helpless. Most pathetic of all were the intellectual leaders of European socialism. In many senses, they were the true heirs of the philosophers. The heroic cause they believed in was that of universal justice. They knew, bitterly, that the struggle which loomed ahead would set worker against worker. However, they had no means of comprehending in advance how much fraternal blood would be shed.[42]

The workers had been nationalized and they would shed their blood profusely for the nation. That blood would join them more profoundly to the nation. The battlefield was a kind of altar, and their sacrifice upon it would bond them to one of the oldest communities of all: *comrades at arms.*

## THE GREAT WAR, THE BLOODY SACRIFICE

Around the bloody sacrifice of war, national societies unleashed, organized, and directed—by word and deed, myth, propaganda, and police—great conformities of resentment, hatred, and anger. Consecrated by the deaths and injuries of millions, those dark, elemental emotions were transformed into forces that have been inimical ever since to the philosophers' conscience.

The Great War taught cruel truths, truths that contradicted all progressive hopes. Humanity had not transcended war as a means of settling human differences. Reason and philanthropy, though powerful in their influence upon mind and institutions, did not command states, especially states at war. As the Great War developed into a prolonged, violent encounter of wounded armies, only victory mattered. Victory alone promised to give a meaning, however illusionary, to the bloody sacrifice.

All was systematized for victory.[43] Conscience itself was conscripted, and dissent was universally denied legitimacy. Resistance to the war effort was interpreted to be the first treacherous step on the road to disloyalty. Even England, with the strongest tradition of civil liberties, immediately passed upon its entrance into the war an Aliens Registration Act. Parliament instituted an Official Press Bureau and eventually enacted the Defense of the Realm Act, that gave the representative of Majesty in Council the power to secure the public safety.[44] Neither traditional nor constitutional rights were allowed to interfere with what Asquith called "fighting for the principles whose maintenance is vital to the civilized world."[45]

The other side of the conscription of conscience during World War I was the mobilization of minds and enthusiasms.[46] Young men had to be induced to sacrifice their lives for the nation. They, and all who loved and cared about them, had to find in the national good a reason for the offering of young innocence. All sacrifice, in effect, had to be given a moral justification. Words, rhetoric, songs, and propaganda generously furnished by ministers, politicians, and professors were used not just to set banners a-waving and armies a-marching, but to harness all hearts and energies to the cause of the nation at war. Guilt and gratitude were "needed tools" of government. Indeed, one English war-time poster pictured a tender-eyed young girl asking every passerby, "Daddy, what did you do in the war?"

The war brought elemental laws of human exchange into play. The more the state asked from the people, the more the state had to promise to give them in return. Gifts call for gratitude; investment demands a return. The sacrifice of human life demanded the highest return of all. The "suffering theory of value" was also at work here. As the war dragged on, the sacrifice of men, materials, ideals, and even hope itself was greater and accordingly the debt owed to the people was ever higher. In a sense, it can be said that the twentieth century was given over in sprritual mortgage during the First World War. Each state had accumulated a terrible debt of innocent blood to repay.

An elemental exchange occurred at the heart of the war. The more people paid for the war with their sufferings—their losses and disillusionments—the more they came to feel that they belonged to the nation and the nation belonged to them.[47] The war was a savage crucible. In it people and nation were fused together. The war was a bloody baptismal rite.

The war for the entire society—soldiers, workers, peasants, teachers, and merchants alike—was a rite of passage into national life. In Europe and America entire new groups enrolled themselves for the first time in the national ethical community. The national unity which teachers, political parties, and railroad tracks began, the war completed. Nationality became universally a part of conscience in the West.

With the war, one of the oldest laws of ethical discourse took hold of twentieth-century public life: *Blood demands blood.*

The war put military sacrifice at the center of all national life. All participated in the sacrifice. The veterans—the legionnaires—became the high priests of this new church. The war called forth millions of "soldier-Christs." These martyr-founders, these fallen soldiers, became more powerful in their deaths than they were during their lives. Cults, shrines, and memorials were erected in their names, vengeance was called for, wars were justified, and new armies were set to marching. Official cults of gratitude were formed.

The war was a blood rite. It was proclaimed by some to be the holiest national sacrament. It established new elders. The conception of the nation at war was now more potent and influential than the philosophers' ideal of humanity's progress which, in the aftermath of four years of carnage, appeared a sheer abstraction.

Pacifists cautioned against the cruel gods of war. They cautioned that killing deadens the conscience, that one goes blood-blind—as butchers supposedly do—from too much killing. They said that the demands of wronged innocence can never be satiated, that blood in the mouth of power causes great death. They tried to enlighten. But these pacific voices, echoing the philosophers, were unheard against the blood-thirsty sirens of the heroic dead.

## FASCISM, BLOODY WAYS TO REMAIN LOYAL TO THE BLOODY WAR

Out of the First World War came the new ethics of national sacrifice, and out of that ethics came fascism, the greatest enemy of the philosophers and their conscience. No doubt the war's mobilization, regimentation, and fervid nationalism set the stage for fascism which sprang up in various forms throughout Europe.[48] The war prepared the actors and audience alike for the dramatic, pathetic plots as well as the insane monologues of fascism. It created an atmosphere in which callow, cruel people could set forth their demands upon society at large. In his "Second Coming," Yeats wrote of this climate, in which the philosophers' disciples lost their bid to command Western conscience, as a time when a "blood dimmed tide is loosed," and "innocence is drowned."[49]

Fascism cynically traded in the blood of the war. It simplified public discourse; its rhetoric was of bloodshed, loyalty betrayed, national honor lost and avenged. It was *a religion of soldier and nation* around whom was erected *a cult of gratitude.*

Fascists were pledged not to forget the war. Indeed they could not do otherwise, for it was the fundamental experience by which they knew and valued themselves. A member of the German *Freikorps* (an active interwar paramilitary group composed of radical right-wing veterans, students, and others) expressed his abiding loyalty to the war in these terms: "People told us that the war was over. That made us laugh. We ourselves are the war. Its flame burns strongly in us. It envelopes our whole being and fascinates us with the enticing urge to destroy."[50]

In the postwar period a collision became inevitable between the consciences of the veterans of the war and the veterans of labor.[51] The two groups simply valued the world differently. They believed in different sacrifices and heroes, and they had different loyalties, cults, and communities. Labor's explanations of World War I denied it all value. The war, for labor, served only the interest of the ruling elite. It was not a matter of valor, heroism, or sacrifice. It was a gigantic death mill. This view, for the fascists in particular and the entire nationalist right in general, was a sacrilege. It desecrated the highest national sacrament. It impugned the ethical core of the national community. The struggle between fascism and labor, which marked the entire period from 1919, through the Spanish Civil War, and until the Second World War itself, was a battle of ethical world views. It was a contest for conscience, with labor carrying the philosophers' ideal and fascism articulating the violent nationalism created around the suffering of the war.

Veterans, who for the most part came from the toiling and laboring classes, had to choose upon their return home between the languages of labor and nationalism. They were confronted with two radically opposing conceptions of society's giving and taking. The soldiers who returned home—expecting a show of gratitude but finding themselves without work, their families in misery, and their neighborhoods and cities in disorder—were often filled with rage. It was the combination of this rage and their demands for immediate justice that made them dedicated fascists. Salvemini wrote of them:

> These "Fascists of the first hour," as afterwards they were termed, were convinced that the country, which owed victory to them, had the duty of providing for them now, not in proportion to their ability to work, but in proportion to their glory. The war was the sole foundation of their claims. The acts of military valor which they had performed—or boasted they had performed—were their titles of nobility. They hated the Socialists and all those who had opposed the war, as they would have hated a personal enemy who was trying to deprive them of all their honors and rights. The Socialists, furthermore, were the leaders of the workers, who were then earning high wages, while they—the "saviors of the Fatherland"—were unable to find employment.[52]

Hitler's and Mussolini's National Socialisms appealed to the consciences of those resentful veterans who returned from the front to find their idealized society torn by inflation and scarcity and on the verge of insurrection. They were revolted by what they experienced. One returning soldier who joined the Nazis clearly expressed his outrage:

Troops were once again returning to the Fatherland, yet a disgusting sight met their eyes. Beardless boys, dissolute deserters and whores tore off the shoulder bands of our front-line fighters and spat upon their field gray uniforms. At the same time they muttered something about *liberty, equality* and *fraternity.* Poor, deluded people! Was this liberty and fraternity? People who never saw a battlefield, who had never heard the whine of a bullet, openly insulted men who through four and a half years had defied the world in arms, who had risked their lives in innumerable battles, with the sole desire to guard the country against this horror. For the first time, I began to feel a burning hatred for this human scum that trod everything pure and clean underfoot.[53]

Hitler's appeal to the members of the *Freikorps* as well as the *Stalhelm*, the largest German veteran organization, was his fervent nationalism.[54] Further binding Hitler and the military veteran was the Nazi party's use of its own armed guard, the S.A. (The purpose of the S.A., in the words of one comrade, "was to dominate the street," and "the street," another comrade said, "was our trench.")[55]

The battle between fascism and labor began immediately after the First World War. Society's transactions were severely disrupted and disordered. Strikes and protests abounded, as did paramilitary groups. Communism, inspired by the Russian Revolution, spread. Successful revolutions in Russia and Hungary, and an abortive December 1918 attempt in Germany itself, caused many to hope for the possibility of a new world of justice, brotherhood, and internationalism. Yet others were filled with terror at the possibility of communist revolution. To them it meant barbarism, a new reign of terror, the loss of property and freedom, the destruction of the national community. Fears flew like sparks from a fire as Europe seemed to verge on anarchy. The first country to succumb to fascism was Italy, which emerged from the war having incurred monumental human and economic losses without any compensation for its part in the victory or any means for its renewal.[56]

Once in power, fascism demanded total support from society as a whole and attacked all opposition. The individual's struggle, Mussolini contended, could only have a true meaning when it was in harmony with the nation: For in the nation,

individuals and generations are bound together by moral law, with common traditions and a mission which, suppressing the instinct for

life closed in a brief circle of pleasure, builds up higher life, founded
on duty, a life free from the limitations of time and space, in which
*the individual by self-sacrifice, the renunciation of self-interest, by
death itself can achieve that purely spiritual existence in which his
value as a man consists.*[57]

Fascism denied all conscience, except as it served the nation.
Mussolini wrote of the fascist state: "It is all-embracing; outside of
it no human or spiritual values can exist, much less have value."[58]
"Fascism, in short," he continued, "is not only a lawgiver and
founder of institutions, but an educator and a promoter of the
spiritual life. It aims at the refashioning not only the forms of life
but their content—man, his character, and his faith."[59]

At the same time, on a scale and with an intensity beyond anything Mussolini ever conceived, Hitler was developing National
Socialism, the German version of fascism. National Socialism attacked conscience and all its sources of independence. It tolerated
no institutional, social, or spiritual opposition to the State. Law,
parties, churches, professions, labor organizations, intellectual
traditions, press, institutions, the market were all molded in ac-
cordance with the party's ever-changing ends. No spiritual independence of mind, art, or culture was permitted. (The Nazis, for
example, raided the theatres where *All Quiet on the Western Front*
was showing. They obviously wouldn't tolerate the pacifist thesis
that Germany's youth had been senselessly sacrificed in the war for
the good of the fatherland.[60]) "The prolific German mother," to cite
another example of Nazi intervention into culture, was declared by
official propaganda "to be accorded the same place of honor in the
German Volk community as the combat soldier, since she risks her
body and gives her life for the people and the Fatherland as much as
the combat soldier does in the roar and thunder of battle."[61]

Their intention was to create a "national socialist" culture.[62]
They even went as far as to accuse the German people of having
forgotten how to hate. "Virile hate had been replaced by feminine
lamentation," proclaimed Nazi ideology. "Fanatical love and
hate—there kindles flames of freedom. . . . Only passion gives
knowledge and creates wisdom."[63] Their aim was to have conscience belong to the state.

Nazism's mixture of the expedient and the mythological was
another cruel legacy of the First World War. High culture, so important for the philosophers' ideas of reason and humanity, had

been breached at all levels by violent activisms. The most nihilistic forms of philosophy—the types we might identify with Fichte, Schopenhauer, and Nietzsche—were made integral parts of Nazi ideology. Progress and its allies, reason, science, freedom, and democracy, were directly attacked. After four years of an insane war there was no longer any prima facie basis to defend traditional high Western culture. "What the war did was to destroy the ties of German culture, both to the usable past and to the congenial foreign environment, for all but the most determined cosmopolitans," explained one German historian.[64] Humanist culture was under full attack, not just in Germany but throughout Europe. Nothing seemed to stand irreproachably above the battlefield of ideology and propaganda; everything, including philosophy, religion, and art, was understood to be a matter of combat.

Culture and conscience for the Nazi leaders were considered to be battlefields upon which they had to carry out their struggle for total dominance.[65] Their goal was to have the nation, the state, the party, and the leader understood to be the source of all power, creation, and gifts. Conscience was allowed no basis for objection, no other object of loyalty, no recesses for retreat. Revealing this, a Nazi official wrote: "There are no more private citizens." Another said: "The only person who is still a private individual is somebody asleep."[66]

At the heart of this nihilism was Adolph Hitler, the archetypical expression of the degradation of twentieth-century conscience, and the living antithesis of the Christians' and the philosphers' ideals. He was a person devoid of gratitude. Indeed, he was a person of gratitude's opposite, resentment. It was as if he had received only insults, never gifts, throughout his life. Charity, sympathy, love, humanity, tolerance—none were in that thankless, angry spirit.

Of the whole breed of twentieth-century politicians of resentment and hatred, Hitler was master. Hitler—an artiste déclassé, a postcard painter, a nobody until the war rescued him with its glory from his poverty and ignominy—suffered Germany's betrayal as his own. He spoke with the furor of wronged innocence, the anger of a betrayed soldier.

His *Mein Kampf* voiced his resentment. It is a spiteful, hateful, vengeful work composed of calculated scheming and uncontrolled ravings. Its theme is the story of "a good man and pure people" caught in "an evil, deceiving, and humiliating world." "If at the start [of World War I] we had held under poison gas twelve or fifteen thousand of these Hebrew subverters of our people," he wrote, "then the sacrifice of a million Germans at the front would not have been in vain."[67] *Mein Kampf* nursed grudges. It called to account those "liberal, humanitarian makers" (those disciples of the philosophers) of the Treaty of Versailles whose "altruism" led them to amputate Germany for the sake of France's revenge. It articulated "the stab in the back" myth, which was first used to denounce the civilian government that signed an armistice based on Germany's unconditional surrender while it still had an undefeated army in the field. Then it was used to indict the Weimar government for signing and complying with the humiliating terms of the Treaty of Versailles. Eventually "the stab in the back" myth came to mean how the Jews of Germany conspired against that country for the international causes of Zionism, capitalism, and communism.

George Orwell's portrait of Hitler seemed to grasp his inner essence as the man of resentment: "It is a pathetic doglike face, the face of a man suffering under intolerable wrongs." "He is the martyr, the victim, Prometheus chained to the rock, the self-sacrificing hero who fights single-handed against impossible odds."[68] Hitler raged against everything that had once humiliated him and he spoke for the whole lower-middle class and other Germans who were filled with rancor and hostility. Hitler took himself to be the prophet of a biological order from which conscience would be banished forever. He would use all the power of the public realm to destroy the interior ethical foundation of the person. "Providence has ordained me," Hitler reasoned, "that I should be the greatest liberator of humanity. *I am freeing man from the restraints of an intelligence that has taken charge; from the dirty and degrading self-mortification of an illusion called conscience and morality, and from the demands of a freedom and personal independence which only a very few can bear.*"[69]

Hitler's drive seemed to be the absolute purification of existence. There would exist, if he were to have his way, only a perfectly homogeneous community: *Ein Volk, Ein Reich, Ein Fuhrer!* (One People, One Country, One Leader!). This Nazi chant sought to conjure the diverse peoples of a modern society back into a primitive tribe.

Hitler's National Socialism attacked Western values of peace, reason, and humanity. In their place it proposed an extreme Social

Darwinism which, on the international level conceived all states to be locked in a life-and-death struggle, and at the domestic level supported the most vicious principles. One Nazi expressed some of their new principles in these terms: "not to use force against the enemies of the regime, not to smash their windows, not to destroy them—these were evils."[70] Novelist Franz Werfel neatly characterized this upside-down conscience when he wrote of Nazi Germany, *"Not the murderer but the murdered person is guilty."*[71]

Perhaps we seriously err if we do not recognize in ouselves, at least in some measure, the identical quest for a homogeneous community. A constant temptation of twentieth-century modern consciousness is the wish to return to simplicity. The desire to abolish all but that which comforts us is strong in human nature.

## ANOTHER BLOODY SACRIFICE

War was the only transaction that remained with Nazi Germany. Everything had to be asked once more in sacrifice for a second national all-or-nothing struggle. War was again the bloody sacrament of the nation.

The spiritual consequences of a war for conscience are too many to count, too profound to fathom. We still live in their shadows. Yet certain consequences are clear. The nation-state was uncontestably the most powerful form of human organization. At one and the same time, it defined, engulfed, and divided secular humanity. Its government, institutions, bureaucracies, ideologies, and official culture formed the public life; and nowhere were men and women any longer entirely free of it. Their guilts and gratitudes became entangled with the public life. Universally the nation-state real and supported, or the nation-state imagined and struggled for, was looked to for *earthly* happiness. By what now could be considered to be a worldwide imperative, the nation-state was expected to secure justice, material plenty, a fair distribution of goods, and equality of opportunity, not to mention a constitution of rights and responsibilities drawn up in accord with the dignity of each human being.

Culminating the process of a century and a half, the Second World War marked the universal triumph of the principle of nation-state. As everything in society was given a political equivalent, so conscience itself was increasingly taken up with public considerations. To suggest this by exaggeration, the universe was politicized; and conscience, in some corresponding degree, was nationalized.

The paradox cannot be overlooked. Despite the tragedies of war and revolution, as well as other injustices so intimately associated with nation-states, the great majority look to their own country with the expectation of greater happiness and a better future. Nation-states, which have imposed, and no doubt will continue to impose, such bloody demands upon their peoples, set the horizons of the contemporary search for the good.

If one paradox is that the nation-state, the transmitter of the philosophers' ideal of humanity as its own fulfillment, has proved to be savagely antihuman at times, there is an additional paradox for the conscience of citizens of Western democratic societies. In war we must fight as our enemies fight. There is no choice. Our nationalism, mobilization, use of weapons, and sacrifices cannot be limited. We, as paradoxical as it may be, are led to be savage in the defense of reason and efficient in the destruction of others, for the cause of humanity. This paradox (embodied for Americans in their use of the atomic bomb) cynically eats at conscience.

We have discovered in the twentieth century that even the good must use evil power. The philosophers' dreams of humanity are transmitted by class and by nation-state. Both are terrifying teachers of division and powerful engines of violence. The nation-state, in particular, has made us the secular humans we are. Yet its power forces us to ask: Are we fortunate survivors, or victims kept hostage for future sacrifice?

Once having tasted this bitterness, we might wish to forsake the philosphers' ideal and the public life altogether. We might wish to save our conscience for, and restrict our guilt and gratitude to, family, friend, and God. But power intrudes, and we neither escape the realities of class and nation nor totally dismiss the ideals of humanity. So in a conscience composed of the voices of peasant, Christian, and philosopher, we must suffer our givings and takings in a world that moves between great promise and terrible threat.

## NOTES

1. The distinction between "folkways" and "stateways," as the essence of the opposition of traditional versus modern worlds, belongs to William

Graham Sumner's *Folkways* (Boston, 1906). For this distinction as well as several classic attempts to distinguish traditional and modern mentalities, see Brian Berry's *The Human Consequences of Urbanization* (New York, 1973), esp. 7–15.

2. Europe's population was estimated to be 188 million in 1800 and 401 million in 1900, according to Peter Stearn, *European Society in Upheaval* (New York, 1967), 58. In 1800, approximately 80 percent of France's population and 95 percent of Russia's were rural, ibid., 3. Specifically for France, Robert Mandrou says that in the seventeenth century less than a million of its 14 million inhabitants lived in cities, and on the eve of the French Revolution 22 to 23 percent of its 25 million inhabitants could be classified as rural, *La France aux XVII^e et XVIII^e siècles* (Paris, 1974), 76–77. For a brief but illuminating study of life in pre-Revolutionary France, see Pierre Goubert, *The Ancien Régime, French Society, 1600–1750*, (New York, 1973).

3. Black, *The Dynamics of Modernization*, (New York, 1966), 1–2.

4. This traditional prayer of the eighteenth century is found in Robert Mandrou's *La France aux XVII et XVIII^e siècles* (Paris, 1967), 98. For a provocative introduction to the faiths of the ancien régime, see Robert Mandrou's *De la culture française aux 17^e et 18^e siècles* (Paris, 1964).

5. Two useful guides to the migration of nineteenth-century European peoples are Philip Taylor's *The Distant Magnet: European Emigration to the U.S.A.* (New York, 1971); and Frank Thistlewaite's "Migration From Europe Overseas in the Nineteenth and Twentieth Centuries," in *XI^e Congres International des Sciences Historiques, Stockholm 1960, Rapports, 5: Histoire Contemporaine* (Stockholm, 1960), 32–60.

6. Mircea Eliade, *Rites and Symbols of Initiation*, trans. William R. Trask (New York, 1968), xi.

7. I intend, in a forthcoming manuscript tentatively entitled "A History of Pain and A Suffering Theory of Value," to define and contrast the ethics of traditional and modern mentalities in relation to the matters of pain and suffering.

8. Barrington Moore, *Injustice: The Social Basis of Obedience and Revolt* (White Plains, N.Y., 1978), 47. See my review of this work, *World View* (April 1979), 53–55.

9. For an introduction to the growing body of literature concerning the mentality of the old order and the character of its revolts, see George Rudé's *Ideology and Popular Protest* (New York, 1980), which I reviewed for a forthcoming issue of *World View*. Also worth noting are Moore's *Injustice*; E. J. Hobsbawm's *Primitive Rebels: Studies in Archaic Forms of Social Movement in the 19th and 20th Centuries* (New York, 1959); E. P. Thompson's "Eighteenth-Century English Society: Class Struggle Without Class," in *Social History*, vol. 3, no. 2 (May 1978), 137–65, and his "The Moral Economy of the English Crowd of the Eighteenth Century," in *Past*

and Present 50 (May 1971): 76–136; Michel Vovelle's "Le tournant des men-
talités en France 1750–1789: la sensibilité pré-revolutionnaire," in Social
History (May 1977), 605–29; Robert Darnton's "The History of
Mentalités," in his Structure, Consciousness and History (Cambridge,
Mass., 1978), 106–36; and Le Roy Ladurie's Carnival in Romans (New
York, 1979). Also see footnote 11 in this chapter.

10. The idea of a moral economy is taken from Thompson's "The Moral
Economy of the English Crowd." It included not only a demand for price
but also justice in all social and economic dealings that affected the people's
well-being.

11. For a start on the subject of what motivated the preindustrial crowd
in the countryside and city, see, for an introduction, such classics as
Hobsbawm's Primitive Rebels; and Rudé's The Crowd in History:
1730–1848 (New York, 1964). For more theoretical considerations of
peasants in rebellion, see Barrington Moore, Social Origins of Dictatorship
and Democracy: Lord and Peasant in the Making of the Modern World
(Boston, 1966); and Eric Wolf, Peasant Wars of the Twentieth Century
(New York, 1969).

12. Thompson is cited in Rudé, Ideologies and Popular Protest, 144.

13. Ignazio Silone, Fontamara (Zurich, 1933; 3rd ed., Milan, 1971).

14. Progress and Disillusion (Garden City, N.Y., 1968), xvi.

15. For a short overview of the Cahiers, see Georges Lefebvre, The
Coming of the French Revolution (Princeton, N.J., 1947), 62–65.

16. For a classic study of the administrative centralization of the ancien
régime, see Alexis De Tocqueville's, The Old Regime and the French
Revolution (1856; reprint ed., Garden City, N.J., 1955). For one study of
the resurgence of the nobility's power in the eighteenth century, see
Franklin Ford, Robe and Sword: The Regrouping of the French Aristocracy
After Louis XIV (New York, 1965). For a study of Western political theory,
especially in early modern England, as it was developed around the
dominance of the father as the head of the family, see Gordon Schochet,
Patriarchalism in Political Thought: The Authoritarian Father and Political
Speculation and Attitudes Especially in Seventeenth-Century England
(New York, 1975). The awesome social and political conflicts in which
France was trapped upon the eve of the revolution are clearly explored by
de Tocqueville in The Old Regime; George Lefebvre in The Coming of the
French Revolution; and R. R. Palmer in his two-volume Age of Democratic
Revolution (Princeton, N.J., 1959–1964).

17. Georges Lefebvre, The French Revolution from 1793 to 1799 (New
York, 1964), 266.

18. In his recent Growing Old in America (New York, 1978), David
Fischer has provocatively traced how culture in this era shifted in favor of
the new and the youthful. See especially Chapter 2, "The Revolution in
Age Relations, 1770–1820," 77–112.

19. If any one painting expresses the public order's *new power* over conscience it is Jeurat de Bertray's *Allegory of the Revolution*. Of particular interest, in considering the new inner order brought by the public world, is Raymond Firth, *Symbols: Public and Private* (New York, 1973). Also of use for understanding artists as the conscience of the public world is Ralph E. Shikes, *The Indignant Eye* (Boston, 1969).

20. See Chapter 2, footnotes 17 and 19.

21. Amintore Fanfani, *Catholicism, Protestantism, and Capitalism* (New York, 1935), 22.

22. Thompson attacks paternalism as a term that is vague and laden with nostalgia, implying human warmth and a mutually assenting relationship. He writes: "Paternalism as myth or as ideology is nearly always backward-looking. . . . It has considerably less historical specificity than such terms as feudalism or capitalism; it tends to offer a model of the social order as it is seen from above; . . . it confuses the actual and ideal," "Eighteenth-Century English Society," 135. For a more positive assessment of the community of the old order and its paternalism, see Peter Laslett, *The World We Have Lost* (New York, 1965).

23. Elinor Barber, *The Bourgeoisie in the Eighteenth Century* (Princeton, N.J., 1955), 36.

24. Cited in Eugen Weber, *The Western Tradition: From the Enlightenment to the Present*, third ed. (Lexington, Mass., 1972), 585.

25. Ibid., 586.

26. Rudé, *Ideology and Popular Protest*, 114. "The *sans-culottes*," Moore noted, "directed much of the parasitic upper class in the popular mind, one without any of the redeeming features of the paternalist systems," *Injustice*, 42. Also very useful for understanding the elemental issues of fairness and resentment at play in the Revolution is Richard Cobb, *The Police and People: French Popular Protest 1789-1820* (New York, 1970); Rudé, *The Crowd in History*, 93-134.

27. For Marxist historian E. P. Thompson, the 1790s marked the final decade in which traditional culture no longer held and the old paternalism and the gentry's cultural hegemony gave way. Thereafter, he wrote, "We move out of the eighteenth century field-of-force and enter a period in which there is a structural reordering of class relations and of ideology. It is possible, for the first time, to analyze the historical process in terms of nineteenth century notations of class," in "Eighteenth-Century English Society," 165.

28. For an excellent collection of historical essays dedicated to the formation of class consciousness, see John Merriman, ed., *Consciousness and Class Experience in Nineteenth Century Europe* (New York, 1979). For two classic theoretical considerations of class and class consciousness, see Karl Marx, *The Eighteenth Brumaire of Louis Bonaparte* (Moscow, 1963); and Max Weber, "Class, Status, Party," *From Max Weber* (New York, 1958),

180–95. Also worth seeing for the formation of class and class consciousness is E. P. Thompson's *The Making of the English Working Class* (New York, 1966); and Peter McPhee's "Popular Culture, Symbolism and Rural Radicalism in Nineteenth-Century France," in *Journal of Peasant Studies*, vol. 5, no. 2 (January, 1978), 238–53. For two works that offer empirical inquiries into the American situation and the formation and limits of class consciousness, see Stephan Thernstrom's *Poverty and Progress: Social Mobility in a Nineteenth Century City* (Cambridge, Mass., 1964); and Alan Dawley's *Class and Community: The Industrial Revolution in Lynn* (Cambridge, Mass., 1976).

29. Carlo Cipolla, *Before the Industrial Revolution: European Society and Economy, 1000–1700* (New York, 1976), 276.

30. For a brief discussion of the interrelation of the new philosophy of prosperity and material progress, so visibly embodied in the Crystal Palace, see Chapter 3, "The Philosophy of Prosperity and its Critics," and Chapter 4, "The Culture of Prosperity and its Critics," in W. E. Mosse, *Liberal Europe: The Age of Bourgeois Realism, 1848–1875* (London, 1974), 41–80.

31. Max Weber wrote: "Thus every class may be the carrier of any one of the possibly innumerable forms of 'class action,' but this is not necessarily so. In any case, a class does not in itself constitute a community. To treat 'class' conceptually as having the same value as 'community' leads to distortion," in "Class, Status, Party," 184.

32. One useful historicist approach to Marx's thought is offered by George Lichtheim, *Marxism: An Historical and Critical Study* (New York, 1961). For the education and formation of Marx, see Karl Löwith, *From Hegel to Nietzsche: The Revolution in Nineteenth-Century Thought* (New York, 1964); Sidney Hook, *From Hegel to Marx* (Ann Arbor, Mich., 1962); Jean Hyppolite, *Studies on Marx and Hegel* (New York, 1969); Shlomo Avineri, *The Social and Political Thought of Karl Marx* (Cambridge, 1968); Ziyad I. Husami, "Marx on Distributive Justice," in his *Marx: Justice and History* (Princeton, N.J., 1980), 42–79. A convenient collection of the young Marx's writing is Loyd Easton and Kurt Guddat, eds., *The Writings of the Young Marx on Philosophy and Society* (Garden City, N.Y., 1967).

33. Cited in Avineri, *Karl Marx*, 107; last emphasis is mine.

34. Cited in David McLellan, *Karl Marx* (New York, 1975), 28–29.

35. Husami, "Marx on Distributive Justice," 78.

36. David Binkley, *Realism and Nationalism* (New York, 1935).

37. For nationalism and its transition from the language of progress to that of national exclusiveness, competition, and war, see Carlton Hayes, *The Historical Evolution of Modern Nationalism* (New York, 1931); Boyd Shafer, *Nationalism: Myth and Reality* (New York, 1955); and Hans Kohn, *Nationalism: Its Meaning and History* (New York, 1955). Particularly useful for Germany's new nationalism in this period is Fritz Stern, *The*

*Politics of Cultural Despair: A Study in the Rise of Germanic Ideology* (New York, 1961); and Hajo Holborn, *The Political Collapse of Europe* (New York, 1965), 37–54.

38. To understand forces in need of integration into national life, see Karl Polyani, *The Great Transformation* (Boston, 1957); Cyril Black, *The Dynamics of Modernization* (New York, 1966); and Sidney Pollard, *European Economic Integration, 1815–1970* (London, 1974).

39. For two different approaches to the integration of national life see Eugene Weber, *Peasants into Frenchmen* (Stanford, Calif., 1976); and Merle Curti, *The Roots of American Loyalty* (New York, 1968).

40. The psychological dimensions of labor's demands are at the center of Barrington Moore's discussion of the pre–World War I German labor movment, *Injustice*, 173–274. Highly useful for understanding some of the psychological dimensions of French labor is Joan W. Scott, *The Glassworkers of Carmaux* (Cambridge, 1975).

41. There is no doubt that between 1848 and 1890 nationalism ceased to be essentially democratic and revolutionary and became fundamentally reactionary and aggressive. For totalitarian dimensions of the *Action Française Nationalism*, see Ernest Nolte, *The Three Faces of Fascism*, (New York, 1966), 29–144; and Carlton Hayes, *Modern Nationalism*, 164–231.

42. For a touching account of the last international socialist meeting, which gathered such giants as Juárez and Guesde of France, Adler of Austria, Hasse of Germany, and their helplessness before the coming war, see Angelica Balabanoff, *My Life as a Rebel* (1938), excerpted in Alexander Baltzly and A. W. Salomone, eds., *Readings in Twentieth-Century Europe* (New York, 1950), 17–19.

43. For a work on World War I as the test of mobilization, see Raymond Aron, *The Century of Total War* (Boston, 1954).

44. For the nonlibertarian responses to the war, see Arthur Warwick, *The Deluge: British Society and the First World War* (Middlesex, Eng., 1965), 35–39.

45. Cited, ibid., 32.

46. For a discussion of the mobilization of enthusiasm, a phrase of Élie Halévy, see Jack Roth's conclusion to his *World War I: A Turning Point in Modern History* (New York, 1967), 82–133.

47. For insight into the war as matter of myth, imagination, memory, and art, see Paul Fussell, *The Great War and Modern Memory* (New York, 1975).

48. For three guides to fascism as a general European movement of the interwar years, see Eugen Weber, *Varieties of Fascism* (New York, 1964); Hannah Arendt, *The Origins of Totalitarianism* (New York, 1958); and Ernst Nolte, *Three Faces of Fascism*.

49. William Butler Yeats, "The Second Coming," found in *The Varorium Edition of the Poems of W. B. Yeats* (New York, 1940), 402.

50. Cited in Robert Waite, *Vanguard of Nazism: The Free Corps Movement in Postwar Germany* (New York, 1969), 42.

51. One useful discussion of the postwar moral dialogue in Germany is found in Moore's *Injustice*, 53–55.

52. Gaetano Salvemini, *The Origins of Fascism in Italy* (New York, 1973), 129.

53. Moore, *Injustice*, 413.

54. Among the declared goals of the *Stalhelm* was "the fight for the German *Volk*," "the renewal of the German Race," and "the elimination of foreign racial influences from the nation," George Mosse, *Nazi Culture*, (New York, 1960), 102.

55. George Mosse, *The Crisis of German Ideology* (New York, 1964), 255.

56. For a useful collection of sources on Italian fascism, see S. W. William Halperin, *Mussolini and Italian Fascism* (New York, 1964). For useful collections of interpretative essays, see A. W. Salamone, ed., *Italy from the Risorgimento to Fascism* (Garden City, N.Y., 1970); and Roland Sarti, ed., *The Ax Within* (New York, 1974). For a short essay placing Italian fascism in its postwar context, see F. L. Carsten, *The Rise of Fascism* (Berkeley, Calif., 1969), 45–81. For the convergence of the military and fascism on the need for discipline, national preparedness, and the uselessness of parliamentarianism, see Giorgio Rochat, "The Fascist Militia and the Army, 1922–1924," in Sarti, *The Ax Within*, 43–56.

57. Cited in John Weiss, *The Fascist Tradition* (New York, 1967), 424–25; emphasis is mine.

58. Benito Mussolini, *The Doctrine of Fascism*, cited in John Sommerville and Ronalyd Santoni, eds., *Social and Political Philosophy* (New York, 1963), 426.

59. Ibid., 428.

60. The incident is cited in Peter Gay, *Weimar Culture* (New York, 1968), 137.

61. Mosse, *Nazi Culture*, 45.

62. For an introduction to Nazi culture, see Friedrich Meinecke, *The German Catastrophe* (Boston, 1963); Fritz Stern, *The Politics of Cultural Despair* (New York, 1965); and Mosse's three works, *The Crisis of German Ideology*, *The Nationalization of the Masses* (New York, 1975), and *Nazi Culture*.

63. Mosse, *Nazi Culture*, 102.

64. Peter Gay, *Weimar Culture*, 8.

65. In his classic critique, *The Revolution of Nihilism* (New York, 1939), early Nazi follower Hermann Rauschning grasped the Nazis' absolute bid for total dominance. In his *Three Faces of Fascism*, Nolte analyzed the traditions that led fascism in general and National Socialism in particular to deny conscience all transcendence.

66. Cited in Henry Grosshan, *The Search for Modern Europe* (Boston, 1970), 357.

67. Cited in Peter Viereck, *Metapolitics: The Roots of the Nazi Mind* (New York, 1961), 317. Emphasis of *held under poison gas* is Viereck's literal translation of Hitler's phrase *"unter Giftgas gehalten."*

68. Cited in Grosshan, *The Search for Modern Europe*, 362.

69. Cited ibid., 363; emphasis is mine.

70. George Mosse, *The Culture of Europe* (Chicago, 1961), 352.

71. Cited ibid; emphasis is mine.

# 4

## Humanity, A Failed God: Intellectuals in Search of a Moral Way in a Guilty Era

During the second half of the 20th century the judgment of history has been abandoned by all except the underprivileged and dispossessed. The industrialised, "developed" world, terrified of the past, blind to the future, lives within an opportunism which has emptied the principle of justice of all credibility.

John Berger, *About Looking* (New York, 1980), 54.

Sartre: The intellectual and the worker were very close for a hundred, a hundred and fifty years. That has changed by virtue of the evolution of the working class and now they are drawing nearer precisely because the intellectual can polish the worker's thought, but just polish it, not produce it.

Marcuse: I am not yet convinced. . . . The problems which pose themselves in a revolutionary society, the problem of love, the problem of passion, the problem of all the erotic conflicts, the problem of the demand for the eternity of joy, all that is formulated by the intellectuals of the old type. Do you want to suppress all that?

Sartre: I want to change all that. Personally I feel myself still an intellectual of the old type.

Marcuse: I also, I do not contest that.

Sartre: But me, I contest myself!

Marcuse: No, I do not have a bad conscience. Excuse me, but I am sincere.

Sartre: And I do not have a bad conscience. For me, the classical intellectual is an intellectual who ought to disappear.

1974 dialogue between Sartre and Marcuse, cited in Ronald Aronson, *Sartre: Philosophy in the World* (London, 1980), 322–23.

If the philosophers and their disciples' dreams had come true, a Copernican Revolution in ethics would have occurred. Humanity would have become its own end, the source of its own good, the reason for its own guilt and gratitude. Of course, that revolution did not take place. Twentieth-century experience defied eighteenth- and nineteenth-century hopes; and in this defiance one explanation for the diffusion of guilt in twentieth-century consciousness can be found.

In abstract terms, humanity can be understood to have made itself God in the nineteenth century, and then in the twentieth century suffered the guilt of not only being God but also that of being a failed God. This diffuse guilt, born of great presumption and great failure, was immense. Every societal flaw, fault in justice, political error, historical tragedy, missed opportunity, expression of potential left undeveloped—everything less than perfect—was one of a thousand glaring indications that humanity had failed its responsibility. Humanity was God of its own defective universe.

As we have seen, responsibility came not just with the philosophers' claims, but resided in the new material forces and ideologies of the French and Industrial Revolutions. In less than a century and a half, humanity had altered its essential relation to nature. As man was once the victim of nature, he now was its victimizer. Democracy accounted for a gigantic increase in the human sense of responsibility. Society no longer was conceived as unchanging; it now had to appear before the people's tribunals of reason, equality, justice, and aspiration. The state also enhanced humanity's sense of power. The state no longer was understood to be an instrument of authority but was conceived instead as being a creative instrument for realizing the good of nation, human destiny, and the sum of human possibilities. Technology, democracy, and the nation-state each fed, and was fed by, the unprecedented assumption that man was responsible for making his own history.

It was this assumption, which forms the very core of modern mind and conscience, that was tested by twentieth-century events. These events challenged humanity's lordship. They put at issue the question of the existence of a faith that could guide humanity's ever-growing powers.

It increasingly appeared that man both had and did not have the power to make himself. It appeared he had power to do all but save himself. Diffuse guilt was one of the consequences of this paradoxical situation.

As discussed earlier, there were other sources of diffuse guilt which came with the spread of the modern mentality. The new mentality proposed an ethic that set men and women upon the guilt-producing path of seeking to find the good in the future instead of in the past; in possibilities rather than in tradition; in criticism and even defiance rather than in gratitude, piety, and reverence.

The modern mentality carried with it an altogether unprecedented attack upon traditional conscience. It denied that the good had its source in the past; it denied that imitation was the primary means to achieve the good. This permanently sentenced the contemporary mentality to feeling the guilt of seeking to validate the good of one's life without the fixed point of past example and tradition. The good was no longer in what was to be established but in what was to be realized.

The logic of this negation caused a somersault of morality. The good now depended on future revelation. No sooner was the good affirmed and embodied in the present than its very negation was already confirmed, insofar as it anticipated the greater good yet to come. The present was sentenced guilty before the tribunal of future possibilities. Perpetual negation, the exact opposite of traditional imitation, became the good, the way of the true spirit.

The events of the twentieth century, which were announced universally by the First World War, brought further diffuse guilt to contemporary man. They taught the possibility of humanity's failure. In one century it seemed humanity's lordship had risen and fallen.

This sense of failure pervades the contemporary spirit. With the concept of *rivoluzione mancata* ("failed revolution"), A. W. Salomone examined the persistent tendency of twentieth-century Italians to survey their past under the rubric of failure. They question their past with one single question: What revolution did we fail to make?[1] In general terms we can understand the attitude of failed revolution as describing that pervasive tendency of the contemporary mind to survey the past as a matter of failure and guilt.

From this perspective, today's wrongs constitute standing inquisitions into the past; all legacies are assumed to be flawed. The past is refused its powers over the present. Its heroes, sufferings, and sacrifices are made into mute monuments, placed in the shadows of suspicion. All inheritances, whether social, scientific, religious, or political, are potential matters of guilt.

This attitude constitutes a violent attack against gratitude. Piety, the reverential form of gratitude which was the highest virtue of the old order, is stripped of meaning. Critical negation—the activity of denying the given in the name of the possible—which is acclaimed as liberating by Hegelian and Marxist alike—is promoted as the new noble way.[2] This sense of history as defective only further intensifies the ethical obligation of the modern mentality to use the present to transcend the past. All the gifts of the past, even the very engines of progress, technology, science, and democracy that have won our freedom from what was worse in the old order, do not win the contemporary person's gratitude. We have been trained to be suspicious, as our most frightful antiutopian literature intimates, that these gifts themselves are turned against humanity. In this era of totalitarianism, all gifts are to be scrutinized. Nothing is without consequence. It is this attitude that justifies saying the period of time extending from the First World War to the present is a guilty and ungrateful era.

## A CRISIS OF CIVILIZATION

It was the intellectuals who most consciously suffered the guilt of the failed lordship of humanity. Unlike the majority they had lost their ties to the old way. They had been politicized even when they professed to be apolitical. In contrast to the majority, they could not cherish material goods and status advancement as ends in themselves. They could not live ethically by a plurality of uneven loyalties—like those to family, friends, neighborhood, church, work, and so on—nor could they see life simply as belonging to nature, God, fate, or luck. The intellectuals lived by words, opinions, ideas, and ideologies; they gave abnormal attention to their thinking. Inescapably, by their reading, writing, friendships, and identity, they made themselves part of the public order and its sensibilities and ideologies. They, so to speak, were "plugged into their times"—its events, feelings, happenings, trends in the arts—and this made them intellectuals.

The intellectuals were not alone in consciously anguishing over new realities.[3] However, as to no others, the debate over the public life belonged to them. They promoted science, created religious revivals, spoke of new moving spirits, and furnished parties with leaders. From the French Revolution on, as wealth, leisure, education, ideologies, and public cultures grew, the number of intellectuals multiplied. Although conceit, nonsense, self-interest, and the powerful human demand simply to be different shaped their vocation, especially among the political intellectuals, they took up the prophet's mantle in great numbers and with the sincerity of self-sacrifice.

In some terrible way the First World War made everything a matter of contention. It licensed everyone to have an opinion. The war made public discourse more intense and a matter of conflicting extremes. Accusations of blame and guilt became universal. Millions of dead, four years of official craziness, administrative violence, and rational insanity all went a long way toward lending a certain legitimacy to ideas, however insane they were. Virulent mental infections, such as nationalism, fascism, anti-Semitism, and communism, took on epidemic proportions as a consequence of the war. Concepts were inflated to compensate for the devaluation they had suffered at the hands of the overwhelming violence. Accusations, charges, indictments, and guilt filled the landscape. Myths abounded. Political rhetoric, ideologies of sacrifice, and talk of sacred missions, unforgivable betrayals, and blood-thirsty revenge became common. Rhetoric, indeed, propaganda, was used especially by the fascists to form an ersatz national culture and a political ideology that made the nation a moral entity, undoubtedly which was judged to be "more sinned against than sinning."

Like the parties of the right and left, intellectuals pushed their ideas to extremes. This was necessary, if one was to have "something to say" in an era when "everything" had already been "said by action." As rich as nineteenth-century social criticism and literature were, something was needed other than their repetition. Defining the spirit of the 1920s, intellectuals, artists, and bohemians took word and art to their limits. It was dramatic to announce the death of reason and progress, and from all sides this was heard. It was not without theological, literary, and psychological interest to "discover" the subconscious and the irrational. Freud was welcomed into the mainstream of twentieth-century life; and everyone, at least indirectly, inherited more guilt and a greater interest in themselves. In addition, some intellectuals turned against high culture, the West, and art itself. Taking up what the Italian Futurists had initiated, the Surrealists threw themselves on the side of the future against the past. Although posturing, showing their difference, and having the fun of "shocking the middle class" were not without importance, the Great War gave them their justification.

The 1920s, characterized by new aesthetic and literary movements, and by theological and philosophical revivals, appear to have been a last festival of Western high culture before the onset of a dark time, when terrible events, mass society and cultures, grim ideologies, and dour prophecies ruled. The period from 1929 to 1933, initiated by the Great Depression and culminated by Hitler coming to power, marked a veritable crisis in Western civilization. The international free economy, internationalism, constitutional democracy, and democratic and socialist politics appeared to perish before the sea of anarchy and the tides of tyranny. Humanity was coming undone. There was no longer a single, good God; His providence had become erratic, violent, that of a cruel, fickle demon. Of these three years and their effects on the intellectuals, H. S. Hughes perceptively wrote:

> As Europe experienced its second great crisis of the century—as depression and fascism added their shocks to the psychological damage that the First World War and its aftermath had inflicted—people began (like Spengler, Croce, Meinecke, Bloch, and Toynbee) to turn towards historical speculation and to ask themselves in the broadest terms to what end the modern world was moving. This mood of cosmic questioning had already been widespread in the post-war years; the experiences of the 1930s revived it and increased its range.[4]

This mood of cosmic questioning focused on the destiny of man and Western civilization. The names of such contemporary thinkers as Husserl, Heidegger, Jaspers, and Tillich and the names of Malraux, Marcel, Berdyaev, and Shestov in themselves evince this new note of existential guilt and anxiety about man, culture, and civilization that spread across Europe. The increasing importance of Freud and Jung for European intellectual life, no less than the ever-growing number of supporters of Nietzsche and Kierkegaard, were symptomatic of a culture in crisis. This dark brooding concern over humanity and the West fused with, and further radicalized and universalized, nineteenth-century criticisms of society. No past criticism of European life went unvoiced; no past attack against European culture was considered to be without relevance to the contemporary world.

European reflection reached a new level of global speculation in the years from 1929 to 1933. At this point the European dialogue shifted its axes from the fundamental nineteenth-century questions of progress versus decadence, science versus religion, and reform versus order to the more universal and guilt-inducing question of the very survival of Western civilization. It was no longer possible for a serious thinker to discount the First World War, the Russian Revolution, and Italian Fascism as tragic, but ultimately only temporary aberrations in the mainstream of Western historical progress. During these years it became obvious that these were the very headwaters of the century. As unwanted as these reflections were, sensitive Europeans everywhere came to revoice the awesome, anguish-filled lines of Paul Valery: "We later civilizations . . . we too now know that we are mortal."⁵

Both the extremes of the political right and left consciously made the bourgeoisie and its civilization a target. They held it responsible for the disorders of industrial capitalism as well as all the spiritual malaise they themselves suffered as highly conscious members of a changing urban-industrial order.

The fascists, who defined one significant part of the atmosphere of the period, accused the bourgeoisie of destroying community and of breaking the true organic ties of family, region, and nation. The bourgeoisie, in fascist depictions, were guilty of creating the unjust international order, the corrupt parliamentarian democracy, the destructive capitalist economies, the inhuman urban order, and all else they felt was wrong in modern industrial life. The fascist indictment of the bourgeoisie was also "ethical": The bourgeoisie was judged to be materialistic, rationalistic, skeptical, heartless, and nonvital.

Above all else, the fascists accused the bourgeoisie of betraying the homeland. They were like the Jews, the communists, and all other aliens who blighted the nation. In France, for instance, the bourgeoisie were accused of lacking a true sense of French grandeur; they were not of the same spiritual family as Joan of Arc. In Rumania the bourgeoisie should have been moved by the same sense of sacrificial expiation that Codreanu's Legionnaires were. In

Spain the bourgeoisie, the fascists contended, were alien to the vital unities of church and state, hidalgo and romance, that gave Spain its soul. In Germany the bourgeoisie were taken by the National Socialists to be those who had not suffered during the war and were indifferent to the need for German restoration. In every Western nation the fascists used the bourgeoisie as an anti-ideal. "To the materialism of a grubby, bourgeois world, the Fascists," wrote Eugen Weber, "opposed a doctrine of sacrifice, abnegation, and entire devotion to the cause, similar to that which the good Bolshevik must accept; a doctrine to which they often added the mystical idea of transcendence by expiation."[6] The fascists overwhelmed weakened societies with their suspicions and accusations. There is no wonder that everyone became guilty. Innocence no longer existed, except by permission of the party.

Disillusionment pervaded all levels of Western intellectual life. Its unifying theme was hatred of the bourgeoisie and its civilization.[7] By indicting the bourgeoisie, intellectuals found a way to react to the crises of the era. They found a way to unleash their anxiety, resentment, and guilt about a world which was not all it should be. Hating the bourgeoisie in one or all of the many detestable forms, such as banker, parliamentarian, narrow individualist, or Philistine, was part of the standard rhetoric of the era. It was a spiritual passe partout, useful for small talk in elite artistic circles as well as beerhall political agitation.

The radical left was joined to this climate of accusation. Their indictment of the bourgeoisie and its civilization carried with it the whole range of nineteenth-century radical voices. The influence of Marxism, which provided an array of economic, social, and ethical criticisms of the bourgeois civilization and predictions of its inevitable collapse, was pervasive. The events from 1929 to 1933 intensified all radical left criticisms. The prediction that the present civilization was on the verge of disintegration became commonplace.

Indeed a new hour seemed at hand, but for the intellectuals of the left this was no time to rejoice. They were in a quandary. They felt the powers of the growing right. Unlike the extreme right, they had no "mystical past" to retreat to or "sacred nation" to shelter them from the collapse.

More importantly, more than they knew or would admit, the civilization based on reason, freedom, material goods, ambitions for self, and aspirations for reform was in truth not only the bourgeoisie's but also their civilization. The intellectuals of the left were, in truth, the heirs of the philosophers who themselves had articulated the values of the aspiring eighteenth-century bourgeoisie. The intellectuals like the philosophers were the advocates of internationalism, reason, and progress. If one civilization was to fall, so their optimistic theory ran, the one to replace it should be a superior civilization that would be more humane, fraternal, equal, and free. Yet for many this optimistic faith, which once had protected the left from the ravages of history, was now strained beyond belief. It appeared to be as bankrupt as the civilization itself.

The left's indictment of the civilization carried with it the responsibility to find a better future. The responsibility in turn created guilt, a guilt which was not always conscious. It gave rise to questions they had to ask: What should humanity be? What could it be?

The Russian Revolution, unlike any other event of that period, was understood to address those questions. For some, its answers were, and remained, authoritative; for others of the left, the answers given by the Russian Revolution and the Soviet Union only increased their pessimism about the condition of twentieth-century humanity and their self-assumed role as humanity's leaders. There were obvious, painful truths: The Soviet Union was as cynical as any other state; its apparatus was party, propaganda, police, and terror. The Soviet state not only betrayed workers and the revolution it claimed to lead, but it slaughtered millions, from the most politically indifferent to its most devoted of servants, in the name of progress. The Soviet Union sent forth dark, contradictory, guilt-laden messages to those who believed that revolution was the road to liberation, and that the state, once captured by the right class, would serve the advancement of humanity. The Soviet Union was "a failed god" for many of the left, and buried with that god (of worker, history, and revolution) were the highest progressive beliefs of eighteenth- and nineteenth-century secularism.[8]

One intellectual who found communism a failed god was Ignazio Silone. Silone, brought up in the poverty of southern Italy, came to communism as a convert.[9] To serve the poor, humanity, and communism was one and the same mission for him. To be a communist in Mussolini's Italy was to belong to a persecuted church; it was to have the opportunity for martyrdom. Being at the top of the Italian Party in the 1920s also led Silone to Moscow where he saw at firsthand Stalin's cynical treatment of Trotsky and the Chinese Revolution.[10] Silone's dissillusionment was profound.

The only position left to Silone was to resist fascism, communism, and liars everywhere and to continue, if only by his writings, his service to downtrodden humanity. His helpless political position was expressed by the oppressed peasants of his fictional *Fontamara*. They had lost everything, their water, the one leader who cared about them. Their position, established by millenia of oppression, had not been altered, they had not experienced the fruits of progress. Expressing Silone's own sense of helplessness, they could only ask in rage (making bitter parody of Lenin's confident, militant tract, *What is to be Done?*):

> They have taken away our water. What is to be done? The priest won't bury our dead. What is to be done? They rape our women in the name of the law. What is to be done? Don Circonstanze, a false ally of the peasants, is a bastard. What is to be done?[11]

The dilemma of commitment, finding a revolution that served humanity, which Silone faced in the 1920s and 1930s, Albert Camus confronted in the 1940s and 1950s. Educated by the Second World War and the Resistance experience, Camus and his generation of young French intellectuals affirmed that man was his own history and that he was the consequence of his own actions.[12] Therefore, the greatest evil was indifference; the greatest good, idealized at the time by the martyred lives of communist Antonio Gramsci and Christian Dietrich Bonhoeffer, was to lose one's life for the cause.

The young Camus of pre-World War II did not share this conscience of active commitment. He conceived the world with the pessimistic formula that man is condemned to act in a hopeless world.[13] His goal, then, was to find a meaningful way to exist in a meaningless, "absurd" world.[14] With the Second World War, however, Camus gave himself unreservedly to the Resistance. A new question appeared at the center of his work: How can men and women act together for the good in a world infested by evil? He replied with this moral imperative: "Once the war has come, it is cowardly to stand on one side under the pretext that one is not responsible. Ivory towers are down. Indulgence is forbidden for oneself as well as other people."[15]

In the postwar period, Camus found himself in the guilt-inducing situation which has continued to confront so many young contemporary European intellectuals. He had no politics to match his ideal of commitment. This was not simply a consequence of Camus' true predeliction for the private versus the public life, it was essentially so because the world had changed. Events no longer counseled clear lines of action. Politicians again ruled, and the age of heroism was over.

Camus also could find no path of action because of his understanding of power. Camus, moralist that he was, understood four truths about power in the world of contemporary politics. First, politics can mean accepting, even wanting, the death of one's adversary. Second, social change costs blood. Indeed, he wrote, "it requires bucketsful of blood and centuries of history to lead to an imperceptible modification in the human condition. Such is the law. For years heads fall like hail, terror reigns, Revolution is touted, and one ends up by substituting constitutional monarchy for legitimate monarchy."[16] Third, men often become mass murderers for their causes. Those who cause the most blood to flow, Camus argued, are the people who believe that history is on their side. (In his play The Just Assassins, the revolutionists demand the insane commitments to tomorrow to prove their authenticity today. For the perfect community of tomorrow, they must stand ready today to shed the blood even of innocent children. "Not until the day comes when we stop sentimentalizing about children," one character says "will the revolution triumph, and we be the masters of the world.")[17] The fourth truth Camus understood was that men with revolutionary ideas are dangerous when they gain power. They create "a socialism of the gallows":

> States laden with too many crimes are getting ready to drown their guilt in even greater massacres. One kills for a nation or a class that has been granted divine status. One kills for a future society that has likewise been given divine status. Whoever thinks he has omniscience imagines he has omnipotence. Temporal idols demanding an absolute faith tirelessly decree absolute punishments. And religion devoid of transcendence kills great numbers of condemned men devoid of hope.[18]

In The Rebel (1951), which put Camus at odds with fellow French intellectual Jean-Paul Sartre, Camus called the spiritual criminals of the last two centuries "metaphysical revolutionists."[19] Camus wrote that "these revolutionists confounded the immanent with the transcendent." They proposed earthly substitutes for God: Sade did this with sexual perversity, Lautremont with art, Nietzsche with will, Rousseau with society, Hegel with history, and Marx with the future. Cruelest of these new "gods," Camus argued, have been the gods of history: They make the present a perpetual struggle to dominate tomorrow and "the entire history of mankind nothing, but a prolonged fight of death for the conquest of universal prestige and absolute power."[20]

Camus's ethics left him without a politics. He conceived of the very hope of revolution conspiring with the state to produce the greatest evils of this era. Expressing an awesome repudiation of revolution, which Sartre so severely criticized, Camus wrote:

> All modern revolutions have ended in a reinforcement of the power of the State. 1789 brings Napoleon; 1848, Napoleon III; 1917, Stalin; the Italian disturbances of the twenties, Mussolini; the Weimar Republic, Hitler. . . . The strange and terrifying growth of the modern State can be considered as the logical conclusion of inordinate technical and philosophical ambitions, foreign to the true spirit of rebellion, but which nevertheless gave birth to the revolutionary spirit of our time. The prophetic dream of Marx and the over-inspired predictions of Hegel or of Nietzsche ended by conjuring up after the city of God had been razed to the ground, a rational or irrational State, which in both cases, however, was founded on terror.[21]

Camus's and Silone's loss of faith in communism and revolution suggests the sense of historical impotence that overcame the twentieth-century left-wing intellectuals. They could create journals, seek out new coalitions, and take up arms against fascism, as they did in Spain and throughout Europe in resistance movements, but they could not escape the diffuse guilt of failure and impotence that engulfed progressive conscience in twentieth-century Europe. This guilt specifically was tied to three profound factors: First, humanity had proven no substitute for God; second, no longer were there any clear means to serve man—revolution, party, class, ideology, and state had all betrayed man—and finally, the vocation of being a committed intellectual proved to be the most superfluous when measured against events.

This diffuse guilt carried special torment for the intellectuals. They lived by and for their minds, and as a result they confused their worth with their opinions. Their guilt, however, is of particular interest for two reasons. First, to a significant degree, we have all come to resemble intellectuals. Increasingly all members of mass, democratic industrial society are convinced that our feelings, sensibilities, opinions, and ideas are serious business. Second, as Americans we share by national culture a sense of responsibility for humanity's progress. This means that not only the intellectuals' diffuse epochal guilt, but also the guilt arising from a sense of authentic humanistic responsibility, are ours. To learn of their guilts is to understand our own.

## JEAN-PAUL SARTRE,
## ETHICAL EXPERIMENTS IN SELF-DEFINITION

As no other, Jean-Paul Sartre expressed the guilt-filled plight of twentieth-century intellectual life.[22] By his prose and fiction, and the intensity and range of his ethical commitments, Jean-Paul Sartre is the paramount example of a twentieth century intellectual.[23] Sartre's preoccupation was with literature and philosophy. His existentialism was the result of a marriage he made between the philosophies of Heidegger and Husserl and modern introspective literature. Sartre's course to political commitment was slow. However, with the Second World War, Sartre began his engagement with the public life by what he called "la force des choses." Thereafter he was committed. Commitment became for him a primary moral duty. His conscience took shape around what he defined to be the authenticity of his own and others' commitments.

Since the war, Sartre's commitment—his profound need to take a moral stand on the issues of the hour—passed through several stages. In 1945, along with Merleau-Ponty, he founded the journal Les temps modernes.[24] It was predicated on the proposition that man is and creates his own conditions. Man alone must save or damn himself. History is a vast courtroom in which his freedom and responsibility are absolute. They have no boundaries in nature to limit them; there exists no fixed ideal to guide them. The most diffuse anxiety and guilt, revealed so clearly by Sartre's existentialism, have their source in a world in which man is totally free and yet absolutely responsible.

The desire to intervene directly into the politics of France led Sartre in 1947 to found the party *Rassemblement du Peuple Français*. Attracting only intellectuals, the party was short-lived and of no significant consequence. As sole editor of *Les temps moderns*, in the period from 1952 to 1956, Sartre increasingly lent his support directly to the Communist Party at home and abroad, and his writings became more dependent on Marxism. This commitment shaped his understanding of human historical responsibility.

Reacting against the 1956 Soviet invasion of Hungary, Sartre resumed the role of critic of the Soviet Union and of the subservient French Communist Party. In the late 1950s and early 1960s, Sartre took up the cause of the peoples of the Third World. He supported the native Algerians against the French colonists and in the same period lent his support to Castro and the Cuban Revolution. Sartre was the left's most prominent critic of American capitalism and worldwide imperialism. In harmony with, and not without significant influence upon, the emerging new left in the United States, Sartre supported the black Civil Rights movement in the United States and condemned American involvement in Vietnam. At the 1967 Lord Russell War Crimes Trial in Paris, Sartre took a leading role in judging America guilty of genocide in Vietnam.[25] No doubt, the mature Sartre had become, as in measure all political intellectuals are, a judge of the world, and his fame gave his sentences and the guilt they imputed a kind of official character in left-wing circles across the globe.

Sartre gave his full support to the 1968 student uprising in France, *les événements de mai*. His support of the most radical students led him to the final stage of his political development.[26] He indicted his past commitments as mere literary *engagements*, which allowed him to express his moralism without sacrificing his career and the other benefits he derived from his sophisticated "bourgeois subjectivity." Sartre, like some kind of perpetual enfant terrible, now put himself entirely at the service of France's militant Maoist youth.[27] Indeed, he not only worked for them with a remarkable intensity, putting in nineteen-hour days, but consciously allowed his reputation to be exploited by them.

The evolution of Sartre's commitment didn't follow the more common paths that led intellectuals in the 1940s and 1950s from left to right, from greater to less intensity. Instead, his evolution anticipated and shaped the new left of Europe and the United States.

His essential premises were in accord with the new left. He felt that technology would not necessarily liberate humanity or that history itself guaranteed any certain victories. Further, Sartre increasingly believed that revolution and the future existed with the nonwhite colonial people. With the sensibilities of the new left, Sartre's world view was psychological and moral instead of social, economic, and political. In further conformity with the new left, Sartre's preference gravitated consistently toward searching for the meaning of the self.

This trait, so common to the French self-reflective tradition, was manifested by Sartre's abiding concern for the victim and especially the victim's psychology. Although one meets, in Sartre's writings, victims of economic exploitation and racial prejudice, the majority of his victims are the spiritually abused, the pariahs of society whose ideas, sexuality, or crimes make them outcasts. They are judged to be guilty by official, established society. Sartre, Molnar observed, is the ally of the bastard.[28] His favorite hero-victims, whom he makes the subject of separate biographical studies, are intellectuals like Baudelaire, Nizan, and Genet.[29] They all are, to an extent, like Sartre himself, young men without fathers, secure families, or certain social definition. They share a common alienation and are without a real presence in society. They live poorly, as students and artists often have, alone in small rooms, along the sidewalks of the impersonal city. They look for relief for themselves. Like Dostoyevsky's Raskolnikov, and so many other antiheroes of modern depth literature, they occupy small, dark spaces. They sense themselves to be estranged, besieged, not belonging to anything or anyone. Commerce and politics are alien to them. They want or have no respect, honor, status, or place. Sartre's characters have been given nothing. No tradition, love, or memory sustains them. They are without gratitude. They are, to use Sartre's language, "sequestered," walled off from social life. They have only their own thought, which must be used against themselves and others for what meaning they can gain. Their entire being turns upon their self-consciousness, or more precisely, it pivots upon that guilt-inducing consciousness of being aware of one's constant "dialogue" with oneself.

These phantom creatures of sheer mind, who are without community and know neither gift, nor reciprocity, nor exchange, are artifices of Sartre's philosophy. Particularly as formulated in his major treatise, *Being and Nothingness*, his philosophy envisions the individual as absolutely alone and totally free in an existence which, in itself, has no meaning. Sartre's philosophy admits the existence of no governing order of ideas, natural laws, or principles of knowledge, nor does it acknowledge any binding human reciprocities. There is, in Sartre's view, only the free, solitary individual who must struggle for his meaning against himself and others. In this Manichean perspective, betrayal is always possible. Within the individual there exists the ever-present temptation to betray one's freedom by identifying oneself entirely with one's condition or role, instead of accepting the freedom and responsibility one has for self-definition. Sartre labeled the false objectification of oneself, the defining of oneself as a thing, "bad faith." Bad faith is the attempt to escape the terrible anxiety of freedom, the need to choose constantly what one wishes to be. (Is not anxiety itself one form of diffuse guilt for all who labor under the burden of having to choose constantly in a world in which one is unsure of the value of agents, means, and ends?)

Outside himself, the Sartrean individual is engaged in a permanent battle. He must constantly struggle against the others who attempt to take possession of him, to define him as simply an object for their existence. "Everything which holds for me," Sartre formulated in his Hobbesian epistemology, "holds for him. While I attempt to free myself from the hold of the Other, the Other is trying to free himself from mine; while I seek to enslave the Other, the Other seeks to enslave me."[30] The very glance of the Other ignites in the self the consciousness that one is being turned into an object, denied one's own inner subjectivity. The glance of the Other, and the shame it ignites, establishes the fact that "I am this self which another knows. And this self which I know—this I am in the world which the Other has made alien to me."[31]

To translate Sartre's vision into the terms of this work: In Sartre's world every eye judges. Every eye is the all-seeing eye of God and its metamorphosis, the all-surveillant eye of public life. By the very fact that one can be seen, one is judged: one's worth is reduced simply to the glance of the other. Guilt, in this compassionless Sartrean world, is as diffuse as humanity is universal; it is as profound as the terrible threat that one is nothing other than what others see one to be. This guilt, revealing severe social fragmentation, suggests that one is real only insofar as one can cherish one's private illusions free of others. Guilt, too, exists in knowing the lie of one's private illusion.

Sartre saw no escape from these interior and exterior threats to the self. There is only the truth of one's superfluousness, and gratuity which one's freedom nurtures. "In anguish," Sartre wrote, "I apprehend myself at once as totally free and as not being able to derive the meaning of the world except as coming from myself."[32]

To the man of such a consciousness there comes the anguish of knowing that he is the sole source of all values. As Orestes, the afflicted protagonist of Sartre's *Flies*, said: "And there was nothing left in heaven, no Good, nor Evil, no one to command me."[33] "Man," Sartre continued, "is condemned to be free . . . to carry the weight of the whole world on his shoulders; he is responsible for the world and for himself as a way of being."[34]

As if to carry this spiritual masochism to its furthest limit, Sartre wrote of the ultimate meaninglessness that shadows all human meaning:

> Every human reality is a passion in that it projects losing itself so as to found being and at the same time to constitute the in-itself which escapes contingency by being its own foundation, the *ens causa sui,* which religions call God. Thus the passion of man is the reverse of that of Christ, for man loses himself as man in order that God may be born. But the idea of God is contradictory and we lose ourselves in vain. Man is a useless passion.[35]

As Sartre's literature mirrors his philosophy, so his philosophy is autobiographical. All Sartre's writing is ultimately autobiographical, or narcissistic, according to Victor Brombert:

> The fact that Sartre, perhaps more than any other contemporary writer, is a victim of a peculiar mirror-disease of thought. A special narcissism compels him to stare at his own image at the same time as he resents that confining and defining glance. Young Hugo in *Les Mains Sales*, carries photographs of himself in his suitcase. They represent the burden of his past, as well as the eye of the self which allows the Sartrean intellectual hero no respite. Roquentin is thus trapped by himself, trapped by the mobile refractions of his own accusing eye. Intelligence, above all, is in Sartrean terms a form of life imprisonment.[36]

The truth of Brombert's insight into Sartre's narcissism is confirmed by Sartre's own *Words,* his autobiography of the early years of his youth.[37] There Sartre describes himself as being a lonely, fatherless child. He was in love with his mother who, since the death of her husband, had to return to live with her parents. There she lived as if she too were a child, and thus Sartre's own sister. Her father, Sartre's dominating grandfather, Charles Schweitzer, is the quintessence of that detestable, domineering, cultured bourgeois whom Sartre hates. This hatred manifests itself in much of Sartre's fiction and nonfiction.

The young Sartre was the child who learned to live for the show he put on, he explained, "who respected adults on the condition they idolized me."[38] "Books," Sartre wrote of his secluded childhood, "were my birds and my nests, my household pets, and my countryside."[39] His first adventures were in libraries. His first and ultimately last ambitions were to write, to make his words a gift to the world, to be immortal. "I discovered that in *belles lettres* the Giver can be transformed into his own Gift, that is, into a pure object. Chance had made me a man, generosity would make me a book."[40] Sartre, who was always looking at himself, knew himself to be a pretense and therefore expected the rest of the world to be a sham.

> I was a fake child. . . . Play-acting robbed me of the world and of human beings. I saw only roles and props. Serving the activities of adults in a spirit of buffoonery, how could I have taken their worries seriously? I adapted myself to their intentions with a virtuous eagerness that kept me from sharing their purposes. A stranger to the needs, hopes, and pleasures of the species, I squandered myself coldly in order to charm it.[41]

Of all the literary figures Sartre wrote about, he most resembled Baudelaire. Like Baudelaire, he lived, suffered, and sought to construct a life out of and against his sense of sheer gratuitousness. As with Baudelaire, an unresolved Oedipal complex, a profound solitude, and a desperate need for self-definition all warred within him. Engaged in self-revelation, Sartre wrote of Baudelaire:

> People have taken every opportunity of attributing an unresolved Oedipus complex to him, but it matters little whether or not he desired his mother. I should rather say that he refused to resolve the theological complex which transforms parents into gods. He refused to resolve it because it was necessary in order to evade the law of

> solitude and find in other people a remedy against gratuitousness, to
> confer on other people, or rather on certain other people, a sacred
> character. What he wanted was neither friendship, love, nor rela-
> tions on equal terms: He had no friends or at most a few intimates
> among the riff-raff. He wanted judges—beings whom he could
> deliberately place beyond the fundamental law on contingency,
> beings who existed simply because they had the right to exist and
> whose decrees conferred on him in his turn a stable and sacred
> 'nature.' He was ready to appear guilty in their eyes; and 'guilty in
> their eyes' meant absolutely guilty. But the guilty man has his func-
> tion in the theocratic universe. He has his function and his rights. He
> has a right to censure, to punishment, and to repentance. He co-
> operates with the universal order and his misdoing invests him with a
> religious dignity, a place apart in the hierarchy of beings.[42]

Sartre's ultimate lineage was no doubt that of Rousseau and the
Romantics. Self-consciousness dominated his being. He sought his
meaning in mind and words. They served him as heart, family, life,
and immortality, and as a defense against the impermanence of
things. Like Rousseau, Sartre lived within the infinity and the
finitude of his self, and therefore he was his own curse and blessing.

Sartre knew all this about himself; and the awareness was his
burden. It made him vividly experience how superfluous his life
was, how vain his art. He was both fascinated and sickened by his
own self-awareness. At times he mocked, despised, and hated
himself for it. Therein exists part of the explanation for the intensity of his hatred for his own background. He repeated André
Gide's spiteful dictum, *"Famille, je vous haïs!"* The slightest palpi-
tations of his spirit were in succession his anguish and pleasure, his
torment and pride, and always his most absorbing preoccupation.
Sartre felt guilt when he thought about himself and when he did not
think about himself. The examined life, for Sartre and the
twentieth-century intellectuals like him, carried with it the curse of
obsessive introspection.

Sartre invariably was led, for reasons of self-hatred, self-
preservation, and a range of other motives, to attack his own narcissism. Sartre was driven to look to others for his meaning, even
though he often despised them for the meanings they gave and
denied him. At times, he unreservedly cast all his moral support to
the masses. They, he judged, were real, embodied, authentic in a
way he, and intellectuals like him of the safe secluded world of

words, could not be. They were sincere; he was insincere. They were potent; he was impotent.

The logic of this brutal self-judgment led Sartre at times to prefer deed over word, action over thought, combat over philosophy. In his preface to black Algerian Frantz Fanon's *Wretched of the Earth*, Sartre went so far as to reconstruct, sympathetically, Fanon's argument: Killing whites was essential for black psychological liberation. This process of counteridentity served to aid Sartre in his escape from his own nihilistic self-circlings. It also gave him a public identity, a commitment, and an ethics: He made the liberation of the downtrodden his end. Upon that elevated territory, Sartre, if only momentarily, stood above the narcissism of his own subjectivity; and, in a sense, he also regained the high grounds of nineteenth-century progressive humanism. His life, in this role, served not the idlings of his mind but the historical progress of humanity.

Sartre held that ground with difficulty. The self, with its anxiety, guilt, and its fascinating attraction was always the temptation. Sartre, perhaps despite himself, commonly converted the affairs of men in society into backdrops for a celebration of solitary hero-victims. Among Sartre's hero-victims were Orestes, the Resistance fighters, all the individuals who—not that differently from Camus' Sisyphus—"by sheer force of will set limits to the torturers; power to negate his autonomy as a free man."[43] In the words of Germaine Brée, "All Sartrean 'free' men are participants in a mystic sacrifice."[44]

Sartre had one additional altruistic exit through which he would escape the valueless preoccupation with his inner self. Sartre would sacrifice himself for the sake of his writing, he would make himself "a martyr-comedian" of ideas. He would put all his "senseless picking" at himself in the service of mankind. By making his mind a kind of purgatory he would suffer in some intense, conscious way what the rest of mankind suffered. He would be the bridge to a new spiritual order. He would be the dead-end sign marking a broken trail. He would be what Baudelaire declared himself to be: *"Je suis la victime et le bourreau"* ("I am the victim and the executioner").[45]

He would be a Romantic Socrates. He would have his value by suffering for others. As an intellectual he would assume for himself the contradictions of the whole society. In "A Plea for Intellectuals," he wrote:

We find that the intellectual's contradictions are the contradictions inherent in *each* one of us and in the whole society. . . . The intellectual, because of his own contradiction, is driven to make this effort for himself, and consequently *for everyone*—and it is this that becomes his *function*. In one sense he is suspect to all, since he is a disputant from the outset and thus a potential traitor, but in another sense, he makes an effort to achieve consciousness *for all.*[46]

Sartre declared that to carry out this responsibility he would strive to reach "the bottom." He would assault himself. Expressing that terrible abiding ambivalence of his thought, Sartre wrote, in the conclusion of *Words*, of the necessity yet futility of his assault:

I took my pen for a sword; I now know we're powerless. No matter. I write and will keep writing books; they're needed; all the same, they do serve some purpose. Culture doesn't save anything or anyone, it doesn't justify. But it's a product of man: he projects himself into it, he recognizes himself in it; that critical mirror alone offers him his image. Moreover, that old, crumbling structure, my imposture, is also my character: one gets rid of a neurosis, one doesn't get cured of one's self. Though they are worn out, blurred, humiliated, thrust aside, ignored, all of the child's traits are still to be found in the quinquagenarian.[47]

## GUILTY INTELLECTUALS

Sartre was of the spiritual lineage of Jean-Jacques Rousseau: the marginal man, the terrible solitary thinker, the first intellectual in whom we all see ourselves. Rousseau ceaselessly, and nearly always guiltily, sought an identity. He pursued it, simultaneously and contradictorily, in the authenticity of the self (his sincerity) and in the approving eye of the other; and even in being one with nature in the idyllic countryside. When we read Sartre we think of the Rousseau who announced a new moral order of individualism. (In the opening lines of Rousseau's *Confessions*, he called all who dared to stand openly in moral comparison to him. There he declared himself to be "as good as all and no better than anyone else.") Also not to be forgotten is the Rousseau who, at one point near the end of his life, was so tormented by what he took to be a universal plot against his reputation that he took to the streets of Paris, distributing at random a letter declaring his innocence. Sartre was of that lineage and that guilt.

Sartre, too, is joined to all the intellectuals, writers, and thinkers who live by consciousness and create by artifice of word. Their art, at least when not officially recognized, makes their lives marginal. It makes them protean. They become, in a certain sense, all they write. They also mold themselves to the fame they seek. They empty themselves of almost everything but their will and claim to be a writer. Books, as Sartre knew, become the writers' costumes. Sartre, like all writers, lived in the kingdom of words, and he inevitably suffered the diffuse guilt of having his identity be that elusive kingdom and what fame he could steal from it.

In another sense, Sartre, by his oscillations between art and politics, commitment and nihilism, righteousness and guilt, and the sheer breadth of his writings, was above all the archetypical intellectual of the twentieth century. Sartre was joined to all the intellectuals who believed that humanity is historical and that it is for man to make his own meaning.

The belief that man is the exclusive agent of his own historical making expoded in the crucible of twentieth-century events. For all progressive humanists there mushroomed forth the terrifying recognition that man verges on becoming either his own saviour or his own executioner.[48] With this recognition came the guilt of identifying oneself as being either god or demon of this existence.

The spiritual condition of intellectuals like Sartre in the postwar world is described by Jean Guitton: "Around 1880," with the belief in the historical inevitability of progress, "one could say: *Even the guilty are innocent. In 1950,*" with the belief in progress severely crippled, "it is necessary to reverse the terms of that formula and say: *Even the innocent are guilty.*"[49] Continuing to embrace the guilt-laden proposition that humanity is responsible for humanity, these intellectuals held themselves and their civilization to be guilty for having failed to realize the highest dreams of the eighteenth and nineteenth centuries. This made them guilty before the world for all that was not perfect in it.

As post–World War II intellectual culture testifies, this guilt could be blinding and even presumptuous; it was always diffuse. Some intellectuals personalized it. Others exploited it for art, while still others transformed it into the service of their favorite ideologies. In all cases, this guilt led the intellectuals to judge the world severely. The Nazi experience and the atomic bomb seemed to sustain all indictments and to make culpability universal.

Following the tradition of intellectual discourse in the interwar years, the postwar intellectuals surveyed the past under the rubric of failure. Their interrogations were as predictable as they were relentless: With the premise that the past has universally failed the present, no gratitude was owed any tradition, no respect was to be given to any authority.

This guilt-laden logic, at its extremes, conceives all compromises as betrayals. It views all present institutions as potential betrayers. Further, in the most Puritanical fashion, it considers existence itself as the perpetual temptation to do wrong.

Understanding this logic, which commands so much of the mentality of the left, accounts for its proclivity to judge negatively all that is part of the Western world, all that is of its own "failed" guilty self. Also, understanding this logic explains how so much of contemporary Western literature reads as an extended act of atonement: it seeks inwardly to make compensation for what has not been realized historically. It might be argued that all those who are of the same progeny as Sartre are engaged, ironic as it is, in ancient rites of sacrifice. In spite of their professed secularism, they believe that good and bad are inseparable from human suffering and that, by their suffering and self-punishment, they purify themselves and the world.

Only a minority of intellectuals are willing to denounce equations that join morality and politics, ethics and the public life, their vocation and humanity's destiny. Only a minority adopt the position recently expressed by Michel Foucault: "From the death of God in the philosophy of Enlightenment to the disappearance of Man (and the Cartesian *cogito*) only two centuries had elapsed: time enough for the experiment of putting Man in God's place to have exposed its inherent dangers."[50] The majority of intellectuals of the left have not accepted the death of man. With or without justification, they will continue to believe that their prophetic vocation has relevance to humanity.

From one point of view, these "prophets" are of little significance when measured by their direct influence. Eugen Weber gives one revealing explanation of the irrelevance of the French intellectual left wing to France's politics.

> There were always too many people who had too much to lose for
> extremist gambles to stand a serious change. Recurrent crises were
> resolved by surrenders, mutual surrenders, for no one wished to rock

the boat too hard, least of all the great mass of conservatives. And, while moderation prospered, the radicals, stranded by such unsuitable conditions, were left to sing and shout and strut on a little promontory of their own.[51]

Zeldin, even more pointedly than Weber, suggests the separation of intellectuals from the sense of nation in France in the postwar period when he notes that, in 1951, only 42 percent of the French could identify, much less care about, Jean-Paul Sartre—who was France, Europe, and the contemporary world's most famous philosopher.[52]

Surely the intellectuals are too different from the great majority of people to have much direct influence upon them. The majority's interests, feelings, and ideals are far more concrete and far less conscious, abstract and systematic than the intellectuals'. Neither by free time, nor education, nor desire is the majority prepared to live by a cultivated consciousness. Even those who have been participants in the great events of this era are hardly likely to make their conscious identity a central matter of their existence, or their responsibility to humanity a high moral duty. Obligations to family, work, neighborhood, church, and other local associations—even occasionally to nation—are felt to be pressing enough. Adding to one's conscience such an intangible thing as humanity's welfare seems an unnecessary burden.

However, the intellectuals of the left warrant our attention for reasons other than their social influence. Aside from the obvious reason that they form our language, and thus the understanding of our experience, they shed light on our conscience: They are the harbingers of the conditions and sensibilities to come.

First, they reveal the diffuse guilt which pervades all members of contemporary society, not just the transmitters of ideas or the politicians but to all of us who consciously seek an identity. In measure the demise of the traditional world, coupled to the spread of democracy, education, and leisure, have made us all intellectuals. We consciously experience with guilt and anxiety the eclipse of traditional culture and religion, and the onset of mass, commercial, national culture. None of us can escape the presence of human power, the sense that somehow mankind has become its own destiny. We all suffer the feeling of being lords of a vacant universe. In the simplest terms, to know intellectuals, the guiltiest of the guilty, is to know ourselves.

Finally, the intellectuals of the left are the disciples of the eighteenth-century philosophers. They believe that humanity makes itself; and thus these intellectuals are not just "the guilty," but "the man of guilt."

## NOTES

1. A. W. Salomone, "The Risorgimento between Ideology and History: The Political Myth of 'Rivoluzione Mancata,'" in *American Historical Review* 67 (October 1962), 38–56.

2. The standard work praising dialectical thought as freeing and positivism as enslaving is Herbert Marcuse, *Reason and Revolution: Hegel and the Rise of Social Theory* (New York, 1941). In the *Dialectical Imagination* (Boston, 1973), Martin Jay offers a guide to the thought of Max Horkheimer, Theodor Adorno, and others who formed the Marxist-inspired, and very influential, interwar German Frankfurt School, out of which Marcuse came.

3. Useful for a general discussion of twentieth-century intellectuals are R. Alberés, *L'aventure intellectuelle du XXᵉ siècle* (Paris, 1950); Rolland Stromberg, *European Intellectual History Since 1789* (Englewood Cliffs, N.J., 1981), 243–300; Victor Brombert, *The Intellectual Hero: Studies in the French Novel, 1880–1955* (Philadelphia, 1961); Peter Gay, *Weimar Culture* (New York, 1968); H. S. Hughes, *Consciousness and Society* (New York, 1961); and my *Mounier and Maritain: A French Catholic Understanding of the Modern World* (Ala., 1975).

4. H. S. Hughes, *Contemporary Europe* (Englewood Cliffs, N.J., 1961), 264.

5. Paul Valéry, "The Crisis of Mind," in his *History and Politics* (New York, 1962), 23. The ellipses in this quotation are Valéry's.

6. Eugen Weber, *Varieties of Fascism*, 40.

7. For the climate of this period, see Jean Louis Loubet del Bayle, *Les non-conformistes des années 30* (Paris, 1969); and David Caute, *Communism and French Intellectuals, 1914–1960* (New York, 1960).

8. A post–World War II volume titled *The God That Failed*, Richard Crossman, ed. (New York, 1949) is the personal testimony of several European intellectuals, such as André Gide, Stephen Spender, Arthur Koestler, and Ignazio Silone, who once believed in, and then became disillusioned with, Soviet Communism.

9. For a thorough guide to Silone's writings, see Luce d'Eramo, *L'Opera di Ignazio Silone: Saggio critico e guida bibliografica* (Milan, 1971). Also of use is Ferdinando Virdia, "Silone," *La Nuova Italia*, no. 6 (Guigno, 1967), 1–145. Useful guides to Silone in English are Irving Howe, "Ignazio Silone: Politics and the Novel," in Sergio Pacifici, *From Verismo to Experimentalism: Essays on the Modern Italian Novel* (Bloomington, Ind., 1969),

120-34; and Robert George, "Silone's Use of Folk Beliefs," in *Midwest Folklore* 12 (1962), 197-203.
    10. Ignazio Silone, *Bread and Wine*, trans. Harvey Fergusson (new ed., New York, 1962).
    11. Ignazio Silone, *Fontamara*, 3rd ed. (Milan, 1971), 256. Translation is mine.
    12. For the pervasive concern for commitment by European intellectuals, see Michel-Antoine Burnier, *Choice of Action* (New York, 1968).
    13. Useful introductions to Camus are Philip Thody, *Albert Camus: A Study of his Work* (New York, 1957); Conor Cruise O'Brien, *Albert Camus of Europe and Africa* (New York, 1970); and Germaine Brée, *Camus* (New Brunswick, N.J., 1961).
    14. For Camus's articulation of the absurd, see his *The Myth of Sisyphus and Other Essays* (New York, 1960).
    15. Albert Camus, *Notebooks: 1935-1942* (New York, 1963), 143.
    16. Albert Camus, *Notebooks: 1942-1951* (New York, 1965), 119.
    17. Albert Camus, *Just Assassins, Caligula and Three Other Plays* (New York, 1966), 256.
    18. Albert Camus, "Reflections on the Guillotine," *Resistance, Rebellion and Death* (New York, 1960), 228.
    19. Sartre's "Reply to Camus" from *Les temps modernes* is available in *Situations* (Greenwich, Conn., 1965), 54-81. Two useful discussions of this debate are found in Burnier's *Choice of Action* and Brée's *Camus and Sartre* (New York, 1972), esp. 1-14.
    20. Albert Camus, *Rebel: An Essay on Man in Revolt* (New York, 1956), 139.
    21. Ibid., 177.
    22. For a useful bibliographic guide to Sartre, see *Yale French Studies* 30 (1963): 108-19; and Benjamin Suhl, *Jean-Paul Sartre* (New York, 1970), 273-86. Helpful introductory studies to Sartre are Philip Thody, *Sartre: A Biographical Introduction* (New York, 1971); Edith Kern, ed., *Sartre: A Collection of Critical Essays* (Englewood Cliffs, N.J., 1962); R. D. Laing and D. G. Cooper, *Reason and Violence: A Decade of Sartre's Philosophy, 1950-1960* (New York, 1971); and Mary Warnock, ed., *Sartre: A Collection of Critical Essays* (Garden City, N.Y., 1971). Two works of different inspiration but both highly critical of Sartre are Raymond Aron, *History of the Dialectic of Violence: An Analysis of Sartre's Critique de la Raison Dialectique* (New York, 1975); and Thomas Molnar, *Sartre: Ideologue of our Time* (New York, 1968).
    23. For works useful for an understanding of the development of Sartre's thought and his growing tie to the left, see the autobiographical works of his life-long companion, Simone de Beauvoir, *The Prime of Life* (New York, 1962) and *Force of Circumstances* (New York, 1965). Stanley Hoffman, "The Paradoxes of the French Political Community," in *In Search of*

*France* (New York, 1963), 1–117; H. S. Hughes, *The Obstructed Path: French Social Thought in the Years of Desperation, 1930–1960* (New York, 1968), esp. 153–226; George Lichtheim, *Marxism in Modern France* (New York, 1966); Raymond Aron, *The Opium of the Intellectuals* (New York, 1962); and Mark Poster, *Existential Marxism in Postwar France* (Princeton, N.J., 1975).

24. For Jean-Paul Sartre's relation to Merleau-Ponty, see "Merleau-Ponty," in Sartre's *Situations,* 156–226. For Ponty's shared philosophy of an historical commitment that led to justification of the Communist Party, see Maurice Merleau-Ponty, *Humanism and Terror* (1947; reprint ed., Boston, 1969). To understand the general transformation of European thought from idealism to existentialism and historicism, see George Lichtheim, *Europe in the Twentieth Century* (New York, 1972), 211–39.

25. For examples of pieces reflecting Sartre's commitment to causes, see his *Sartre on Cuba* (New York, 1961); "Vietnam: Imperialism and Genocide," "Czechoslovakia: The Socialism that Came in from the Cold," "France: Masses, Spontaneity, Party," in his *Between Existentialism and Marxism* (New York, 1974), 67–137; *On Genocide* (Boston, 1968); and Sartre's preface to Frantz Fanon, *The Wretched of the Earth* (New York, 1968), 7–31.

26. For Sartre on *les evénéments de mai,* see "Itinerary of a Thought," in *New Left Review,* no. 58 (November-December 1969), 43–66; and his *Les communistes ont peur de la revolution* (Paris, 1967).

27. For Sartre's own expression of political support of Maoism and the most radical youth after 1968, see his interviews in *New York Review of Books* (March 26, 1970), *Esquire* (December, 1972), and *L'Espresso* (February 11, 1973).

28. Molnar, *Sartre,* 47.

29. Sartre, *Baudelaire* (Paris, 1947), *Saint-Genet; comédien et martyr* (Paris, 1952), and his preface to Nizan's *Aden arabie* (Paris, 1961), 9–62.

30. From *Being and Nothingness,* excerpted in Robert Cumming, ed., *The Philosophy of Jean-Paul Sartre* (New York, 1965), 209.

31. Ibid., 199.

32. Ibid., 129.

33. Sartre, *Flies,* ibid., 240.

34. Excerpted from *Being and Nothingness,* ibid., 277.

35. Ibid., 352.

36. Victor Brombert, "Jean-Paul Sartre, Techniques and 'Impossible' Situations," in *Modern Language Quarterly,* vol. 30 (Summer 1969), 442.

37. Jean-Paul Sartre, *The Words* (Greenwich, Conn., 1964).

38. Ibid., 20.

39. Ibid., 30.

40. Ibid., 121.

41. Ibid., 53.

42. Sartre, *Baudelaire* (New York, 1950), 55–56.

43. Brée, *Camus and Sartre*, 161.

44. Ibid., 161–62.

45. Sartre, *Baudelaire*, 26.

46. Sartre, "A Plea for Intellectuals," in his *Between Existentialism and Marxism*, 265.

47. Sartre, *Words*, 159.

48. For a discussion of how the terror of man's historicity affected the high culture of post–World War II Europe, see Lichtheim's *Europe*, 358–72.

49. Cited in Jean Lacroix, *Les sentiments et la vie morale* (Paris, 1952), 23. Emphasis is mine.

50. Lichtheim here paraphrased Michel Foucault, *Europe*, 370.

51. Eugen Weber, "France," in Hans Rogger and Eugen Weber, eds., *The European Right* (Berkeley, 1966), 126.

52. Theodore Zeldin, *France: 1848–1945, vol. 2: Intellect, Taste and Anxiety* (Oxford, 1977), 30.

# 5

# The Test of a National Conscience: From Philosophers' Republic to World Empire

Men resemble their times rather than their fathers.
    Henry Loyn, "Marc Bloch," *The Historian at Work* (Boston, 1980), 133.

    The present leading actors are hardly the ablest God could lay his hands on, but the element of sacrifice is undoubtedly present.
    Conor Cruise O'Brien, "Politics as Drama as Politics," *Power and Consciousness* (New York, 1969), 228.

The United States is officially the land of philosophers. It is, in fact, a political creation of eighteenth-century philosophers. By its official national culture, the United States is neither a part of nor in history. It transcends history. The United States is a unique amalgam of two transhistorical myths. It is both the new Israel and the new leader of humanity. Its official culture, fusing the myths of America's seventeenth-century religious-pilgrim foundings and its eighteenth-century republic beginnings, always depicts America as transcending history. America's mission, whether to God or humanity, belongs to universal redemptive history.[1]

America could never meet the measure of such high expectations. Always intruding themselves were unwanted historical realities. The United States is a nation, more or less, like other nations. Its sinews are power, industry, war, self-interest, and all the rest of that irrational, defective, and human stuff which defies American myths.

In the twentieth century, the conflict between myth and reality has become increasingly severe. The United States, in fact, has encountered the humanity by myth it was destined to save. Americans have had to ask whether or not their nation is really unique. They have had to consider opinions like that expressed by Pitirim Sorokin:

> In spite of some three or four centuries of geographical separation, there has been for a long time and still is only one culture, the Western or Euro-American culture, identical on both continents in all its essential traits. Being essentially identical, it is of the same age on both continents, not a bit younger in America than in Europe. As such, it changes along similar lines on both continents, and passes in this change through the same main phases and exhibits similar tendencies. So it was during the seventeenth and eighteenth centuries, and has continued to be up to the present time. . . .[2]

The United States in this period also had to test itself on a new scale. The test abroad involved sustaining international capitalism and liberal democracy, as well as fighting two world wars. At home, the test meant the burden of reconciling freedom and social justice amid the mounting complexities of industrial society. This gave ample reasons for guilt and disillusion about America's supposed universal mission.

Nevertheless, the myths of America as the innocent servant of God and humanity did not perish. Rather, they survived, even thrived, for several reasons. The United States had been spared from being engulfed by the tragic events of the first half of the century. In addition, those who propagated official American culture, from high politician to grade school teacher, did not falter in their service of the official culture. Further, and most significantly, the great majority of Americans knew that their lot had improved dramatically in the last few generations, and that improvement, or at least the promise of it, was inseparable from America's progress.

In the aftermath of the Second World War, the myths of official America were tested more rigorously than ever before. The United States could not retreat from the world it was committed to save. It could not avoid the awesome transformation from republic to empire, from a small, rural, democracy to an international, capitalistic, industrial world power. The country had entered onto the stage of universal history. To exempt its actions from that role was no longer possible. Indeed, the United States was the decisive power in fighting and settling the Second World War.

The marriage of America to humanity, which was contracted in myth, now was consecrated in fact. On a scale never precedented, one nation had made itself the protagonist of world history.

To be the hero of history was to assume awesome responsibility. That which most elevates also most condemns. The diffuse guilt of fearing failure is exceeded only by the worse guilt of failure itself.

The formulation of national responsibility and guilt began during the Second World War and further developed during the debates of the Vietnam War. An ethical identity was being sought at a time when the nation had passed from the traditional to the modern world and from republic to empire. In light of this new national responsibility and guilt, what has come of the philosophers' faith in the contemporary world? And what has been the role of national culture in the formation of our conscience?

To know ourselves we must know our history. American national culture is descended from the philosophers. To see that culture tested against the reality of the twentieth century is to measure the ideals of our own conscience.

## THE PASSAGE OF GUILT FROM
## THE OLD WORLD TO THE NEW WORLD

Nazi Germany, for contemporary Western conscience, is the epitome of evil. It stands not just as the antithesis of the West's secular humanistic hopes, it is, at least for many, undeniable proof that the demon has been resurrected in our midst, that all the dark forces the philosophers and their followers sought to drive out and banish forever from the Western kingdom have returned sevenfold.

Like a great plague, Nazism infects with its guilt. "One misses much of the post-war mood," wrote Rolland Stromberg, "if one fails to understand *how the monstrous guilt of the Nazis was transmitted into a sense of general guilt of the human race.*"[3] In *The Question of German Guilt*, German philosopher Karl Jaspers helps us define that guilt. In addition to criminal, political, and moral guilts, Jaspers speaks of a metaphysical guilt:

> Metaphysical guilt is the lack of absolute solidarity with the human being as such—an indelible claim beyond morally meaningful duty. The solidarity is violated by my presence at a wrong or a crime. It is not enough that I cautiously risk my life to prevent it; if it happens, and if I was there, and if I survive where the other is killed, I know from a voice within myself. *I am guilty of still being alive.*[4]

Hannah Arendt, German Jew and a student of Jaspers, further generalized this guilt:

> For the idea of humanity, when purged of all sentimentality, has the very serious consequence that, in one form or another, men must assume responsibility for all crimes committed by men and that all nations share the onus of evil committed by all others.[5]

In fact, Arendt believed that only those who sense this guilt should be trusted with the affairs of man.

> Perhaps those Jews, to whose forefathers we owe the first conception of the idea of humanity, knew something about that burden when each year they used to say "Our Father and King, we have sinned before you," taking not only the sins of their own community, but all human offenses, upon themselves. Those who today are ready to follow this road in a modern version do not content themselves with the hypocritical confession, "God be thanked, I am not like that," in horror at the undreamed of potentialities of the German national character. Rather, in fear and trembling, have they finally realized of what man is capable—and this is indeed the precondition of any modern political thinking.[6]

This general guilt for mankind, however defined, is not easily controlled; it can be dynamic. It can demand myths, ideologies, rituals, and actions to express it and to exorcise it. It can be cynically manipulated as a powerful source of moral leverage. This guilt can also turn to self-hatred, denying all inheritance. In the guise of revolutionary passion, nihilistic art, or cynical individualism, it attacks nearly everything about the West—Europe, America, the white man, the middle class, reason, freedom, and progress. Those moved by this self-hatred write the West's history as a story of failure and guilt.

The way out of this guilt-induced self-hatred is often found by critical negation: One rejects all that one has inherited and is associated with. One establishes a new moral identity with the underdogs, the outcasts, the exploited, the homeless—all the real and supposed "innocent" victims of the present order. These pariahs have the innocence of being sinned against, and of not sinning; they suffer, but they do not cause suffering. They are idealized to be free of the evils of intellect and power; and therefore are considered to be simpler, healthier, more natural. As in Hegel's idealization of the slave, the special greatness of "these innocent ones" is found in the undefined freedom of their potential. They also offer community in "this communityless era." "In these dark times," Arendt wrote "the warmth, which the pariahs substitute for the light, exerts a great fascination upon all those who are ashamed of the world as it is that they would like to take refuge in invisibility."[7]

Given how abundantly this logic of guilt operated in the 1960s, one might assume mistakenly that the universal guilt associated so closely with Nazi Germany spread directly from there to the rest of Europe and from Europe to America. There is a certain truth to this. No sooner does one hear of the Nazis' horrible deeds, than one participates in their guilt. In measure, we become what we hear; we do in spirit what we discover others have done in body. This view of the diffusion of guilt, however, implies a distortion of American experience.

By virtue of their national culture and experience, Americans had immunity against this virile guilt. The United States was not only different from Nazi Germany, but had defeated it in four years of war. Also, there was no reasonable basis for believing that the United States would succumb to Nazism. There were ways, however, in which Americans were not completely invulnerable to that guilt. After all, the United States was part of the West. If progress had backfired in Europe, which it was generally conceded that it had, what would one expect from the United States, the epitome of the West? In addition, there were memories of slavery, genocide, class warfare, jingoism, virulent nativism, racist immigration policies, and much else, which were heard to say "America, you too are mortal." Never to be forgotten was the fact that America had been the first to use the atomic bomb.[8]

Guilt also entered into America when a small number of educated Americans adopted Europe's culture, and thus its tragedies, as their own. With unprecedented enthusiasm, increased numbers of Americans took to books, universities, art, museums, travel abroad, and other forms of high culture, which literally and figuratively put them upon European cultural territory.[9] In dramatically increasing numbers in the interwar years, Europe's best minds migrated to the United States. These "illustrious immigrants," representing all Western cultural traditions, taught Americans to know themselves and their responsibilities.[10] Aided by a host of visiting European scholars and rapidly multiplying translations, these immigrants preached their anticommunism, neo-Marxisms, and philosophical conservatisms. They initiated American thinkers into historicism and historical sociology; they infected Americans with their "depth theologies," new scholasticisms, and existentialisms—Christian and nontheistic alike. Though they were not "serpents in the garden," they made legitimate an anguish, a despair, a guilt, and even a nihilism which had its source in European tragedies. In a few instances, with the help of Dostoyevsky, Kierkegaard, Nietzsche, Rilke, Kafka, Sartre, Bernanos, Marcel, Heidegger, Jaspers, and Arendt, Americans were taught to assimilate European guilt about man's place in existence.

This high intellectual road of guilty anguish over the human condition, nevertheless, was alien to the American conscience of the postwar period. The majority's first preoccupation, as was the case in Europe itself, was with matters of family, self, and local community. Also, the official view still held that America was the ally of humanity. Its people were understood to be generous and humane, its government free, its resources abundant. Indeed, these contentions were supported in fact. As was true of no other, America was an owed nation. During the First World War, the United States had passed from being a debtor to a creditor. By the end of the Second World War, the United States was owed as no other nation had been owed. It could count the world's indebtedness not just in dollars, but in dead.[11] America, it was officially claimed, deserved gratitude, not accusation; its gifts should never be forgotten. The majority, especially the veterans, wholeheartedly agreed.

It was this ruling ethical consensus of the 1940s and 1950s that was challenged openly in the 1960s.[12] The Vietnam War, a long, degrading process of political error, military defeat, and immoral and political arrogance, undercut the faith of many. At the extremes, accusers called America fascist. Vietnam, like some kind of American Syracuse, seemed to reveal a republic madly and self-destructively at war for the sake of the empire. The ignorance, lying, and violence associated with the war evoked guilt. Daniel Ellsberg was not alone in believing that, in Vietnam, America looked into the abyss, and the abyss looked back into America.[13]

The Vietnam War, the Watergate affair, the energy shortage, the onset of a seemingly uncontrollable inflation-depression cycle, and Congressional corruption on the one hand and lassitude on the other all served to acquaint every sector of the American population with national limits. America was becoming, despite the assumptions of the national culture and its most vociferous defenders, far less the shining city on the hill and far more an arena of conflicting forces. Americans grew to be far less confident about their public givings and takings, and altogether less sure about their gift to humanity. This change in national conscience is not, however, just an American matter. Being questioned is the result of the highest eighteenth- and nineteenth-century Western ideals to guide the aspirations, machines, and states of contemporary man.

## SONS' GUILT VERSUS FATHERS' GRATITUDE IN THE 1960s

At issue in the decade of the 1960s was America's service to humanity.[14] The decade was initiated by John F. Kennedy's announcement of America's determination to bring a new era of justice, freedom, and abundance to humanity. The decade ended with Richard M. Nixon seeking adroitly to extract the nation from a lost war abroad and unprecedented protest at home.

The Vietnam War cut the decade in two. It swallowed Lyndon Johnson's presidency. From 1965 onward, Johnson's administration increasingly was preoccupied with the war. To that most demanding of human gods, he sacrificed more and more materials, ideals, and men. Yet in the end, defeat was not escaped. Progress and the good of humanity had again been lost to war.

Aside from death and destruction, harvested from the Vietnam War were the emotional consequences that resulted from a disastrous collision between an expanding optimism (fostered by the liberal presidencies of Kennedy and Johnson) and the dark realities of fighting a costly, prolonged, shameful, and manifestly un-winnable war—indeed, a war that had never even been declared. The war imposed the theme of tragic waste upon the decade. Material goods were squandered. Moral authority was depleted; and in certain quarters, the very link between America and human-ity's progress was broken. The war caused a great debate over America's givings and takings. Guilt and gratitude were the essen-tial emotional terms of that debate, which was, above all else, a debate between fathers and sons.

The 1960s debate over American national culture can only be retold by resorting to the theme of the conflict between fathers and sons and between mothers and daughters.[15] The theme of intergen-erational conflict revolved around the existence of the military draft for the most advertised and the least popular war in American history. It was tied to the simple demographic fact that there were more youth, and more youth in relation to adults, than ever before. Likewise, the theme could not be separated from the burgeoning college populations and the conflicts that filled the campuses from 1967 onward. Changes in sexual practices, marriage, and childrear-ing also seemed to be matters of intergenerational conflict.

Influenced by the era, Margaret Mead gave the intergenerational conflict a cosmic dimension. In her *Culture and Commitment: A Study of the Generation Gap*, she hypothesized the most awesome estrangement imaginable between generations.

> We have to realize that no other generation will ever experience what we have experienced. In this sense, we must recognize that we have no descendants, as our children have no forebearers. We elders are a strangely isolated generation. No other generation has even known, experienced, and struggled to incorporate such massive and rapid change—has watched while the sources of energy, the means of com-munication, the certainties of a known world, the limits of the ex-plorable universe, the definition of humanity, and fundamental im-peratives of life and death have changed before their eyes. . . . At this breaking point between radically different and closely related groups, both are inevitably very lonely, as we face each other know-ing that they will never experience what we have experienced, and that we can never experience what they have experienced.[16]

Robert J. Lifton and Kenneth Kenniston shared Margaret Mead's belief that protesting students expressed a dramatic turning point in human history.[17] Robert Lifton argued that they were born into a world in which the fundamental boundaries of life were being altered. They were without inheritance; any meaning their lives were to have had to be won by experimentation. Kenniston, using other terms, affirmed this. Youth, he argued, had to try to live in a world in which the cake of custom had long ago crumbled. Standing midway between adolescence and adulthood, the youth carried the burden of forging a new culture.

Richard Flacks also helped to explain protesting youth. He specifically argued that they, the protesters in the developed countries, cannot be treated as an expression of the disassociations which youth of the underdeveloped countries experience under the cultural strains of modernization.[18] The protesting youth of the United States and Western Europe must be understood in reference to the sociology of developed, abundant, and democratic societies.[19] Characteristically, he remarked, they were students at colleges and universities, with better than average academic records. The majority came from upper class, educated families in which "values," careers, and public matters were taken seriously, conventional religion and morality were treated with considerable skepticism, and education was regarded and valued for its own sake rather than in utilitarian terms. Political liberalism, distrust of conventional and mass culture, and a commitment to encouraging independent and self-expressive children were additional values held by these families. According to Flacks, protesting youth's focus was threefold: They found the jobs offered personally meaningless and morally repugnant; they expected more from American society for themselves, the poor, and the world than it gave; and they grew progressively disillusioned by the war until eventually they saw America as an active threat to humanity's future.

Additionally, it should be mentioned that these students knew little or nothing of the hardships of the old order. Therefore they could not be expected to be truly grateful for what they had received. They had been raised in the shadow of the bomb, so for them there was always the sense that everything they had been given might be taken away instantly. The heroism of the Second World War did not belong to them, nor could they claim with pride the traditions of having suffered through the Great Depression. Above all else, they identified with the future they were supposed to make. Thus, the war threatened to take away from them what they most cherished, their potential.

This portrait, of course, is not a complete description of the conscience of the protesting students and their movement, for they were not the product of a single mind, group, theory, or strategy.[20] Rather, they and their movement developed between consciousness and event, culture and change, actor and audience, leader and followers. The movement was marked by paradoxical demands: There was, on the one hand, a quest for the creation of a new consciousness and, on the other hand, the demand for immediate action to end a specific war. There was an initial idealistic commitment to nonviolent action, and there developed a belief that violent revolution alone was sufficient. Further, there was initially a demand for national reform and, at the end, increasing criticism of international capitalism. Increasingly, like the generation of European intellectuals of the political left who came to maturity in the late 1920s and early 1930s, they came to believe that the collapse of the whole of civilization was at hand.[21]

It took the war to create these students and their movement. There were reasons in the 1950s for not being satisfied with America. More readers, more universities, more radios, more television sets and more leisure time were putting Americans in contact with a perplexing world. Sophistication alone, predicated naturally on an ample taste of European ideas and sensibilities, demanded that one show disdain for the consumer society and the advantages of middle-class life. Aside from the well-traveled roads of cultural dissent—from existentialism to anguishing religion, from readings of decadent French poetry to negro jazz spots to folkish sociologies—there were other bases for discord. As was popularly shown by Michael Harrington in *The Other America*, there were many people in America who were not yet getting their fair share.[22] The struggle for civil rights for the blacks in the South showed that justice was not perfect in the nation. Some still remembered the 1930s and were allied to its causes of justice.

Even more significant in the increase of dissent from the national culture was the fact that the United States had become the world's greatest single power. At its disposal were weapons that could eliminate global life itself. Critical questions about this could not entirely be repressed: Wasn't it for God to give and take life? Might

not the United States actually destroy the humanity it was supposed to save? What exchange could there be, what covenant could
be established, with a state that gave a great deal but threatened to
take everything in return? Hans Morgenthau argued that nuclearism, the ultimate defense of a country, was incompatible with
patriotism:

> It is the distinctive characteristic of the nuclear age that this moral
> foundation upon which the legitimacy of democratic government has
> rested in the past is no longer as firm as it used to be. A government
> armed with nuclear, biological and chemical weapons of mass de-
> struction still intends to protect the life of its citizens against a gov-
> ernment similarly armed. But in truth it cannot defend its citizens, it
> can only deter the prospective enemy from attacking them. If deter-
> rence fails and it attacks, the citizens are doomed. Such a govern-
> ment, then, bears the two faces of Janus: insofar as it is able to deter,
> it is still its citizens' protector; if it fails to deter, it becomes the source
> of their destruction. This new quality of modern government, pre-
> cariously poised at the edge of the abyss of self-destruction, is
> vaguely felt, rather than clearly understood, by the man in the street.
> He beholds with awe and without confidence that gigantic machine
> of mass destruction which is anachronistically called the Department
> of Defense, and he wonders whether it will not cause his own de-
> struction while destroying the enemy, and he also wonders whether a
> government so constituted still deserves the obedience and loyalty it
> claims and once deserved. If it is true that *ubi bene, ibi partria*,
> (where the good is, is where one's fatherland is) where is his father-
> land?[23]

These dilemmas of patriotism in a nuclear age—the guilt they
propagated, the disillusion they threatened—however, did not
jeopardize the national official culture significantly. America,
afterall, just had been, and was now again, at war against the
world's worst enemy. This time the enemy was communism. The
vast majority of Americans unquestionably acknowledged the
moral superiority of the United States. Its power had not grown out
of self-interest but, they believed, it had resulted from their heroic
pursuit of the good. Further, no amount of sociological theorizing
about the growth of American bureaucracy and power elites could
have jeopardized the ruling consensus, whose first assumption was
that America was doing the work of God and humanity.

If dissent from the national culture was to occur, if the new responsibility and the guilt it caused was to give rise to a different conscience, power would have to be the midwife. Power opens and shuts the chambers of human sensibilities. At this point, John F. Kennedy held power's keys.

Kennedy invited America to responsibility.[24] He was, in truth, an eighteenth-century philosopher reincarnated. He set aside the cautious traditionalism of the Eisenhower years. He was America's, indeed the philosophers', response to Castro, De Gaulle, Pope John, and Krushchev. Rational and beneficial, dramatic and heroic, his message was one of mastery of the future. He called Americans to put themselves on the stage of world history, to let all humanity judge their performance.

"Let the word go forth from this time and place, to friend and foe alike," he began his memorable inaugural address, "the torch has been passed to a new generation of Americans—born in this century, tempered by war, disciplined by hard and bitter peace, proud of our ancient heritage—and unwilling to witness or permit the slow undoing of those human rights to which this nation has always been committed, and to which we are committed today at home and around the world."[25] He moved between gifts and threats. He made positive pledges to the poor (especially those of Latin America), to disarmament, and to the cooperative attempt "to explore the stars, conquer the deserts, eradicate disease, tap the ocean depths, and encourage the arts and commerce."[26] Yet, he reminded us, "We are willing to pay any price, bear any burden, meet any hardship, oppose any foe to assure the survival and success of liberty."[27] He concluded with a reminder of our blood inheritance of sacrifice.

> Since this country was founded, each generation of Americans have been summoned to give its testimony to its national loyalty. The graves of young Americans who answered the call to service surround the globe. . . .[28]

He called Americans to be responsible for a heroic, religious, millenial struggle:

> Now the trumpet summons us again—not as a call to bear arms, though arms we need—not as a call to battle, though embattled we

are—but a call to bear the burden of a long twilight struggle, year in and year out, "rejoicing in hope, patient in tribulation"—a struggle against the common enemies of man: tyranny, poverty, disease and war itself. . . . *And so, my fellow Americans: ask not what your country can do for you—ask what you can do for your country.*[29]

JFK was exhilirating. For a thousand days he made the liberal education universal. Americans would be responsible for humanity; its condition would be part of their obligation. He promised the sky without once losing touch with the earth. He was both a prophet of a new world and a priest of the old order. He equipped America militarily to an extent Eisenhower had never even dreamed. He equipped America for every imaginable kind of war, relied on the CIA, and drew hard nuclear lines—*"Ich bin ein Berliner!"* He gambled humanity on the Cuban Missile Crisis and was not above carrying out political-military experiments in Vietnam. Kennedy was a mixture of energizing dreams and terrible nightmares. He invigorated American public conscience by pressing to its limits the myths of America as the ally of humanity.

He excited youth. Like their liberal parents, they too tied their conscience to public affairs. They would help "get the country moving again," fight apathy on their campuses, go South to help in voter registration, join the Peace Crops to serve in distant lands. They enrolled themselves in Kennedy's expectations and shared the responsibility and guilt for a "New Frontier."

One group that reflected this newly invigorated conscience was the Students for Democratic Society (SDS). In their 1962 founding address, "The Port Huron Statement," they took up "the torch which had been passed."[30] As young aspiring intellectuals of the left tend to do, they apologized for their social class and education ("bred in at least modest comfort and housed now in universities"). Predictably enough, they called for students to be active rather than passive citizens and they catalogued problems, such as degradation in the South, underemployment in the North, undernourishment in the world, and "the enclosing fact of the Cold War." In accord with the concerns of their intellectual elders, they worried about commercialization, massification, and bureaucratization; denounced Soviet Russia; called for dialogue rather than revolution; and declared that the old left was dead. At no point did they lose contact with the tenets of America's progressive faith. They were the children of the philosophers.

However, their tone was different from that of JFK and their liberal fathers. They declared that the national leaders' idealism rang hollow when measured by the realities of black-American life and national investments in the Cold War. They even postulated, as the national culture never could, that America was an engine of death; that they "might be the last generation to experiment with living"; that politics must be courageously creative, not guided by cliché or by "vague appeals to posterity justifying the mutilation of the present."[31]

In the years immediately following the Port Huron Statement, the SDS, still only representative of a very small cross section of university youth and the political left, broadened its criticism of America. By 1963, in a major statement it made its disagreements with the liberal democrats explicit: The Cold War was denounced as a pretext for increasing militarization. Kennedy and the New Frontier's men were labeled servants of the "Establishment," that amoral system of managerial rule whose primary interest is the preservation of corporate capitalism. Liberals were judged to be more adroit than honest, more at home in cocktail parties and seminars than with the people's causes. At home liberals engaged in "aggressive tokenism." Already the authors of this 1963 document were certain that "America would meet revolution with force if necessary, and this means the sure devastation of country after country in the Third World, as Vietnam, for instance, is now being destroyed."[32] America, for them, was guilty.

By 1965 the War in Vietnam was the SDS's central issue. At an antiwar march in Washington, SDS President Carl Oglesby said of the ruling elders: "They are not moral monsters. They are all honorable men. They are liberals."[33] Oglesby believed that the liberal establishment had put before America the choice of "corporatism or humanism." To those who accused him of sounding anti-American, Oglesby replied: "Don't blame *me* for *that*! Blame those who mouthed my liberal values and broke my American heart."[34]

While the SDS was youth's first effort at critical theory, the Free Speech Movement, which developed in 1964 at the University of California in Berkeley, was their solo flight in dissent.[35] The Free

Speech Movement also anticipated the bitter dialogue between youth and elders which lay ahead: Youth asked about America's complicity with evil, and the elders interpreted their very question as an act of disloyalty.

The Free Speech Movement divided first Berkeley, then California, and then, in a certain sense, the United States. On one side were the Berkeley students—who were veterans of recent campaigns to save Caryl Chessman, to abolish the House Un-American Activities Committee, and to win full civil rights in the South—as well as members of the San Francisco beat culture and still others who loved, what later were to be called, "happenings." On the other side were liberal President Clark Kerr, the regents, and all the other legislative, political, and economic forces that shaped the administrative policy of the University of California in the fall of 1964. The encounters between the two sides in the next six months established the classical model of a university crisis.

The vast majority of the citizens of California perceived no substance in the students' demands. They only felt ingratitude. "We pay the bills, provide the opportunities for an education, a future better than we've had, and they say no to it. They break the law and denounce the country. Their disrespect must be punished." The more sophisticated liberal fathers, while not above the plaint of gratitude ill-paid, first sought to "understand" the students' concerns and were reluctant to prescribe punishment. But, in time, they declared the students to be irresponsible, a threat to the economic benefits and academic freedoms just recently secured for the university. Some faculty accused the students of destroying "the free market place of ideas," of being fascist in their activism and totalitarian in their conception of knowledge. That interpretation put the sons on the side of the fathers' worst enemies, Nazi Germany and Soviet Russia.

The youth sought more than better teaching and less grading. They wanted what American official culture in general, and Kennedy in particular, said they should have: the right to enter the heroic, noble, and moral creation of the world. Their models were the revolutionary leaders of Cuba and the black Civil Rights leaders in the American South. Conversely, they did not want to be what they guiltily judged themselves to be: the future beneficiaries of the present system; the suburban-dwelling managers of "the odious system." They resented, feared, and felt guilt about their place in the university, which they defined as "a knowledge factory which processes us to process others"; "a highly efficient industry which produces bombs, other war machines, a few token 'peaceful machines,' and an enormous number of safe, highly skilled, and respectable automatons to meet the immediate needs of business and government."[36] Defying what traditional culture perennially assumed, they refused to believe that they should have their well-being secured at the cost of the well-being of others. There may have been a profound altruism here; there may also have been a sentimental romanticism. Surely there was a conscience at work here that judged humanity's responsibility to be humanity.

Up to a point the fathers sympathized with the sons. But reluctantly, they judged the sons' to be destroying the education, the very great gift, they had given them. The sons, on their side, judged the fathers to be guilty of reneging on the promise of America to humanity, as well as denying the sons' gift of heroic dedication. Exchange between fathers and sons was broken. They were no longer a moral community; they had split over the value of their nation, its legacy and its responsibility.

On March 3, 1965, a solitary student stood on the steps of the Berkeley Student Union with a sign that read "Fuck!" Again sides were taken on that campus. The notorious "Filthy Speech Movement" had begun. Californians of all classes formed a new opinion of students: They were selfish, lazy, foul, irreligious, immodest, ungrateful, and anti-American. Things, they said, had gone too far.

The consciences that made the SDS and the Free Speech Movement were still a minority. It took the war to give those types of consciences any significance for the nation at large.

One could chart the burgeoning antagonism between fathers and sons from 1965 onward: The good fortunes of American democratic liberalism, which at the moment had its embodiment in and was epitomized by LBJ's presidency, stood in reverse proportion to America's involvement in the Vietnam War.[37]

"The Great Society," LBJ's effort to be loved as a great President, disappeared in Asian jungles. He was the liberal President par excellence. By generous legislation he sought to realize the people's full potential. However, "guns and butter" meant inflation; righteousness about such a costly, dubious project as a war in Asia resulted in tragedy.[38] For three years from 1965 to 1968, LBJ made the war a loyalty test which he administered to more and more Americans. The test had three stages: "We're not in a war!" "We're in it and winning!" "We're not losing the war, in fact we're still winning it. As soon as the other side admits we haven't lost, we'll leave." Moral calistenics became increasingly contortional as the government sent 500,000 troops to fight an "Asian boys' war." Dean Rusk set forth his changing explanations for American presence in Vietnam, such as democracy, the domino theory, free villages, South Vietnam's territorial integrity, SEATO; and mental congestion from the Pentagon intensified with such terms as "defoliation," "pacification," and "preemptive protective retaliation strikes." An American general even went so far as to say it was "necessary to destroy a village in order to save it." Such violence and ignorance were radicalizing protesters' consciences, and thus making America, in contradiction to its deepest official myths, a matter of inhumanity and guilt.

In changing its 1964 position from "Part of the Way with LBJ" to open opposition to LBJ in 1965, the SDS was only responding to the evolution of radical student opinion. That evolution expressed itself in the growing teach-in movement. Although the Senate Internal Security subcommission postulated communism to be the cause of the teach-ins, their source was more obvious. Many educated sons and daughters were profoundly repulsed by the war. They found it morally outrageous. America was supposed to do good for the world. Mixing short lectures, moral accusations, and professions, the night-long teach-ins, which joined students and teachers in new communities, were tedious and long-winded, as well as fervent, compelling, and altogether exhilarating by their novelty. Where one occurred, at least in the early stages, the climate of the campus was altered. There America was on moral trial, and there was a new responsibility for youth in particular and the academic community as a whole to listen and to speak out.

As teach-ins became more common, so accusations became more extreme. America was being judged. "America," some shouted out, "has put property rights over human rights." Others jeered, "Hey, hey, LBJ! How many kids did you kill today?" The duty to disassociate oneself from America intensified; God, humanity, or simple decency required it. There was a strong sense of betrayal. America was betraying itself—its life, its ambitions—and youth were being senselessly sacrificed to the blind stupidities of their elders. David

King, a Harvard student, replied to a condescending talk by George Kennan:

> At graduation we face the certainty of some kind of death, moral, if not physical, and we must hence do all our living, endure all our agony and ecstasy in four short years. We dwell with horrible feelings of being a pawn caught in someone else's chess game. . . . Is it any wonder that we do not go gentle into that good night.[39]

Protesting youth had the test of the draft. This was the measure of their conscience. Starting in 1965 with David Miller of the Catholic Worker, those who openly refused the draft became the conscience of the Movement.[40] They sacrificed themselves to protest. They said no to the system and thus exposed themselves to its punishments. They chose not to associate themselves with the system. They would not hide behind a student exemption or accept conscientious objector status, which in their eyes allowed power to define conscience's legitimacy. In their statement, "We Refuse to Serve," they declared: "The war in Vietnam is criminal and we must act together, at great individual risk, to stop it. Those involved must lead the American people, by their example, to understand the enormity of what their government is doing. . . . The government cannot be allowed to continue with its daily crimes."[41] Their service to humanity put them in opposition to their country, and in risk of imprisonment. In the name of God and humanity, they had chosen to follow their conscience which led them against America.

The spirit of the teach-ins and the conscience of the draft became a truly national matter in 1968. The reason for the diffusion was the year itself. More precisely, by the diversity, awesomeness, and contradiction of its events, no single year following the Second World War could stand in comparison to 1968. We can suggest here only some of the events of that year that opened minds, defied the most precious national myths and ruling authorities, and led great numbers to reorder their consciences.

The year 1968 began with the Tet Offensive, which demonstrated that America's defeat in Vietnam was certain, and followed with federal indictments of nationally known figures Doctor Spock and Reverend Sloan Coffin for conspiracy to counsel draft evasion. The year was filled with unprecedented political changes: The

Eugene McCarthy Campaign, the beginnings of the Peace and Freedom Party, the withdrawal of LBJ from candidacy, the Robert Kennedy campaign, and the full resurrection of Richard Nixon whom
JFK had buried eight years before. The year was marked by the
tremors of the assassinations of Martin Luther King and Robert
Kennedy, the latter of whom was killed on the very eve of his
crucial victory over Eugene McCarthy in the California Democratic
Primary. Of the student protests that year, none were as dramatic
as those at Columbia and San Francisco State. Abroad, in France,
there were *les événements de mai*, a spontaneous student rebellion
which for three weeks tottered the French government. The year
climaxed with the conviction of Spock and Coffin; Nixon's quiet
nomination in Miami; Humphrey's nomination at the dark, violent, war-torn Chicago Convention; and the Russian invasion of
Czechoslovakia.[42]

That was a terrible, incredible year. For many it melted the
founding myths of official American national culture. Many, of
course, from progressive, liberal circles were ready to say America
had been metamorphosed from being an ally into being an enemy
of humanity. Many now were ready to join Susan Sontag in saying, "This is a doomed country. . . . I only pray that, when
America founders, it doesn't drag the planet down, too."[43] In 1968,
some even felt that America was cursed, that it no longer was
blessed with a special covenant. Reacting to the assassination of
Robert F. Kennedy, John Updike remarked, "God might have with-
drawn his blessing from the country." Surely liberalism's decade
ended in 1968.

Those convinced that war was wrong were now confronted with
the task of bearing a conscience in full contradiction to the government. This was an agonizing situation. One's nation was guilty of
wrong; one's responsibilities, once accepted, meant separation
from one's family, home, and American society itself. The choice
increasingly was prison, exile, or an underground existence. Nation
and conscience were at odds.

Dissent, however, was not exclusively the work of people of pure
conscience, "men of guilt." In fact, in 1968, with cultural and political authority so broadly challenged—even now fashionably attacked for the sake of identity in certain groups—the conscience of
protest was confused with what broadly was taken to be "a

counterculture," "a youth revolution," a range of other activities that dissented, or at least were understood to dissent, from the established order of things.[44]

Some protest was sheer insolence. It was bratty youth thumbing its nose at its elders. For instance, Jerry Rubin, the most insolent of Yippies to show up at the Democratic Convention, called every policeman a pig, every soldier a murderer.[45] If the Yippies had a manifesto, it was: "Whenever we see a rule, we must break it. Only by breaking rules do we discover who we are." Defiance itself became the way for some to find authentic selfhood. Some protesters at the Pentagon, for example, urinated on its walls, others prayed for its levitation. A nude female graduate student served a pig's head to Humphrey and Muskie supporters. Jerry Rubin and Abbie Hoffman burned money on Wall Street, appeared before HUAC dressed as a guerilla warrior and Uncle Sam, and designed other infantile charades of insult.

Obviously such protest had little or nothing to do with conscientious objection. In fact, after 1968 protests were increasingly about issues other than the war. Protests often served, as they have throughout modern history, as initiatory rituals for those who wished to identify themselves with radical causes. Protests also meant excitement, a chance to get on the public stage, and for a very small number an opportunity to practice the manipulation of crowds. The one thing protests weren't characterized by, at least in their beginning, was business as usual, the normal course of things. Administrators, city officials, police, and even governors and national guards helped see to that. Protests in the form of parades, sit-ins, and "flower-to-gun confrontations" made streets, buildings, and parks into stages for a moral play. Protests also created a sense of carnival. It was as if the world had entered an irregular time. With classes canceled, grades left ungiven, the disappearance of authorities, all-night mingling, the air of unusual happenings, and unexpected burnings and lootings, students made displays of themselves and there were manifestations of new communities. Protests, therefore, and the atmospheres they created could be moral, dramatic, religious, and communal; adventures not just in conscience but in fun, drugs, and self-celebration.[46]

Youth of all ages and from all sectors of society absorbed the new climate of moral confrontation and festival and distorted it for their own ends. Taught by their peers, professors, the media, "head shops," and rock groups that they were unique—altogether different from their parents—they declared themselves by dress, drugs, music, posters, and jargon to be a new youth. Their ideology, not really coherent, was arrogantly self-righteous. Their basic moral argument was: The old made the war, and therefore they were guilty; whereas they, the youth, were against the war, and thus innocent. The ethics were indeed conscienceless. They shirked responsibility for society, humanity, and principle; everything but being themselves. They had no history, inheritance, or tradition; they were beyond guilt and gratitude.

Some made their biology itself the basis of their innocence and their justification. Michael McClure argued that he was not responsible for any collective crimes, for he was free and innocent, a warm-blooded "mammal." The future, he predicted, will be "biological."[47]

This presumed status of biological innocence put them beyond the canons of reason, work, discipline, and philanthrophy. There was something terribly decadent about this self-venerating youth who divided the world into ogres and saints: The ogres were their parents, laws, moralities, and all other authorities; they themselves were saints, a self-anointed "party of Eros," to use a book title of the era.[48] They were, they thus affirmed, on the side of life and love. Their flight from complex, industrial, urban society to the natural—that is, sex, the folk, folk music, communes—was supported by society's abundance and leisure, and was distastefully remniscent of fascist youth ideology. They smoked pot and played guitars, while others anguished over the politics of effective protest.

Such arrogant disrespectfulness on the part of youth had several sources, all of which cut against national-official culture. There was the scandalous absurdity of the war itself; and there was the whole critical tradition of the country. Youth inherited an entire repertoire of criticisms of modern life—all of which had already been part of the interwar European culture. Youth, to be critical of American society, only needed to repeat existentialism's indictment of the superficiality of contemporary existence. They merely had to recite standard left-wing sociology's indictment of the suburbs, business, the bureaucracy, and the factory system; reissue 1920 Surrealist attacks against the conventions of middle-class life; and paraphrase all the nineteenth- and twentieth-century, conservative and radical, social, economic, and political and aesthetic criticisms of the bourgeoisie and its mass, urban, industrial life. In other words, whole traditions of criticism converged then. Criticizing everything about the United States became commonplace. Criticism was in the air. Abundance had produced the demand for perfection; the war had produced the right of honesty, and protest had given legitimacy to speaking out.

All this criticism taken together seemed to constitute a culture of opposition or, to use the label of the era, a counterculture. In fact, however defined, it was not a culture. It was neither a high nor a traditional, neither a national nor a popular culture. In all ways it was eclectic; it did not exclude anything. There was no past criticism of Western life that, in one form or another, it did not now bring to the surface. It abundantly tested sex, drugs, communes, and "alternate life styles"; it bantered about a plethora of feelings, sensibilities, ideas, and ideologies. Everything was hawked at the teeming fairs of liberation. Personal postures ranged from youthful defiance in the style of Dada to the following of countless non-Western ways; all promised self-fulfillment.

Some broad characteristics describe the sensibility of this counter-culture. In complete opposition to the leaders and the majority of the nation, the counterculture spoke against material progress. Many of the members feigned to be beyond it. They took the side of the primitive—the folk, the guitar, the Indian—against the modern. They chose the small over the big; and they, the children of the most technological nation of the world, made technology one of their favorite targets. Huxley, Orwell, Mumford, Ellul, Seidenberg, and Marcuse were used by the more articulate to say no thank you to American technology.[49] Technology, in their eyes, formed a way of life against life.[50]

Another theme, in fact an ethical principle of the youth, was that life was to be experimented with; one was to get out of it all one could. Even though this should be expected from healthy youth in an abundant nation, in a secular era the attitude violated the majority's sense of what was proper. A corrolary to the principle was the right to pursue pleasure as one could; the sexual was defined as liberating.[51] All this made it appear that one of the very characteristics of the counterculture was to shock America—not just the leaders, but the great majority who lived by work, discipline, and the hope that they and their families would prosper. Perhaps that was the case. There was no question that the people of the counter-culture had learned to shock the majority, and they, like past generations of European intellectual youth, took pleasure in that.

One irony of this cannot be overlooked. The people of the counterculture used the Vietnam War, consciously or uncon-sciously, to prove that all that existed was wrong. Tradition, loyalty, inheritance, gratitude—nothing that was given was worth having; what was different was worth trying.

Guilt and conscience themselves were attacked by the counter-culture. With the help of irrationalists like Norman Brown and others, consciousness itself was considered to be an impediment to life.[52] In this twilight zone of civilization, the counterculture people postulated, nothing any longer seemed to hold; everything was considered to be possible. Indeed, they were not unlike many who reacted to the tragedy of the First World War and the crisis period from 1929 to 1933; they were just more commercial, more popular, and less intellectual. They had turned against the philosophers' ideals of reason, philanthropy, reform, and progress. They pro-nounced America and its official national culture dead. In truth, though, the members of the counterculture were not innocent; they were a "guiltless" people.

In an unprecedented fashion, universities, "the home of 'pro-testing youth,'" became critical of official America. The univer-sities recorded, as never before, the tremors of a society in contest. The insistence that knowledge be morally committed filled the halls of ivory. In tacit agreement with the Free Speech Movement, the whole notion of value-free knowledge—that is, objective under-standing, or understanding free of the duty to act—was challenged at its core by university people.[53] The university, it was repeatedly claimed, could not simply be for careers, nor should it without con-science serve the establishment by making weapons, investing money in racism, or training the CIA people who designed pro-grams to subvert revolution.[54] The university was turning itself into the conscience of the nation.

Elements of each discipline of the Social Sciences were inspired by New Left criticism.[55] The "new economists" reintroduced political economy. Capitalism became the common term for the understanding of American business.[56] The "new political scien-tists" challenged the validity of consensus models of decision

making, as well as the justice of a pluralistic society.[57] The "new anthropologists" found the primitive to be the measure of the advanc-
ing inhumanity of industrial society; they judged the cost of being
modern to be high.[58] The sociologists, representing the discipline
that probably had the most professionals in the service of the New
Left, indexed the victims of American normalcy. By empathizing
with deviants, minorities, and the oppressed, they sought to expose
the underside of prosperous American society.

The new American historians broke with the historiographical
notion of a binding concensus that joined Americans together.[59]
Their "new history" concerned itself with the oppressed and the
protestors of oppression. Historians supplied new voices to the
dead; Indians, blacks, women, religious dissenters, mountain men,
miners, and saloon prostitutes got a chance to speak out to the
whole nation for the first time. Protestors—radicals, reformers,
populists, IWW leaders—and so many others who had once spoken
out against the established order also received sympathetic historical reconstructions. The melting pot was understood to be a fiery
foundry. Violence was understood not as a temporary aberration
but as an abiding element of American history. The social, institutional, and mental structures of genocide were sought, and the
roots of American imperialism were pursued. Revisions were made
regarding the United States' responsibilities for the Cold War.[60]
These historians were seeking to undo the myth that their pre-
decessors had helped to create. National-official identities were being taken apart. In place of America, servant of God and friend of
humanity, there was an America of power, self-interest, victims,
protesters, and much else antithetical to official myth and dutiful
nostalgia. Historians were putting America on trial.

Also the blacks were putting America on trial, calling its myths
to judgment. They voiced an oppositional conscience. Their actions, like the war itself, set the stage for a dramatic reconsideration
of America. In the early 1960s, they placed before America an experiment in nonviolence which was equal to Gandhi's in India.
Their voter registration in the South won them enthusiasm from
many whites. With the courts on their side, the blacks were a
power to be reckoned with. They forced JFK to send troops to integrate schools, caused profound embarrassments at the 1964
Democratic Convention, and were the secret agenda of LBJ's War
on Poverty. The urban riots, beginning in 1964 and cresting in

1967, gave substance to Baldwin and other black writers' prophetic principle that America's destiny was joined to the black man's fate. The blacks made America their classroom. (National television brought scenes of them being set upon by police dogs and firehoses, stories of how a church and children were dynamited. Also there were scenes from 1964 of Blacks burning and looting, carrying guns, and declaring "Black Power!") Every move of the blacks seemed to reveal the moral state of the nation.

## THE BLACK FACE BECAME THE WHITE CONSCIENCE

White liberals and radicals, in most cases denied intimate contact with the realities of the black community, as a matter of reflex conceded the status of innocent victim to the blacks and tended to support whatever claims the blacks made. Some romanticized blacks as daring, exciting, sensual, primitive, more fundamental. (Tom Wolfe felicitously referred to this "romanticism" of "*la nostalgie de la boue*," thus a romanticism of the earthy, the dark.)[61] Most of the liberals and radicals felt guilty to some degree for being the beneficiaries of an exploitive society. Intellectually they were seeking to compensate the black for wrong done him. Yet this often gave birth to a double standard which, on the one hand, granted blacks a moral blank check, and on the other hand, denied lower-class white people any other ethical status than that of being racist.[62]

Of all the radical black intellectuals to take their place at the podium in the late 1960s, Eldridge Cleaver—criminal, rapist, self-educated author, journalist for *Ramparts*, 1968 Peace and Freedom Party candidate for president, and Secretary of Information of the Oakland Black Panthers—marked the black radical consciousness.[63] Cleaver sought a counter mythology to official culture: The white man, "Pig America," and the evil West combined were the universal oppressor. According to his Muslim beliefs, the whites formed "a race of devils, created by their maker to do evil, and make evil appear as good. . . . The white race is the natural, unchangeable enemy of the Black man, who is the original man, owner, maker, cream of the planet Earth."[64] White history was, in Cleaver's view, the uninterrupted tale of a rapacious drive to dominate. All colored peoples know the purpose of white police and armies. They have lost their lands to the whites and had their bodies broken by white rule. Further, they can discover in their minds—and here Cleaver's analysis in *Soul On Ice* is at its best—how centuries of white dominance have led blacks to despise themselves.

For Cleaver, psychological analysis itself did not suffice. Power, he argued, is essential for respect. Upon that premise Cleaver conceived of a coalition including "all" the oppressed peoples of the Third World and the enemies of America and the West. His appeal included the radical white youth, whom Cleaver believed had come to know who the true enemy was and had shown a true willingness to fight him. Cleaver wrote:

> There is in America today a generation of white youth that is truly worthy of a black man's respect. A young white today cannot help but recoil from the base deeds of his people. On every side, on every continent, he sees racial arrogance, savage brutality toward the conquered and subjugated people, genocide; he sees the human cargo of the slave trade; he sees the systematic extermination of American Indians; he sees the civilized nations of Europe fighting in imperial depravity over the lands of other people—and over possession of the very people themselves. There seems to be no end to the ghastly deeds of which his people are guilty. *GUILTY.* The slaughter of the Jews by the Gemans, the dropping of atomic bombs on the Japanese people—these deeds weigh heavily upon the prostrate souls and tumultuous consciences of white youth. The white heroes, their hands dripping with blood, are dead.[65]

Cleaver's hope for a world coalition led nowhere. Cleaver, like all in this century who pursued international coalitions against the power of nation-states, found himself to be a general with an army. The Panthers were hunted down and killed; Cleaver escaped into exile. The international illusions he and other radical blacks held vanished even more quickly than they had been intellectually conjured. If one point need be chosen for their disappearance it was during the ping-pong match arranged by Nixon and Mao. Even China could be had, so it now appeared. For the majority of educated, middle-class blacks, it was now time to consolidate the gains of the 1960s. A post in government or the university was not to be sneered at. In truth, they had in some unequaled way made the injustice done to them a matter of national conscience.

Militant white youth ended in many ways where radical blacks ended. Their new consciousness and conscience led them in the realm of power from nowhere to nowhere. They could indict America as being the country of "the cowboy, the marine, the Bible-toting missionary priest, the businessman, the cop-on-the-beat." They could accuse it of having "destroyed the Indian, enslaved the black, colonized Latin America, A-bombed Japan, invaded Cuba, and napalmed Vietnam." They could charge America as being a war criminal, as the European Left and Jean-Paul Sartre had at the Russell War Crimes Tribunal in Paris, 1966–1967.[66] They did not yet have knowledge of the Pentagon Papers, the 1968 My Lai massacre, the secret and annihilating bombing of the Plain of Jars, or a full inventory of the stratagems and weapons that made up the United States' "automated battlefield"; nor had they yet heard the self-accusatory testimony of returning American soldiers, who formally charged themselves and their superiors with war crimes at the Winter Soldier Hearings in Detroit.[67] But even if they had had that information, what would it mean? They already had the essential truth of the war; and against the power of the nation, that conscience was weak.

With Nixon in power, youth, as well as their supporters turned inward.[68] The "apocalypse" was over. There was no real leadership left.[69] A small articulate elite, who never really guided the movement, was subject to what Carl Oglesby called "vanguarditis" and "galloping sectarianism."[70] The Weathermen, seeking to exert radical leadership in 1969, expressed a raging impotence as well as a violent infantilism.[71] They testified to the state of their own conscience when they declared: "If America hates the devil, fears Manson, speaks in the guise of goodness and decency, then the Weather Bureau embraces the devil, lauds Manson, equates those virtues with softness."[72] The role of saint-revolutionist convinced few. Like anarchists of a century before they tried to make their conscience their deeds.

From time to time youth sallied forth to protest the war that would not end. For instance, in 1970 Nixon made a command decision: with pointer in hand, he showed the nation the Cambodian border across which he had just ordered American troops. The next day, as if a tradition had to be continued and an insult had to be answered, students began their protest. And then, heard across the country, was the scream of a Kent State coed, "My God! They're killing us." Four students had been shot to death by the Ohio National Guard.[73]

Chicago had taught students that the old politics would be protected by force. Kent State and Jackson State taught that protest might be answered by bullets. The majority did not sympathize with the students, even when they were killed. The Harris Poll of April 1969 recorded a hardening of adult opinion since Chicago. (Sixty-eight percent of the American people were hostile to militant campus demonstrations, and even more so in cases in which blacks were involved.) The vast majority believed law breakers should lose scholarships. Almost 90 percent believed that college authorities were right to call the guard when students occupied buildings. Students' ingratitude and disrespect, which the adults found expressed by bizarre dress, long hair, and foul language, would be tolerated grudgingly; law breaking would not.[74]

The majority of Americans wanted respect for America. They believed that the students owed the nation gratitude; the students had no right to transgress against the rights of property or defy authority. The majority saw the students' protests as impious, sinning against the national culture, which for many was inseparable from their personal identity, communal ideas, and religious faith.

As students had passed from guilt to protest and then to disillusionment in the 1960s and early 1970s, so great sections of the American public in the same period went from gratitude to resentment and hostility. To know our own conscience, we must know the voices of the public as well as those of the students. Both speak within us.

## "THE WORKING CLASSES":
## FROM GRATITUDE TO RESENTMENT

Richard Nixon and John F. Kennedy illustrated a difference of men, presidencies, epochs, and sensibilities. They manipulated national culture in different ways. As Kennedy called Americans to a universal mission, so Nixon strove to return America to law and order. As Kennedy sought to put moral energies in the service of what should be done, Nixon dampened them by reminding Americans of what they had done. Kennedy asked Americans to experience guilt over what could be done; Nixon encouraged Americans to expect gratitude for what they had done.

With Nixon in office "the revolution" was over. His first goals were domestic tranquility and international order. To that end he developed a foreign policy based on détente with Russia and the initiation of contact with China. Focusing attention on these two countries permitted the isolation of the Vietnam War, which gave the Nixon administration time to move toward its avowed end of "peace with honor" in Vietnam, while domestic protest at home was first contained and then defeated. With domestic protest curtailed to ever smaller circles of students, war protesters, and blacks, Nixon could boldly affirm that there still existed a moral unity in America. This affirmation, so essential to his presidency, was defined in terms of "the silent majority" and "the silent center, the millions of people in the middle of the American political spectrum who do not demonstrate, who do not picket or protest loudly."[75]

Resentment was the main moral ground upon which Nixon sought to recruit his "silent majority," the forerunner of 1980s' "moral majority." Around this sentiment he sought to join the silent majority to traditional free enterprise Republicans, the people of the new South, blacks who wanted a piece of the action, and all the college-educated, suburban-dwelling whites on the rise. The message was simple: By your intelligence, work, pain, sacrifices you have made the greatest nation in all history. But how is your nation treated? It is shown no respect. Its gifts and services to humanity are denied; everywhere it meets ingratitude. It is "the rejected one"—the good denied.

The myth of the silent majority was used to conjure the existence of a core American people morally superior to all the protesters. This virtuous core, saving host, redeeming remnant, was none other than the majority who worked, supported their family and church, and who, above all else, believed in America and—conveniently enough!—were obedient to established authorities. They were held in a sense to be above the temporary "political fray"; their loyalty did not change because of "specific issues." They would persevere; for they were, in this nativist mythology, the moral stock of the nation.

The silent majority was forged in the foundry of "the politics of resentment."[76] With this myth Nixon fabricated the moral rock upon which he built his church. He used it to appeal to all those who felt ignored, were afraid, were worn out by ceaseless do-gooders' litanies and the maddening rush of words, events, and changing cultural fashions that engulfed the nation and threatened their moral identity with it. This myth, like all myths, strove to return people to fundamentals; this myth, like all myths serving power, aimed at order.

Attorney General John Mitchell and Vice President Spiro Agnew spear-headed the Nixon regime's use of this myth of the silent majority and the politics of resentment. Protest would be silenced. As soon as Mitchell took office he launched actions, both legal and illegal, against protesters. Indeed, in the "conspiracy" trial against the Chicago Eight he took aim at the New Mob, SDS, Black Panthers, Yippies, as well as other groups associated traditionally with the left or specifically now with war protest. Agnew also wasted no time. His coarse oratory was calculated: "For the whole range of deserters, malcontents, radicals, incendiaries, the civil and uncivil disobedients among our young . . . I would swap the whole damn zoo for a single platoon of the kind of young Americans I saw in Vietnam." As to what should be done with them, Agnew advised: "separate them from our society with no more regret than we should feel over discarding rotten apples from a barrel." Further, "A society which comes to fear its children is effete. A sniveling, hand-wringing power structure deserves the violent rebellion it encourages. If my generation doesn't stop cringing, yours will inherit a lawless society where emotion and muscle displace reason."[77]

One group the politics of resentment was intended to please was the working class of the nation. However defined—and there is much debate about who they were, who they followed, and how they voted—the Nixon regime wasn't entirely off target in assuming that a great number of the workers felt like wronged Americans.[78] They believed themselves to be the ones who paid their own way, did their part, served the country well, and yet weren't receiving their fair share of wealth, education, and, above all else, the respect they deserved.

There were many sources of the laboring whites' resentment. The sharpest were insults that denied their sacrifices. Their lives were built around sacrifice; and for them, like their traditional ancestors, sacrifice determined their idea of the good.[79] Everything they had—their family, house, jobs, neighborhood, church, and nation—they had worked for. In effect, their life was made by their sacrifices; and it was their sacrifices that gave them their personal worth.

Their sacrifice included laboring a better portion of their lives, holding up their end at work, obeying the law, paying taxes, doing military service, respecting their parents while rearing their own children properly, as well as continuing to "plug along" in a world in which they were constantly reminded that they were not "the best" and did not have "the best." It was upon that basis of sacrifice that they knew themselves and their ethical worth; upon that basis that they set forth their own claim to authority and respect. They understood their sacrifice as constituting a kind of treasury of merit for their family. What goods, respect, and opportunities they did not receive from their sacrifices, they expected that their children would. Their sense of sacrifice and the good essentially were that of traditional culture. The only significant difference was that they had put a nation, America, at the center of their exchange of sacrifice.

It was this sense of sacrifice that was insulted in the 1960s. Insults seemed to come at them, the working classes, from everywhere. They were called "fascists" and "hardhats." They were told that they were stupid, insensitive, ignorant, and racist. Their neighborhoods, religious values, and work were denied all importance; their own patriotism and military service, a matter of immense pride for them, was debunked. Insults came in the form of protests—the array of ideas, attitudes, clothes, and values associated with the counterculture—and the whole sea of change that inundated traditional ethnic values in the 1960s.

The blacks, in particular, threatened the white working man's sacrifices. The black ideological claim that black suffering was unique and that it alone merited special compensation was understood by the working whites as an attack upon the moral stature of themselves, their families, and their institutions. Consequently, everything connected with the black claims—riots, urban problems, crime, welfare, black culture—became a matter of revulsion. Increasingly, they saw the blacks violating the most elemental law of exchange: they asked for everything and gave nothing; they wanted all the attention and offered no respect.

Protesting youth insulted working people even more sharply. Youth—generally all lumped together as "hippies," "pot heads," "draft-card burners," and so on—were understood to deny laboring peoples' most basic value. They did not work. They did not even value work. They had no respect for family. In fact, they flaunted their disdain for family, sexual control, marriage, and childrearing.[80] The working class was critical of youth for having been given so much and proved to be so unthankful. They judged youth as severely for its ingratitude, shown by its lack of respect for tradition and nation, as youth judged them for their conformity and patriotism.

As youth judged America harshly for its injustice, so the working class, closer to their traditional parents, judged America positively for the justice it rendered their families. They were proud that they were Americans. This was an important identity for them.

It was this conception of America that caused the laboring people to suffer most the insults that came from government itself. They believed the nation, and therefore its government, owed them respect. The respect was owed for their loyalty, work, military service, obedience, and much else that made them feel they deserved the claim to being good citizens. Instead, they felt increasingly insulted and humiliated in the early 1970s by the government. Insults came in the form of court-ordered busing and integration, ranges of legislation that favored others, and an array of directives supporting affirmative action. Affirmative action advocates divided the ethical universe into two moral parts and put the laborers on the immoral side.[81] On one side the advocates placed victims, those who suffered innocently; and on the other side they put victimizers, those who benefited from the exploitation of the innocent. This division outraged the working people. It defined them, their families, their whole tradition on the side of wrong. It denied the risks, work, patience, misery, and sacrifices, in short all the suffering that measured their families' worth. Their entire moral inheritance in suffering was gutted. The working class was sentenced for past wrong-doing which it in no way accepted as its own.

The working classes felt they were losing their place in America. A covenant upon which they had built their whole identity seemed to be coming undone. Their disillusionment, though perhaps not as sharp as that of the war protestors, reached unprecedented levels in the 1970s. Their gratitude to America was strained; their resentment and anger grew.

*       *       *

There is pain, even a special kind of terror, for every generation as it discovers that its sacrifices and accomplishments do not command esteem, that they can even be forgotten or, yet worse, publicly denigrated. For the two generations of Americans who felt they had built this country, who knew they had survived hard times—especially those of the Depression—and who had fought in and won the Second World War, it was horrible to see "their nation" swamped by protest and befuddled in its use of power. Perhaps nothing delivered this unwanted message as forcefully as protesting Vietnam War veterans who felt their own sacrifices to the nation had been betrayed. What could be more poignant than a parade of amputated and battle-decorated veterans throwing their medals back at the Pentagon, as they did in 1972, or veterans publicly confessing their own and their army's atrocities in Vietnam?

Americans of all classes and generations increasingly felt that they were losing their place in America and America was losing its place in the world. A national culture was being put in jeopardy. America was no longer the certain servant of God and humanity. Consciences were less secure. For the majority, a moral shield had been pierced. They felt threatened. They were being divested of their public moral identity, and thus being left naked before an alien, chaotic world.

In the passage from the Vietnam War to Watergate, and the following, America appeared to regress from being *a republic of guilt* to becoming *an empire of shame*. All were forced to watch with mortification as a swelling river of wrong and evil, self-interest, lies, corruption, bribery, sexual debauchery, and so much else threatened to overflow all ethical boundaries. For some, responsibility and conscience no longer mattered. Fate had taken hold. Others turned to religion, nostalgia, and myth to seek to respiritualize the nation. National culture no longer effectively produced consensus.

The vast majority of Americans did not find consolation, much less compensation, in the concept of participation in the public life. As Gary Wills said, few Americans buy that high-brow myth that the fullness of life is found in the politics of participation.[82] Politics at best, in their opinion, might give you a few "kicks," a little to talk about, and get you a job. On the whole, it was just a lot of talking, meeting, and wheeling and dealing. Politics cannot really provide a person with happiness. It cannot speak to the internal mixing of emotion, impulse, disjuncture, ideas, and desires that often give one a sense of individuality, suffering, happiness, worth. It certainly cannot supply a person "with dignity, self-respect or purpose . . . with a stable set of values . . . with a sense of community reciprocated by others. . . . What the schools, the churches, the home cannot do, the political process will not accomplish."[83] What the great majority wants from politics are some benefits and protection, some freedom, nonintervention, and above all a fair deal. What they do not want are words and actions incompatible with their sense of personal meaning, yet it is precisely this that politics has come to mean for them. It filled them with resentment that their sacrifices were forgotten, and with fear that their inheritance would vanish. For the many, the wish was that they could escape from politics and the entire public world.

But politics was not to be escaped. Politics touched everything. Traditional and folk cultures, high and academic cultures, as well as religion were no longer autonomous. Commercial, mass, and national cultures breached every boundary. Conscience had fewer and fewer recesses for its retreat. Every village—every Cottonwood, Minnesota—had been penetrated by the forces and the claims of the nation. Every village was a microcosm of the nation and alive to its national culture.

The power of national-official culture was formed in the eighteenth century and was shaped by the strengthening national experience in this country. To be formed during this period meant on the one hand, it was free of the whole feudal order and all the class, organizational, and ideological impediments that feudalism placed in the way of the formation of national life in continental Europe. On the other hand, national culture was established in advance of mass, industrial society and all the forces that divided national life. American national culture could assume to serve both God and humanity in its early years. The division of the religious and the secular was not yet as severe as it was to become in the nineteenth century, when they increasingly became polarized. Myths still could join Heaven and earth, Providence and progress. The new nation, in some mystic way, could still be understood to serve God and humanity.

Paul Hollander perceptively wrote of this conception in "Reflections on Anti-Americanism in Our Times":

Eighteenth-century values and ideals survive with amazing vitality in the minds of many Americans, who keep judging their society (and perhaps their personal selves as well) in the light of such values. In

few parts of the world, and rarely in history, has there been such a
keen awareness of and concern with the gaps between ideal and actual, theory and practice, collective aspirations and their realization.
This may account for the peculiarly bitter and self-hating quality of
the anti-Americanism of Americans, and American intellectuals.[84]

It was the positive myths of America that came to the center of
the public stage in the 1960s. Kennedy reinvigorated those myths
and brought them to the fore. The Vietnam War forced a debate of
these myths. Their negation and affirmation became more extreme.
The growing possibility that the United States was more imperial
than republican had intensified the debate. Our guilt and gratitude
still are inseparable from this debate. In relation to it we must look
for answers to questions about how much we are Americans, to
what degree are we disciples of the philosophers, and what responsibility do we accept for the public life. The clarity of our conscience and the worth of our guilt and gratitude depend upon our
conclusions to this debate.

## NOTES

1. Worthy of consideration are Richard Neuhaus, *Time Toward
Home: The American Experiment as Revelation* (New York, 1975); and
Robert N. Bellah, "Civil Religion in America," in *Daedalus* 96 (Winter
1967): 1–21. For a recent criticism of Bellah's seminal article see Richard K.
Fenn, "The Relevance of Bellah's 'Civil Religion' Thesis to a Theory of Sec-
ularization," *Social Science History* 1, no. 4 (Summer, 1977): 502–17.
2. Pitirim A. Sorokin, *The Crisis of Our Age* (New York, 1957),
273–74.
3. Rolland Stromberg, *After Everything: Western Intellectual History
Since 1945* (New York, 1975), 4; esp. Chapter 1, "Moods of the Postwar
Years," 1–30. Emphasis is mine.
4. Karl Jaspers, *The Question of German Guilt* (New York, 1947), 71.
Emphasis is mine.
5. Hannah Arendt, "On Totalitarianism," in Roger Smith, ed., *Guilt,
Man, and Society* (New York, 1971), 266–67.
6. Ibid., 267.
7. Hannah Arendt, *Men in Dark Times* (New York, 1968), 16.
8. In *Boundaries* (New York, 1976) as well as in other works, Robert J.
Lifton argued the atomic bomb has changed our very conception of the
boundaries between life and death, therefore giving new psychological

dimensions to human existence. For a critical review of his thought, see a review of his *Living and Dying*, in my "Romanticizing the Void," *World View* (July–August 1975), 48–49.

9. For four different introductions to changing American culture in the postwar period, see Carl Degler, *Affluence and Anxiety: America Since 1945* (Glenview, Ill., 1975); Henry Fairlie, *The Spoiled Child of the Western World: The Miscarriage of the American Idea in Our Time* (New York, 1976); Alvin Toffler, *The Culture Consumers* (New York, 1973); and Jules Henry, *Culture Against Man* (New York, 1963).

10. For surveys of "the illustrious immigrants" who so influenced American intellectual life, see Laura Fermi, *Illustrious Immigrants: The Intellectual Migration from Europe, 1930–1941* (Chicago, 1968); and H. S. Hughes, *The Sea Change: The Migration of Social Thought* (New York, 1975). Jill Kerr Conway specifically wrote, "In the fifties and sixties this sense of lost American innocence was to be still further intensified by renewed contact with European thought and the discovery of elites. The recognition of the existence of elites and the new concern with the nature of leadership came in a decade when the disasters of American foreign policy emphasized in the most unambiguous terms the dimensions of American economic imperialism," *Intellectuals and Traditions* (New York, 1973), 204.

11. For data on American philanthropy see Frank Dickinson, *The Changing Patterns of American Philanthropy* (New York, 1970); useful for American views of their giving abroad is Merle Curte, *American Philanthropy Abroad* (New Brunswick, N.J., 1963).

12. One source to begin a survey of the forms and the motifs of American patriotism is Carl Van Doren, ed., *The Patriotic Anthology* (New York, 1942); to survey some of the extreme forms it took in the 1950s and how national culture seemed increasingly to eclipse all other values, see Douglas Miller and Marion Nowak, *The Fifties* (New York, 1977).

13. In his *Papers on the War* (New York, 1972), Daniel Ellsberg quoted Nietzsche: "Whoever fights monsters should see to it that in the process he does not become a monster. And when you look into an abyss, an abyss also looks into you," 277.

14. Standard historical introductions to the 1960s include: Ronald Breman, *America in the Sixties* (New York, 1968); Harold Hayes, *Smiling Through the Apocalypse* (New York, 1969); Godfrey Hodgson, *America in Our Time* (New York, 1976); William Leuchtenburg, *A Troubled Feast* (Boston, 1973); and Ronald Lora, *America in the 60's* (New York, 1974).

15. For various interpretations of the 1960s, which cast them as a time of struggle between parents and children, see: Erik Erikson, *The Challenge of Youth* (Garden City, N.Y., 1965), and his "Protean Man," *History and Human Survival* (New York, 1970), 316–31; Paul Jacobs and Saul Landau, *The New Radicals* (New York, 1966); Paul Goodman, *Growing Up Absurd*

(New York, 1960); Kenneth Keniston, *The Uncommitted* (New York, 1965), his *Young Radicals* (New York, 1968); and Norman Mailer, *The Armies of the Night* (New York, 1968).

16. Margaret Mead, *Culture and Commitment* (New York, 1970), 78–79.

17. Erikson's interest in youth was already manifested in his near classic *Childhood and Society* (New York, 1964) and *Young Man Luther* (New York, 1958). A contemporary collection of essays by Lifton, Kenniston, and others interested in youth, is Erik Erikson, ed., *The Challenge of Youth* (Garden City, N.Y., 1963).

18. For Richard Flack's interpretation, see his "The Liberated Generation: An Exploration of the Roots of Student Protest," in Richard Flack, ed., *Conformity, Resistance, and Self-Determination*, (Boston, 1973), 104–19.

19. An entire issue of the *Annals of the American Academy of Political and Social Science* (May 1971) was dedicated to "Student Protest" in America and abroad.

20. Useful sources on the New Left include: Michael Ferber and Staughton Lynd, *The Resistance* (Boston, 1971); Christopher Lasch, *The Agony of the American Left* (New York, 1968); and Irwin Unger, *The Movement: A History of the American Left, 1959–1972* (New York, 1975).

21. Stephen Spender, *The Year of the Young Rebels* (London, 1969).

22. Michael Harrington, *The Other America* (New York, 1962).

23. Hans Morgenthau, "What Ails America?" *New Republic* (October 28, 1967), 17.

24. Three critical works of the Kennedy years, which serve as useful introductions, are Richard Walton, *Cold War and Counter-Revolution* (New York, 1972); Henry Fairlie, *The Kennedy Promise* (New York, 1973); and David Halberstam, *The Best and the Brightest* (Greenwich, Conn., 1972).

25. Kennedy's inaugural address is found in Lora, *America in the 60's*, 31–34; citation 32.

26. Ibid., 33.

27. Ibid., 32.

28. Ibid., 33.

29. Ibid., 34.

30. The "Port Huron Statement" is found in Massimo Teodori, ed., *The New Left: A Documentary History* (New York, 1969),163–72. The standard history of the SDS is found in Kirkpatrick Sales, *SDS* (New York, 1974).

31. Teodori, *New Left*, 166.

32. "America, and the New Era, 1963," ibid., 178.

33. Carl Oglesby, "Trapped in the System," ibid., 182.

34. Ibid., 184.

35. Primary documents from his *Free Speech Movement* are found in Teodori's *New Left*, 156–62. One useful critical account of it is Seymour Lipset and Sheldon Wolin, *The Berkeley Student Revolt* (Garden City, N.Y., 1965).

36. Teodori, *New Left*, 156–62.

37. Excellent for the Johnson presidency and his desire for respect and gratitude are Halberstam, *Best and Brightest*, and Doris Kearns, *Lyndon Johnson and the American Dream* (New York, 1976).

38. For a general reaction to the U.S. and the world to Vietnam, see Marcus Raskin and Bernard Fall, eds., *The Viet-Nam Reader* (New York, 1965). Of use for American involvement in Vietnam, see *The Pentagon Papers* (New York, 1971).

39. George Kennan and respondents, *Democracy and the Student Left* (Boston, 1968), 28.

40. For Catholic radicalism of the 1960s, and what can be understood to be a first maturity on the part of a significant part to refuse "official America," see Francine du Plessix Gray, *Divine Disobedience: Profiles in Catholic Radicalism* (New York, 1970).

41. Teodori, *New Left*, 297. To understand the draft protest, see James Finn, ed., *A Conflict of Loyalties* (New York, 1968).

42. For a literary account of the Chicago convention, see Norman Mailer, *Miami and the Siege of Chicago* (October, 1968). For the view of those tried for conspiracy in causing the Chicago "riots," see his *The Conspiracy* (New York, 1969).

43. Susan Sontag, "What's Happening in America?" in her *Styles of Radical Will* (New York, 1969), 203.

44. The word "counterculture" was given form by Theodore Roszak, especially influential was his work *The Makings of a Counter-Culture* (Garden City, N.Y., 1969). The attempt to articulate an opposing culture (not without historical analogy to those who called for new cultures and civilizations in the 1920s) is expressed in such works as Roszak, *Sources* (New York, 1972); Robert S. Gold, ed., *The Rebel Culture* (New York, 1970); Jeff Nuttall, *Bomb Culture* (New York, 1968); and Mel Howard and Thomas Forcade, eds., *The Underground Reader* (New York, 1972). For the international character of the counterculture, see Peter Stanstill and David Mairowitz, eds., *BAM (By Any Means): Outlaw Manifestos and Ephemera, 1965–1970* (Middlesex, Eng., 1971). Daniel and Gabriel Cohn-Bendit, *Obsolete Communism: The Left-Wing Alternative* (New York, 1968); and Daniel Cohn-Bendit, et al., *The French Student Revolt* (New York, 1968).

45. Jerry Rubin, *Do It* (New York, 1970).

46. In *The Electric Kool-Aid Acid Test* (New York, 1969), Tom Wolfe uses Ken Kesey's group to explore drugs, San Francisco, and the premises

and actions of "the new culture." Also useful for a view of "the underground" is Roger Lewis, *Outlaws of America* (Baltimore, 1972).

47. Michael McClure, "Poisoned Wheat," in John Garagedian and Ordre Comb, *Eastern Religions in the Electric Age* (New York, 1969), 11.

48. Richard King titled his work on Paul Goodman, Norman Brown, Herbert Marcuse, and others whose psychology inspired the youth, *The Party of Eros* (New York, 1972).

49. Marcuse, a member of the important left-wing Frankfurt School of Thinkers in Germany in the 1930s, had produced important work prior to his "adoption" by the New Left. They were his studies of Hegel, *Reason and Revolution* (New York, 1941); of Freud, *Eros and Civilization* (New York, 1955); and of Russia, *Soviet Marxism* (New York, 1958). However, it was *One Dimensional Man* (Boston, 1964), that marked Marcuse's adoption by the New Left in Europe and the United States. It was followed by his "Repressive Tolerance," in *Critique of Pure Tolerance* (Boston, 1969), 81–123; *An Essay on Liberation* (Boston, 1969); *Five Lectures* (Boston, 1970); and *Counter-Revolution and Revolt* (Boston, 1972).

50. To the New Left's critique of our technology, Huxley and Orwell respectively furnished the *Brave New World* (London, 1932) and *1984* (London, 1949); Lewis Mumford, *Myth of the Machine*, 2 vols. (New York, 1967–70); Roderick Seidenberg, *Post-Historic Man* (Boston, 1957); and Jacques Ellul, *The Technological Society* (New York, 1964).

51. The belief that they were somehow uniquely liberating themselves through the discovery and the expression of their sexuality ignored the modern person's longstanding and persistent identification of self with sexuality, as well as modern scholarly and institutional attempts to dissect, define, and control it. Sex itself may be experienced as more of a creation of our culture, politics, and commerce than as a function of our biology. A useful work on the modern definition of our sexuality is Michel Foucault, *The History of Sexuality* (New York, 1978).

52. Norman Brown's two most influential works were his scholarly *Life Against Death* (Middletown, Conn., 1959) and his radical *Love's Body* (New York, 1966).

53. For one example of an academician who challenged the traditional nature of objectivity, see Noam Chomsky, *American Power, For Reasons of State* (1973); and his *Problems of Knowledge and Freedom* (New York, 1971).

54. The first of a series of revelations which showed the range of CIA activities in domestic and foreign affairs came in *Ramparts* (April 1966). This article revealed the role of Michigan State University in training special police in Vietnam. In the same year, the CIA was shown to have infiltrated the American student organization, National Student Association, and a major European cultural society, The Congress of Science and Liberty, as well as the prestigious journal *Encounter*. Equally dismaying were the

CIA's intervention into Vietnamese society Project Phoenix, and the celebrated Project Camelot, which on large scale tried to use American university professers' scholarship to help stop revolution in Latin America. The
latter received a full-length study by Irving Horowitz, *The Rise and Fall of
Project Camelot: Studies in the Relationship Between Social Science and
Practical Politics* (New York, 1967).

55. From 1968 onward, radical caucuses emerged openly in the national
associations of historians, sociologists, anthropologists, and political scien-
tists.

56. The following works are a small selection of what can be considered
the radical economies of the 1960s: Murray Bookchin, *Post-Scarcity Anar-
chism* (Berkeley, Calif., 1971); G. William Domhoff, *Who Rules America?*
(Englewood Cliffs, N.J., 1967); Michael Harrington, *The Twilight of Capi-
talism* (New York, 1976); Assar Lindbeck, *The Political Economy of the
New Left* (New York, 1971); Ferdinand Lundberg, *The Rich and the Super-
Rich* (New York, 1968); Morton Mintz and Jerry Cohen, eds., *America,
Inc.: Who Owns and Operates the United States* (New York, 1971); and
E. F. Schumacher, *Small is Beautiful: Economics as if People Mattered*
(New York, 1976).

57. Reflective of some of the charges in political science are Charles
McCoy and John Playford, eds., *A Political Politics* (New York, 1967).

58. Most exemplary of the anthropologist making use of the primitive to
criticize the modern is Stanley Diamond's *Primitive Views of the World*
(New York, 1964) and *In Search of the Primitive: A Critique of Civilization* (New York, 1974).

59. In the 1960s and 1970s, there was a stunning inversion in American
historical writing: national chauvinism had given way to national criticism.
This is explored in Michael Kammen's "The Historian's Vocation and the
State of the Discipline in the United States," in his *The State of the History
Profession* (New York, forthcoming), 19–45.

60. The single most important historical work, which expressed and inspired critical perspectives in American foreign policy, is William Ap-
pleman William's *American Diplomacy* (New York, 1959).

61. For a discussion of the cultural function of black rage and white
guilt, see Tom Wolfe's *Radical Chic and Mau-Mauing the Flak Catcher*
(New York, 1970); for the phrase "*nostalgie de la boue,*" see 38.

62. Michael Parenti wrote of this white pathology: "Way down inside
himself the white liberal wants the Negro to feel indebted to him, and ap-
preciative of him, perhaps to absolve his own sense of guilt for enjoying the
advantages of being white in a racist society. . . ." Berman, *America in the
Sixties,* 87. A most perceptive work on how the logic of white guilt led
them irrationally to make themselves servants of blacks and their causes,
often at great personal price, is Charles Levy's *Voluntary Servitude, Whites
in the Negro Movement* (New York, 1968).

63. Cleaver's writings include his *Soul On Ice* (New York, 1968), and his prison writings and speeches, *Eldridge Cleaver* (New York, 1969).

64. Cleaver, *Soul On Ice*, 66.

65. Ibid., 82.

66. For the *War Crimes Tribunal in Vietnam*, see Bertrand Russell, *War Crimes in Vietnam* (New York, 1967); and Jean-Paul Sartre *On Genocide* (Boston, 1968).

67. For an expression of the awesome illegal bombing of the Plain of Jars, see Fred Branfman, comp., *Voices from the Plain of Jars* (New York, 1972). For the self-accusatory hearing of Vietnam veterans, see Vietnam Veterans against the War, *The Winter Soldier Investigation* (Boston, 1972).

68. Revealing how the war protest did not dominate university youth's interest, H. L. Nieburg wrote: "At Harvard, Buffalo Bob drew 2,300 students. The Black Panther trial at New Haven was still in progress, but it was impossible to get more than a few dozen people to rally on their behalf while at the same time thousands turned out for a Yale revival of The Lone Ranger and Sergeant Preston of the Yukon. In November of 1970, Yale radicals called for a massive demonstration. The rally was attended by 500 persons; 60,000 gathered to watch Yale and Dartmouth vie for the Ivy League football championship," *Culture Storm* (New York, 1973), 248.

69. One work suggestive of the attempt to redefine the left is Michael Lerner's *The New Socialist Revolution* (New York, 1973).

70. Carl Oglesby, "Notes on a Decade Ready for the Dustbin," in his *Underground Reader* (New York, 1972), 183.

71. Harold Jacobs collected a useful set of documents in the *Weatherman* (New York, 1970).

72. Jacobs, *Weatherman*, 311.

73. Three studies of what can only be considered a great crime are Peter Davies, *The Truth About Kent State* (New York, 1973); James Michener, *Kent State* (New York, 1971); and I. F. Stone, *The Killings at Kent State* (New York, 1970).

74. See Jerome H. Skolnick's *The Politics of Protest: Task Force on Violent Aspects of Protest and Confrontation of the National Commission on the Causes and Prevention of Violence* (New York, 1969).

75. Gary Wills, *Nixon Agonistes: The Crisis of the Self-Made Man* (New York, 1970), 73–74.

76. "Politics of resentment" is a section in Wills's *Nixon Agonistes*. Philip Slater wrote two good chapters on those resentful and angered over what occurred in the late 1960s, in his *Pursuit of Loneliness: American Culture At Its Breaking Point* (Boston, 1970), 29–80. Useful for a theoretical understanding of resentment is Nietzsche's *On the Genealogy of Morals* (1887), available in Walter Kaufmann, ed., *Basic Writings of Nietzsche* (New York, 1968), 439–599; and Max Scheler's reply to Nietzsche, *Resentiment* (New York, 1961).

77. Quotations were cited in Wills, *Nixon Agonistes*, 353–54.

78. The white laboring classes were known as the lower-middle class and given an economic definition as those 70 million people in the late 1960s who lived on incomes from $5,000 to $10,000 a year. For income estimates, which ignore the upper levels of unionized and craft labor as well as the increasing prevalent double income working class family, see Richard Parker's "Why They Listen to George Wallace, Those Blue Collar Worker Blues," in *New Republic* (September 23, 1972), 16. For a range of essays on the working class, written in the late 1960s, see Louise Howe, ed., *The White Majority: Between Poverty and Affluence* (New York, 1970); as well as Patricia and Brendon Sexton, *The Blue Collars and Hard Hats: The Working Class and the Future of American Politics* (New York, 1971), esp. 66–69 for data on workers. Leaving aside the issues of busing and affirmative action (profoundly complex to define), on the issue of voting it is clear that it was not urban, unionized, ethnic Catholics who voted for reaction but, by comparison, it was the college-educated, the suburb-dwellers, and small-town white Protestant communities who voted the politics of resentment. Michael Rogin, "Wallace and the Middle Class: The White Backlash in Wisconsin," in his *The Politics of Social Change* (New York, 1971), 400–408. A useful overview of American society is "Patterns of Economic Change, 1960–76," in Peter Carroll and David Noble, *A New History of the United States* (New York, 1977), 383–400.

79. In addition to the just mentioned works, useful explorations into "moral universes" of working America are found in Richard Sennett and Jonathan Cobb, *Hidden Injuries of Class* (New York, 1972); Lilian Robin, *World of Pain: Life in the Working-Class Family* (New York, 1976); Michael Parenti, *Power and the Powerless* (New York, 1978); E. E. LeMasters, *Blue-Collar Workers, Life-Styles at a Working-Class Tavern* (Madison, Wis., 1975).

80. "Since lower-middle-class police are repelled by the uncontrolledness of the lower class from which their families had escaped, they were understandably infuriated by the regression to violence, drugs, and sexuality by the class that expects their deference. The radical students and hippies rejected the values to which the lower-middle class aspired and by which it was able to repress the behavior that the students flaunted." Michael Lerner, "Respectable Bigotry," in Howe, *White Majority*, 205.

81. A provocative introduction to affirmative action is Nathan Glazer's *Affirmative Discrimination: Ethnic Inequality and Public Policy* (New York, 1975).

82. For the majority's rejection of myth of politics of participation, see Wills, *Nixon Agonistes*, 470.

83. Ibid., 470.

84. Paul Hollander, "Reflections on Anti-Americanism in Our Times," in *World View* (June 1978), 51.

*Conclusion*

# A Conscience for This Time

Has the camera replaced the eye of God? . . . The camera relieves us of the burden of memory. It surveys us like God, and it surveys for us. Yet no other god has been so cynical, for the camera records in order to forget.

John Berger, *About Looking* (New York, 1980), 53, 55.

The exploitation of man by state replaces the exploitation of man by man.

Eugen Weber, "Revolution? Counterrevolution? What Revolution?" *Journal of Contemporary History*, 9, no. 2 (April, 1974), 39.

The accumulation of social problems to the point of a potential crisis of species survival is generating a rhetorical conflict that will affect all existing ideologies and induce acute ambivalence in all moral reflections. That conflict is the contest between two justifications for social order. One is the principle of human dignity, the other that of human survival.

Manfred Stanley, "Dignity versus Survival? Reflections on the Moral Philosophy of Social Order," *Structure, Consciousness, and History* (Cambridge, Mass., 1978), 199.

The longing for community and the related hunger for ethical wholeness characterize modern man. These themes appear throughout the extent of modern fiction and politics. They were the decisive motives in the creation of contemporary sociology.[1] Yet they also spawned the most virulent antiprogressive ideologies and parties. This longing and hunger turned man against his future. It seems Theodore Zeldin was right when he suggested that nostalgia moves contemporary man more than progress does.[2] Perhaps nostalgia is best explained as a kind of retroactive utopia that draws us back to our childhood world, a world where things were intimate; a world, in short, in which we were at home. Surely nostalgia, like guilt, is diffuse in the contemporary spirit. No doubt it voices the pervasive yearning for a wholeness which we, in industrial society, sense we are missing.

Among other things, ethical wholeness means that we would have integrity. It would give us confidence in our judgments about our gifts, reciprocities, and sacrifices, our gratitude, loyalty, and allegiances. Communally it would mean being part of a world in which we would know our rights and duties. By tradition, habit, custom, and established ways we would know how to conduct our exchanges, express our thankfulness, vent our anger, and seek our revenge. Although, even in this idealized state, we all would not escape the plight of an Antigone or a Hamlet, we would be free universally of suffering the fate of J. Alfred Prufrock, T. S. Eliot's contemporary man, who shudders before every choice. That constant reexamination of the self would not exist if we were ethically whole. We would pray, cheat, haggle, supplicate, and praise without the damnable self-consciousness that characterizes not just contemporary intellectuals as a group, but all contemporary men and women.

The world of ethical wholeness can never exist in anything close to a pure state. It is forbidden by human nature. It is, furthermore, prohibited by the modern, mass, industrial, national society. In our world, neither ethics nor communities exist autonomously. Rather, a plurality of values, cultures, peoples, and interests, as well as inequalities of power, status, class, and race exist side by side, intermingled, and even sometimes inseparably fused.

Our world belongs to great specializations of knowledge, production, and control. As Michel Foucault has shown brilliantly, all aspects of human existence—even our sexuality—are studied, defined, rationalized, institutionalized, and bureaucratized.[3] Traditional communities are cut into pieces, dispersed, and abolished, and therefore driving the inhabitants inward for the sake of survival. Older communities and individual consciences have no choice but to seek to accommodate themselves to permanent revolution. Yet this revolution, which is not one but many, denies the abiding community and ethical wholeness for which we long.

## PROGRESS, A NEW COMMUNITY IN TIME

Inevitably the community we find ourselves missing in space, we seek in time. As remarked throughout this work, if there is any one faith that gives us the new community, it is the belief in progress that gives value to the revolutionary forces of the modern world. Progress is Providence for earthly man; humanity is the new Israel.

Faith in progress, the belief that we can mutually, rationally, and cumulatively improve our human condition, is not altogether without proof. Its proof is the testimony of its illustrious statist and revolutionary believers, and the great powers of our technology. Under the aegis of progress, man as never before came out from under nature's powerful bonds of scarcity, famine, and plague. Only those who are without appreciation of that liberation glibly dismiss progress and the ideal community in time it provides us.

Progress justifies our greatest material, social, and political enterprises. Yet the very change these enterprises bring about threatens humanity at large with terrifying anarchy. The threat stemming especially from technology, industrial capitalism, and growing statism, promises to destroy all personal, familial, and communal, as well as cultural, social, and political orders we construct. It defies our attempt to impose meaning upon all change.

American patrician Henry Adams, who anguished over the collapse of his eighteenth-century inheritance in the midst of the burgeoning revolution of nineteenth-century American industrial society, found himself without symbols to express this condition that "had broken his historical neck."[4] He found only the pitiless hum of the dynamo expressing this new era of human history. Adams envied the Middle Ages for its ultimate symbol, a divine virgin who cared about suffering humanity.[5]

However, as Adams knew, we must seek to give a different meaning to the change that fills our world. To do this, we must believe that our reason, good will, and conscience will come to dominate the change we unleash. Unless we choose to despair, progress is a necessary wager. It provides us with the hope that humanity is a community with a purpose in time.

Progress, however necessary, is not an easy faith. There are many challenges to it. There is the whole tragic history of twentieth-century war and totalitarianism. There is a pervasive relativism that undercuts the intrinsic value of all faiths, making them mere matters of time, place, and circumstance. Furthermore, the transformation from the traditional to the modern world is not complete; the ethical ways of traditional man still remain within us. Also, Christianity and other supernatural faiths still form fundamental repositories of values: their many supporters resist turning over their final destinies—that of family in particular and humanity in general—to a secular view of the universe. Faiths challenging the fundamental assumptions of progress have come out of the modern era itself. The truth of rationalism, indeed the very existence of reason—so essential to any conception of conscience—has been challenged by an entire range of cultural and political expression.

Progress, too, like any faith has had to bear association with its own believers; and thus it is bent to nearly every purpose. In its name, modern man not only legitimates all his major public, scientific, technological, social, and national enterprises, but he also values his family, career, and self. *Progress serves as the ethical rhetoric of self and politics.* It is expected to organize existence as God's Providence once did.

The burden placed on progress is immense. Unlike the transcendental principle of Providence, it must have its coherence in a temporal meaning. Faith in progress must be sustained against the limits, weaknesses, and sins normal to man. It must be affirmed as a guiding vision at a time when hedonistic individualism, on the one hand, and terror, torture, totalitarianism, and war, on the other hand, have multiplied as rapidly as the fruits of progress. While progress always has the future to support faith, it has no God, Judgment Day, or after life. Against human pain, suffering, and death, progress—and what good men and women can hope for collectively—may not be enough.

## HUMANITY BEFORE THE ALTAR OF STATE

The crisis in the faith of progress has been joined intimately to the crisis of humanism in this century. Humanity, so cherished by all progressive forces from the eighteenth century onward, increasingly seems to be an abstraction when contrasted against the humanity of this century. The more men come to know each other across the barriers of class, tradition, and space, the less they are able to idealize and universalize themselves as members of humanity. They increasingly know themselves to be divided by unique historical periods and differing conditions and circumstances. Knowledge brings awareness of what are taken to be irreconcilable differences, and reasons for war. Every census of available goods, future needs, and power speaks of misery, exploitation, and the growing possibility of increased violence. Man, so to speak, looks into the mirror of mankind, seeing no ideal humanity to love but instead a senseless sea of faces to despise and dread.

The declining plight of humanism is related directly to Western man's diminished confidence in his own technology and politics. His beliefs in his own gifts are terribly weakened.

His finest industrial gifts, for instance, have made the horror of modern war; they have served as justification for plundering, exploiting, and destroying whole peoples.[6] Sensitive Western man, whether merchant, missionary, or politician, can no longer righteously presume the justice of his way. He knows his machinery, culture, and his political ideologies to be dangerous to others. He even fears himself to be the agent of vast systems of evil, the progeny of a flawed and imperiling inheritance. Guilt holds where pride once stood. In sensitive souls yesterday's supposed highest accomplishments are tainted with shame.

The evil revealed by twentieth-century events has cast not just progressive humanisms but all humanisms into doubt.[7] Cruelty, rancor, and war seem to be the new patriarchs. Their conventions appear to deny all conscience. Classical humanism, which advised man to find his dignity in the public life—a humanism so important to elites of the Italian Renaissance, the Enlightenment, as well as the American Revolution and liberalism—seems a remote, utopian, ideal in this age of totalitarianism. Democratic humanism appears to be another utopian ideal when its power is measured against that of ignorance, selfishness, conformities, vindictiveness, and other emotions that motivate modern societies. The "mobs and crowds," so feared by the upper ruling orders of the nineteenth century, have not vanished in the twentieth century. Sanitation, social welfare, education, suffrage, and all the other tools of progressive reform have not yet taken either the suffering or the demons out of the human condition.

All humanisms, whether they are classical or Christian, elitest, populist, aesthetic, or progressive, have been melted down at their core by the revelations of twentieth-century events. The three fundamental assumptions of all humanisms—man's mastery of self, man's mastery of nature, and man's sympathy for man—have been called into question. They appear merely to be ideals of a distant past. Although individual men and women are capable of great sacrifice they seem dreadfully inadequate for the task of taming the beasts of power. Humanity simply may be too angry, too tribal, too docile, too narcissistic, and too self-satisfied for the humanist ideal of self-cultivation. Not without relevance is Nietzsche's description of the tasteless mass who, in his opinion, reduce the good to themselves and their security.[8] Bread and circuses, when available, satisfy the many; only a few, as if their moral selves were like Japanese bonsai, pick at and prune themselves, making themselves in miniature what they take to be a perfect representative of the human species.

Humanism and progress have encountered in this century the terrible, singular reality of the nation-state. No conscience can be indifferent to it. There is no escape from the nation-state even when we have freed ourselves from what Jacques Ellul calls the "politics of illusion": that is, the pervasive tendency of the contemporary world to reduce human existence to a political matter and, therefore, to assume that everything objectionable is a political problem that has a political solution. We cannot escape the issue of the nation-state, for power is felt everywhere.[9] Rightly or wrongly, it defines our sense of justice; it instructs us on what is real and what is possible.

The nation-state raises the most awesome questions for those who seek to serve humanity. Is the nation-state, our most generalized means of expressing our collective human will, inherently flawed? Is the nation-state antithetical to human existence? Is the nation-state, the world's dominant form of power, not only structurally incapable of realizing the good but, by its very nature, an enemy of our common humanity? If these questions are answered in the affirmative, as they must be to some degree, we who would serve progress and humanity must suffer the fact that the institution of our greatest power is our enemy.[10]

The abuses of Marxism, the most recent and vehemently secular of the progressive humanisms, testifies to the destructive power of the state. Marxism, which starts with the presumption that the state is only a neutral medium of class will, finds itself, once power has been captured, the slave of power. Instead of guiding the state, Marxism merely becomes part of the state's ideological repertoire, furnishing justification and propaganda for all occasions. It is used to determine at any given moment who society's class enemies are, how close or far society is from its true end (real socialism), and what is required by way of production or scarcity. In effect, Marxism serves the changing goals of government. In the case of the Soviet Union, Barrington Moore correctly remarked that "these communists are far less compassionate about victims of historical 'progress' (witness the liquidation of kulaks and the purge trials) than were most self-righteous and self-confident nineteenth century capitalists."[11]

The commissar has a portable altar and a calendar of perpetually movable feasts. He decides who should be rewarded and who should be sacrificed. He has arrived in his very bureaucratic function at the point Solzhenitsyn so poignantly described in the *Gulag Archipelago*: he can murder routinely for the sake of "mankind's progress."[12]

We err, however, if we believe that the state wears only Marxism as a mask. The state also disguises itself in the dress of democracy, populism, and nation. The state always insists that it be at the center of society's transactions. Its power depends upon having that central position. To that end, it trades in memories of the dead and in ideals of the future, and sacrifices whole generations, communities, cultures, and peoples.[13] The state insists on a monopoly of violence. During war even the most democratic states limit conscience and forget humanity.

Wherever the nation-state's power is not strongly checked, the state erects "pyramids of sacrifice." Revolution does not destroy the state. Most often it only makes the state stronger, more energetic, and righteous. Eugen Weber perceptively wrote:

> Where once upon a time making a revolution meant overthrowing the state, in the new situation it is the state that makes the revolution, becomes identified with it, so that opposition to the state is opposition to the revolution. A revolutionary state is a contradiction in

terms. But even a socialist state, or one so called, very soon disappears behind administration, institutions, police machinery, bureaucracy—or rather, it becomes simply the flag that flies over the towering office building of the state.[14]

The awesome military appendages of the contemporary nation-state reminds us how distant we are from the era when Mazzini believed that the fatherland would disappear and "every man shall reflect in his own conscience the moral laws of humanity."[15] Nazi Germany and Soviet Russia no longer can be dismissed as purely historical aberrations. They reveal, if not the form certainly the magnitude of the power of the contemporary nation-states, under whose darkening shadows we all live.

## THE STATE WITHIN THE REPUBLIC

The nation-state poses a particular test for the United States, whose founding was a creation of the new conscience of eighteenth-century progressive humanism. American historian Carl Becker, disillusioned by the Great War and its aftermath, commented on the fate of America in this century when he remarked a half century ago in his *The Heavenly City of the Eighteenth Century Philosophers*: The world view of the philosophers, by its clarity, certitude, and ordered rationality, seems to resemble far more the metaphysical vision of medieval churchmen than to accord with the terror-ridden world of twentieth-century experience.[16]

Becker's view, however, still remains that of the intellectual elite. American official culture admits neither the possibility of the nation ever being in the service of the demon power nor the possibility cf it bringing its people to absolute tragedy. The state has no standing in national-official culture. Official belief still joins government, people, freedom, progress, and humanity as if no tragic, unbridgable gaps exist between these goods. America is still depicted as the nation that welcomes millions of immigrants to its shores, makes life decent, gives fair opportunity and just reward, and that fought two world wars for freedom. Its world-wide economic aid, investment, and trade, as well as its ghastliest weapons, are understood by official culture to exist for freedom and humanity. Officially our responsibilities are not yet understood as containing the possibility of irreversible tragedy. Our conscience is not yet torn. America still is officially held to be in the service of the philosophers' dream and within the pale of God's grace.

Nevertheless, it seems that a process of irreversible questioning of official culture is underway.[17] Since the middle 1960s the presumption of America's goodness has become more dubious to ever greater numbers. The Vietnam War attests to that; and since the war there has been no retreat from the world stage. The United States increasingly has had to act, observed by all, in a world characterized by an expanding population, diminishing resources, growing weaponry, and shifting political alliances. It has been less and less able to conceal its fundamental military, economic, and national reasons. Neither its innocence nor its philanthropy can be maintained as easily in the world at large.

Domestically, too, the notion of America as a source of good is in retreat. Inflation-imposed scarcity has been officially declared. Competition mounts among regions, classes, groups, and races. One writer recently referred to this whole process as the "Balkanization of the United States."[18] The two major political parties no longer retain clear majorities; increasing numbers of specialized caucuses, groups, and coalitions draw support away from them. America increasingly appears to be trapped in a permanent war of divergent interests. The whole appears to have given way to its parts.

Of course, the possibility of renewal should never be counted out. American myths are strong. The Soviet Union makes its enemies look good. The wizardry of politicians, the force of nostalgia, and the American desire to believe, singularly and collectively, have great power. However, notwithstanding the election of Ronald Reagan, national-official culture will have to exist (like ideologies in Western and Eastern Europe) in a run-down, broken, and contested world. There is a grim list of sources of divisions. Inflation, unemployment, energy shortage, pollution, crime, and a faltering industrial production all deserve a place on that list. Overseas there is the delicate test of foreign affairs which includes dealing with blackmailers, the question of revolution, the popularity—indeed, the stylishness—of anti-Americanism, the possibility of rekindling an all-out arms race, and, of course, the tension of American and Soviet imperial interests.

What is clear, as explained by Richard Brown, is that Americans are encountering "problems that appear to be intractable. Whether they are fears for the environment, for international politics, for the quality of life . . . we no longer possess the modern optimism that asserted the supreme capacity of human rationality to cope and to solve."[19] What is also painfully evident is that modernization has concentrated and magnified power on a scale far surpassing anything in history. Power on this scale means the inevitability of great tragedy. As a result, the promoters of American national culture will find more suspicion, less respect, and no certain gratitude or allegiance for things done and things promised both at home and abroad. Perhaps it is inevitable that Americans as a whole will discover the state within the republic. Only with increasing difficulty do myths of official America span the growing chasm of twentieth-century experience.

The weakening of American national culture, however, is not to be understood necessarily as a good. A new realism might quickly be translated into indifferent skepticism or, worse, a calculating cynicism. In the end, these attitudes can produce a majority that is both devoid of gratitude for what has been good about the American experiment and is without guilt and responsibility for the vast power of the nation.

It is not easy to conceive how we can abandon the myth of America without throwing out the whole progressive eighteenth-century inheritance. Furthermore, America and the West are inseparable; and they themselves are not to be divided from humanity's progress.

The dilemma of twentieth-century conscience belongs to the whole West. At the beginning of the century, faith in progress commanded the public world of the West. National and international lives were understood separately and mutually in order to advance the good of humanity. Even the socialists, who were most angered by social injustice, did not doubt the truth and the efficacy of the new commanding ethic that we should act for mankind's posterity. Now there is dwindling confidence in ourselves and in the future of humanity.[20] There is dread that catastrophe lies ahead. Ever greater numbers have taken to that grim Socratic wisdom of the twentieth century, so eloquently expressed by Henry Adams: Events only teach us our ignorance and impotence. They teach that there is no certainty about our lives, no necessary good in all we do. We carry no gift for the future.

The notion of being a world citizen cannot console our loss of confidence in our benefaction. As high an ideal as it is, being a world citizen seems a paltry abstraction in an era when nation-states are our primary instruments of giving and taking. To be a citizen of the world may be a way to try to endure morally what we cannot change. It also is to confess what traditional man maintained throughout his existence; mankind is without the means to alter the fundamental nature and course of things. It is to embrace a new fatalism, a fatalism not of nature nor of God, but of man. In this situation, what is to be done, but to pray to God that we be spared from ourselves—not just from our vices, but from our machines, inventions, and humanisms themselves.

## ELEMENTS OF A NEW CONSCIENCE

If we are to have a conscience, humanity—whether in the form of a hurt child, a tortured prisoner, starving masses, or a vanishing tribe—must have a claim upon us. The sympathy we extend to one another establishes our humanity. If we refuse to recognize the existence of others, we deny our own existence. The dead must be buried. Our humanity depends upon our sympathy.

Of course, we cannot open our conscience equally to all people. Only the naive, the presumptuous, the grief collectors, and the victim-manipulators do that. Limiting our sympathy is the act of simple recognition that our hearts are not infinite. We cannot open ourselves to all others, their conditions, suffering, potential, and so forth. There is a point where all must turn their heads aside. Survival dictates that we ignore certain things.

There is one pragmatic measure to determine how much we should open and close the shutter of our spirit to others. We should extend our responsibility as far as our power reaches, that is, our conscience should embrace what we can control. However, this pragmatic guide is severely limited. Our sympathy is no facile servant; it follows its own impulses. The impulses to empathize, to know, to judge, and to flee are not easily stifled. In other words, our mind does not stay inside itself.

Furthermore, the very nature of a modern identity is to be open to a vast, changing world. Literacy, education, the media, class, and citizenship connect us directly to a world far larger than ever was imagined by traditional humanity. Additionally, our citizenship in such a powerful contemporary nation-state as the United States extends our responsibility to the whole world. Our spirit thus finds no clear boundaries marking where conscience should dwell. Our guilt and gratitude are never entirely our own.

Likewise, our empathy is broadened by the first assumption of the modern mentality: Nothing is fixed; nothing is as it needs to be. Modern ideologies encourage us to improve the world. Happiness, not misery, is taken to be natural. Man is measured not by traditions but by possibilities. The good is defined not in terms of what has been but in terms of what could be. The modern spirit, to state this otherwise, measures everything by the question of "what is to be done."

Our expanded imagination and power invite our conscience into all human affairs. We ethically scrutinize all: Why does equality not exist? What is happening to our fellow humans across the globe? What are we doing to nature? There is no end to the questions we ask. Everything is brought within the ken of our conscience. We feel unable to separate ourselves ethically from the movement of humanity in time; it is as if we have become part of the whole.

Our conscience carries within itself the torment of the epoch. Our empathy joins us to this era's highest hopes and foulest deeds, to tragedies that we cannot fathom. Humanity everywhere is cruel, weak, and suffering. We cannot turn away from it. We are part of a humanity that we cannot abide and from which we cannot flee.

In a recent article, "Coming To Terms With Vietnam," Peter Marin offers one sketch of a Vietnam veteran who, in such sharp contrast to the proud legionnaires, lives with the guilt of the war he fought. Veterans "know conscience exists," Marin writes, "they are immersed in it." Noting that they suffer more than guilt, Marin remarked,

> They suffer not only the alienation experienced by the participants of any war but also problems unique to the war in Vietnam: their disappointment at their treatment at home; their anger at the absence of gratitude, attention, respect, or aid; their resentment at having risked their lives and seen men die in a war now regretted or forgotten. But behind all of that, and mixed inextricably with it, is something more, something perhaps not even privately admitted: the anger of the veterans at themselves, their grief at having fought and killed in the wrong war for the wrong reasons in the wrong way.[21]

All of these disturbed veterans—the addicts, the criminals, the depressed, the drifters, the drinkers, the compulsive talkers and weepers—meet guilt on some level of their being. But, writes Marin, "those among them who have consciously tried—as many have—to discover retrospectively the truths of the war find themselves in the predicament of Oedipus: every step they take toward the truth brings them closer to their own guilt."[22]

One story Marin recounted cannot be forgotten easily. In a graduate psychology seminar dedicated to ethics, one black veteran spoke out against the class's ruling consensus that values are relative. He told how one morning in Vietnam, after months of combat, he woke up "weeping and shivering, unable to continue, frightened and ashamed of the killing he had done, full of self-hatred."[23] Only momentarily did his story pierce the smugness of the class. The students soon re-erected their walls. They concurred with the military doctor's diagnosis. He had suffered shellshock; to fit the jargon of the seminar, he had been "conditioned."

The story was not lost on Marin. The veteran had to keep faith with those who experienced the war, even the dead, even if the living kept no faith with him. All the veterans of that war, Marin concluded, must speak the truth for their good and our good. "They know firsthand—as most of us should but do not—that guilt is real, and that men cannot be fully human or whole without coming to terms with their relation to the sufferings of others."[24]

Guilt for the Vietnam War does not belong to American veterans alone. Some of the responsibility for that war lay outside of the United States. Parts of it belong to American politicians who ordered and supported it; and, in some way, the guilt belongs to all of us. Our citizenship alone is reason for such self-indictment. American's role in the war came out of its attitudes, schools, military, factories, politics, and taxes. The war continued as long as it did because it was supported and because it was not protested sooner and more forcefully.

In truth, the Vietnam War was but one war of many in this century. And war is but one form of collective action by which we trade in vast amounts of human suffering. By knowledge, association, or direct participation, twentieth-century people are linked, as individuals and as a whole, to a succession of happenings that have brought profound misery and have radiated immense guilt. As the world becomes one, so our guilt increases, not just for the amount of human suffering caused and for good left undone, but even for the crimes we appear to be preparing: nuclear war and the unprecedented destruction of nature. Our power itself links us to immense exchanges of human happiness and suffering, which in turn identify us with humanity, with victim and victimizer alike.

Diffuse guilt comes out of our very awareness that at every moment vast segments of humanity are dealing—justly and unjustly, generously and mercilessly—in each other's happiness and suffering. Humanity lives by such dealings.

Is there any wonder that guilt is so diffuse in our epoch when power is so great and consciousness so global? How could such distortions as "the guilty man" and "the guiltless man" not occur in such a complex changing world whose transactions often involve the lives and deaths of whole peoples and generations. Our conscience cannot escape, nor yet can it encompass, the exchanges of human life that characterize this era.

## HUMILITY AND TOLERANCE

One conclusion presses itself upon us: Our conscience is not adequate to comprehend our experience. We cannot ethically measure the depths, heights, and perimeters of the world to which we belong. We are witness and participant to transactions that exceed our consciousness by scale, intricacy, magnitude, variety, and sheer incalculability of their consequences. We are joined to a multitude of communities, some by consciously avowed desire, others by habit, benefit, and tradition. Yet these communities are engaged in exchanges, whether political, economic, or social, of which we have inadequate knowledge for assessing even the very responsibility we have for them. Our citizenship in a nation-state is the most illustrative example of such communities. The inadequacy of our conscience in relation to our experience is also shown by our inability to predict the consequences of ideas. In fact, the world is full of great consequences, of which we foresee few and determine even fewer.

From the inadequacy of our conscience we should not conclude in favor of skepticism. Skepticism would eradicate sympathy, deny responsibility, and, therefore, destroy all community by reducing us to being morally isolated beings.

Instead of making the limits of our conscience serve skepticism, we would have it support a kind of humility. This humility would

not be the cowardly, tenderhearted sort which Nietzsche so brut-
ally criticized. It would start with the awareness that we are *in* reality, not *above* it. It would recognize that we humans belong to and
need a range of communities, none of which are perfect. This
humility would carry with it the requirement that we strive to have
our conscience shaped by valid emotions, sentiments, ideas, and
judgments. Particularly we would seek to escape the false bondage
of our guilt and gratitude freeing them as much as possible from
convention and manipulation. We should not expect perfection in
this.

Max Horkheimer defined an essential element of the humility
that should structure our view of existence when he wrote in 1970:
"The longing for perfect justice . . . can never be realized in secular
history; for even if a better society should replace the present social
disorder, past misery would not be righted . . . [and] even if all material needs are satisfied, the fact remains a man must die."[25]

The spirit of humility brings us to the second element of the conclusion: tolerance. Tolerance here is not meant to be a benign acceptance of the status quo, "the established disorder," to use Emmanuel Mounier's critical description of the present order. Nor is
tolerance meant to be a passive spirit that chooses not to discrimi-
nate or fight, arguing by some valueless equanimity that all
humans are, after all, the same by flesh and blood. The tolerance
we ask is not easy. It is the wisdom of experience. It is formed by
paradox around the tension existent between spirit and reality. It is
shaped by a tragic optimism that affirms simultaneously our great
human power and the terrible limits of that power. It asks us to be
responsible for nearly everything, but realizes limits everywhere to
that responsibility in our knowledge, conscience, practice, and institutions.

This tolerance we propose does not flee from an admission of the
dichotomous nature of human life. It acknowledges how much, individually and collectively, we are composed of thought and action, past and future, spirit and body, freedom and habit. This
tolerance realizes that we live amidst a multiplicity of claims upon
us.

This tolerance should make us more generous to those who live
by the values of the traditional world, which in fact are alive in all
of us. No doubt traditional man's conscience can be antithetical to
that of Christian and progressive humanists alike. It can serve the

narrowest parochialisms of family, church, community, and neighborhood. Nevertheless, our tolerance lets us see that at the center of
the traditional mentality there is respect for the values of gift and
sacrifice.

This tolerance extends not just to those who suffer for the sake of
the present and the future, but to those who honor the dead. The
latter affirm that human bonds and values reach beyond, and
should even be asserted against, death. They are loyal to sacrifices
upon which all human communities depend. Likewise, our tolerance should join us sympathetically to those whose hunger for love
and justice is so great that they believe that only the existence of an
afterlife and a god can satisfy that hunger. They know that today
cannot always make compensation for yesterday.

The tolerance we propose also serves ourselves, because the
voice of traditional man, as well as those of humanist and Christian, speaks within us. They make our conscience what it is. Therefore, when we deny others tolerance, we deny ourselves tolerance.
And this denial, this refusal to accept and to listen to ourselves,
makes us angry or, worse, makes us afraid of ourselves. When we
refuse to hear the voices of our inner selves we become strangers to
ourselves. At some point, this alienation puts us into flight from
ourselves and thus from our conscience and humanity.

On these grounds, humility and tolerance constitute our ability
to be honest, which is the first condition of conscience. We must be
willing to join the dialogue that is within us. We must take counsel
from the best voices within us. Our conscience, freedom, and
humanity agree and depend on this.

Integral to this goal of self-knowledge has been an attempt to offer a critical genealogy of contemporary conscience. We have tried
here to understand the guilt and the gratitude that war within us, as
well as the ambiguities, tensions, and contradictions that have
formed around them. To defuse their irrational hold upon us, we
have had to recognize the divisions caused by their opposition
within us. Further, this has been an effort to understanding how, in
our epoch, guilt has become profoundly diffuse and gratitude has
been manipulated. Our endeavor has not been to dissolve these
ethical sentiments upon which conscience itself depends, but it has
been to restore them to health.

In this work we identified a positive guilt and conscience,
specifically in reference to the eighteenth-century philosophers and

their disciples. This conscience alone gives ethical value to that
vast, ever-growing man-made change upon us. This conscience
alone gives value and community to humanity in its passage
through time. We must give human measure and direction to the
forces that encompass us. Short of a progressive vision of the
human community in time, which certainly cannot be that of nineteenth century optimism, we stand naked before the terror of history. We find ourselves ironically to be our own cruel gods; by the
very forces we have created we sentence ourselves to a purposeless
existence.

Our once-boasted freedom to make history, indeed, may prove
to be merely an illusion. But humanity—not just by reason and aspiration, but by technology, economics, and politics—increasingly
insists upon that illusion and the notion that men and women owe
each other justice and mutual help. This help is not just to rid the
world of the bad that exists, but to realize the good that could be.
Our conscience cannot be deaf to that demand.

We have become too much our own makers to surrender ourselves entirely to fortune or Providence. As Americans, Westerners, contemporaries in a secular world, we are compelled to seek
to realize the good. That is our presumption; and with that presumption, in this darkness, we must seek not just to honor God,
parents, and the dead, to make gifts for children and friends, but to
end this terrible strangeness among us—to make humanity more
than the abstraction it presently is.

Thus, if we are to have conscience, we must allow the claims of
guilt and gratitude to struggle within us. Our honesty and dignity
require it.

## NOTES

1. Robert Nisbet explores the connection between the creation of
modern sociology and the sense of loss of community in nineteenth-century
European history in his *Tradition and Revolt* (New York, 1968).

2. Speaking specifically of the Third Republic, Theodore Zeldin wrote,
"Nostalgia was more widespread than optimism. The forces resisting
change were more powerful than those which accepted or welcomed it."
*France: 1848–1945*, vol. 2: *Intellect, Taste and Anxiety* (Oxford, 1977),
1083.

3. In separate works, Michel Foucault has examined how contemporary civilization, with its rationality, specialization, power, institutions, and bureaucracies, has defined, ordered, and controlled human knowledge, insanity, crime, medicine, and sexuality. For his examination of these topics, see *Madness and Civilization* (New York, 1965); *The Birth of Clinic* (New York, 1973); *The Order of Things: The Archaeology of the Human Sciences* (New York, 1973); *Discipline and Punish* (New York, 1977); and *History of Sexuality*, vol. 1: *An Introduction* (New York, 1980). My review of the last work appears in vol. 454 (March 1981) of the *Annals of the American Academy of Political and Social Science*, 239-41.

4. Henry Adams described this effect as his reaction to the Great Exposition of 1900, *Education* (New York, 1931), 382.

5. See ibid., 388-89, as well as his 1905 classic *Mont-Saint-Michel* (multiple English editions).

6. As suggested elsewhere, Michel Foucault speaks of the death of mankind in this era; the most recent of man's myths, man himself, Foucault would have us believe is the most transitory in his *The Order of Things*.

7. Of special worth in discussing the decline of humanism in the face of twentieth-century evils, is Micheline Tison-Braun's *La crise de l'humanisme*, 2 vols. (Paris, 1958, 1967).

8. Almost all of Nietzsche's works can be read as an indictment of mass, industrial society. Among others worth seeing: *The Will To Power* (1901); *Anti-Christ* (1888); *The Twilight of the Idols* (1888); and *The Geneology of Morals* (1887), all of which are available in recent English editions. The outstanding critique of mass society in the twentieth century remains Ortega y Gasset's 1933 work, *The Revolt of the Masses* (New York, 1957).

9. For Elluls' study of contemporary man's pervasive tendency to conceive of all existence as a matter of political problems and solutions, see his *The Political Illusion* (New York, 1967).

10. In my opinion no single volume is as provocative in its exploration of power as Betrand de Jouvenel's *On Power: Its Nature and the History of its Growth* (Boston, 1962).

11. Barrington Moore, *Reflection Upon the Causes of Human Misery and Certain Proposals to Eliminate Them* (Boston, 1972), 71.

12. Aleksandr Solzhenitsyn, *The Gulag Archipelago*, 3 vols. (New York, 1976).

13. A useful recent study of state as engine of sacrifice is Peter Berger's *Pyramids of Sacrifice: Political Ethics and Social Change* (New York, 1976).

14. Eugen Weber, "Revolution? Counterrevolution? What revolution?" in *Journal of Contemporary History* 9, no. 2 (April 1974): 11.

15. Mazzini is cited in Hans Kohn, *Prophets and Peoples* (New York, 1961), 90.

16. Aside from his *Heavenly City of the Eighteenth Century Philosophers*, useful to understand Carl Becker's point of view is his "Progress," in *Encyclopaedia of the Social Sciences* 11 (New York, 1933), 495–99.

17. Richard Brown suggests that traditional ways have been losing ground in America since 1607, and that the Civil War marked "the final surrender of traditional society," *Modernization: The Transformation of American Life, 1600–1865* (New York, 1976), 186.

18. Kevin Phillips "The Balkanization of America," in *Harpers* (May 1978), 34–47.

19. Brown, *Modernization*, 200.

20. Ibid.

21. Peter Marin, "Coming To Terms With Vietnam," *Harpers* 261, no. 1567 (December, 1980), 52.

22. Ibid., 53.

23. Ibid., 55.

24. Ibid.

25. This is quoted in John Galvin's "Schillebeeck: Retracing the Story of Jesus," *World View* 24, no. 4 (April, 1981), 11.

# Selected Bibliography

The works cited here were important in forming, developing, and supporting this book.

The goal of this work is an understanding of contemporary conscience as revealed in the conflict between the ethical sentiments of guilt and gratitude. The underlying premise of this work is historicist: we know ourselves, what we are, by knowing what we have inherited. This historicism, however, is *not* joined to the premise that our ethical inheritance is devoid of all transcendence and truth.

For examples of the multidisciplinary character of this work, see: Conrad Arensberg, *The Irish Countryman* (Garden City, N.Y., 1968); Erich Auerbach, *Mimesis: The Representation of Reality* in *Western Literature* (Garden City, N.Y., 1953); Crane Brinton, *A History of Western Morals* (New York, 1959); Richard Brown and Stanford Lyman, *Structure, Consciousness, and History* (Cambridge, 1978); Numa Fustel de Coulanges, *La cité antique; étude sur le culte, le droit, les institutions de la Grèce et de Rome* [*Ancient City*] (Paris, 1862); Émile Durkheim, *Les formes élémentaires de la vie réligieuse* [*The Elementary Forms of Religious Life*] (Paris, 1912); Edward Engelberg *The Unknown Distance From Consciousness to Conscience* (Cambridge, Mass., 1972); E. E. Evans-Pritchard, *The Nuer: A Description of the Modes of Livelihood and Political Institutions of a Nilotic People* (New York, 1969); Raymond Firth, *Symbols, Public and Private* (Ithaca, N.Y., 1973); Morris Ginsberg, *Essays in Sociology and Social Philosophy* (Baltimore, 1968); Erving Goffman, *The Presentation of*

*Self in Everyday Life* (New York, 1959); Alvin Gouldner, *The Coming Crisis of Western Sociology* (New York, 1970); Edward Hall, *The Silent Language* (New York, 1959); Georg Wilhelm Hegel, *Grundlinien der Philosophie des Rechts* [*Philosophy of Right*] (Berlin, 1821); David Hume, *Inquiry Concerning the Principles of Morals* (London, 1751), Hume, *A Treatise of Human Nature* (London, 1739); Arthur Lovejoy, *The Great Chain of Being* (New York, 1936); Henry Sumner Maine, *Ancient Law: Its Connection with the Early History of Society and its Relation to Modern Ideas* (1861; reprint ed., Boston, 1963); Walter Moblerly, *The Ethics of Punishment* (Hamden, Conn., 1968); A. R. Radcliffe-Brown, *Structure and Function in Primitive Society* (New York, 1965); Adam Smith, *The Theory of Moral Sentiments* (1759); Melford Spiro, *Buddhism and Society* (New York, 1970); William Curtis Swabey, *Ethical Theory from Hobbes to Kant* (New York, 1961); Arnold Van Gennep, *Rites of Passage*, trans. Monika Vizedom and Gabrielle Coffee (Chicago, 1960); Christoph von Furer-Haimendorf, *Morals and Merit: A Study of Values and Social Control in South Asian Societies* (Chicago, 1967); Edward Westermarck, *Ethical Relativity* (Paterson, N.J., 1960); and Westermarck, *The Origin and Development of the Moral Ideas*, 2 vols. (London, 1917).

For works on guilt, see: Hannah Arendt, *Dark Times* (New York, 1968), Arendt, *Eichmann in Jerusalem* (New York, 1969); Ernest Becker, *The Denial of Death* (New York, 1973); Ruth Benedict, *The Chrysanthemum and the Sword: Patterns of Japanese Culture* (New York, 1946); René DuBos, *So Human an Animal* (New York, 1968); Sigmund Freud, *Moses and Monotheism* (New York, 1939), Freud, *Totem and Taboo* (New York, 1946); Erich Fromm, *Escape from Freedom* (New York, 1941); J. Glenn Gray, *The Warriors* (New York, 1970); Jules Henry, *Culture Against Self* (New York, 1963), Henry, *On Shame, Vulnerability and Other Forms of Self-Destruction* (New York, 1973); Karl Jaspers, *The Question of German Guilt* (New York, 1947); Franz Kafka, *Selected Stories*, ed. Philip Rahv (New York, 1952); Søren Kierkegaard, *Fear and Trembling* (1843; reprint ed., Garden City, N.Y., 1955), Kierkegaard, *Sickness unto Death* (1849; reprint ed., Garden City, N.Y., 1955); Joseph Conrad, *The Heart of Darkness* (1902; reprint ed., New York, 1970); Helen Merrel Lynd, *On Shame and the Search for Identity* (New York, 1958); Herbert Marcuse, *Eros and Civilization* (Boston, 1955); Don Martindale, *Institutions, Organizations, and Mass Society* (New York, 1966); Herbert Morris, *On Guilt and Innocence* (Los Angeles, 1976); Gerhardt Pier and Milton Singer, *Shame and Guilt: A Psychoanalytic Study* (New York, 1971); Theodor Reik, *In Myth and Guilt: The Crime and Punishment of Mankind* (New York, 1957); Philip Rieff, *Freud: The Mind of the Moralist* (Garden City, N.Y., 1961); and Roger Smith, *Guilt: Man and Society* (Garden City, N.Y., 1971).

For materials pertaining to gratitude and related matters of reciprocity, fair exchange, and sacrifice, see: Ralph Waldo Emerson, "Gifts," in Brooks Atkinson, ed., *The Selected Writings of Ralph Waldo Emerson* (New York, 1940); Melvill Herskovits, *Economic Anthropology* (New York, 1940); Arthur Hocart, *Social Origins* (London, 1954); Ziyad I. Husami, *Marx, Justice and History* (Princeton, N.J., 1980); E. O. James, *Beginnings of Religion* (London, 1958), James, *Comparative Religion* (New York, 1961), and James, *Sacrifice and Sacrament* (London, 1962); A. Loisy, *Essai historique sur le sacrifice* (Paris, 1920); M. Mauss and H. Hubert, "Essai sur le sacrifice," in *Année Sociologique* (1898); Mauss, *Essai sur le don* [*The Gift*] (1925); John S. Barrington Moore, *Injustice: The Social Basis of Obedience and Revolt* (White Plains, N.Y., 1979); Friedrich Nietzsche, *Beyond Good and Evil: Basic Writings of Nietzsche*, ed. Walter Kaufmann (New York, 1968); Kurt Wolf, ed., *The Sociology of Georg Simmel* (New York, 1964); Marina Tsvetaeva, "On Gratitude," in *Fifty Years of Russian Prose*, vol. 1 (Cambridge, Mass., 1971); Hans von Hentig, *Punishment: Its Origins, Purpose and Psychology* (London, 1937); and Roger Wescott, "Of Guilt and Gratitude: Further Reflections on Human Uniquesness," in *Dialogist*, vol. 2 (1970).

An assumption still alive in the majority's conscience are values from the traditional world. For a discussion of the mind and values of the traditional world, which for me has been dependent on the fruit of the new social history and recent concerns for ethnicity, see: Richard Cobb, *The Police and People: French Popular Protest, 1778–1820* (New York, 1970); Robert Darnton, "The History of Mentalités," in his *Structure, Consciousness and History* (Cambridge, Mass., 1978), Pierre Goubert, *The Ancien Régime, French Society, 1600–1750* (New York, 1973); E. J. Hobsbawm, *Primitive Rebels: Studies of Archaic Forms of Social Movement in the Nineteenth and Twentieth Centuries* (New York, 1959); LeRoy Ladurie, *Carnival in Romans* (New York, 1979); Peter Laslett, *The World We Have Lost* (New York, 1965); Robert Mandrou, *De la culture française aux 17ᵉ et 18ᵉ siècles* (Paris, 1964), and Mandrou, *La France aux XVIIᵉ et XVIIIᵉ siècles* (Paris, 1974); George Rudé, *The Crowd in History, 1730–1848* (New York, 1964), and Rudé *Ideology and Popular Protest* (New York, 1980); E. P. Thompson, "Eighteenth-Century English Society: Class Struggle Without Class," in *Social History* vol. 3, no. 2 (May 1978), and Thompson, "The Moral Economy of the English Crowd of the Eighteenth Century," in *Past and Present* 50 (May 1971).

In many ways, the protagonist of this work is modern, progressive, secular conscience. For works that suggest the formation of that conscience in eighteenth-century high culture, see: Irving Babbitt, *Rousseau and*

*Romanticism* (Boston, 1919); Elinor Barber, *The Bourgeoisie in the Eighteenth Century* (Princeton, N.J., 1955); Carl Becker, *The Heavenly City of the Eighteenth Century Philosophers* (New Haven, Conn., 1932); Nicholas Berdyaev, *Bourgeois Mind* (New York, 1934); Louis Brevold, *The Natural History of Sensibility* (Detroit, Mich., 1962); Ernst Cassirer, *The Philosophy of the Enlightenment* (Boston, 1955), and Cassirer, *The Question of Jean Jacques Rousseau* (Bloomington, Ind., 1967); Henry Commager, *The Empire of Reason: How Europe Imagined and America Realized the Enlightenment* (Garden City, N.Y., 1977); Robert Darnton, "In Search of the Enlightenment: Recent Attempts to Create a Social History of Ideas," in *Journal of Modern History*, vol. 43 (March 1971); Peter Gay, ed., *The Enlightenment: A Comprehensive Anthology* (New York, 1973); Norman Fiering, "Irresistible Compassion: An Aspect of Eighteenth Century Sympathy and Humanitarianism," in *Journal, A History of Ideas*, vol. 30, no. 2 (April–June, 1976); Bernard Groethuysen, *Les origines de l' esprit bourgeois en France* (Paris, 1927); Élie Halévy, *The Growth of Philosophic Radicalism* (Boston, 1955); Norman Hampson, *The Enlightenment* (Baltimore, 1968); Arnold Hauser, *Rococo, Classicism, Romanticism, vol. 3, Social History of Art* (New York, 1958); Erich Kahler, *Man the Measure* (New York, 1961); James Leith, *The Idea of Art as Propaganda in France* (Toronto, 1965); Frank Manuel, *The Enlightenment* (Englewood Cliffs, N.J., 1965); Robert Mauzi, *L' idée du bonheur dans la litterature et la pensée au XVIIIᵉ siècle* (Paris, 1961); Robert Mollenauer, ed., *Introduction to Modernity: A Symposium on Eighteenth Century Thought* (Austin, Tex., 1965); Wilson Carey McWilliams, *The Idea of Fraternity* (Los Angeles, 1973); Friedrich Nietzsche, *The Genealogy of Morals* (New York, 1956); Robert Palmer, *Catholics and Unbelievers in Eighteenth Century France* (Princeton, N.J., 1947); Renato Poggioli, *The Oaten Flute* (Cambridge, Mass., 1975); Franco Venturi, *Utopia and Reform in the Enlightenment* (Cambirdge, 1971); and Eric Voeglin, *From Enlightenment to Revolution* (Durham, N.C., 1975).

For works that suggest the spread of the modern conscience to society at large, as well as the popularizations, distortions, and manipulations of that conscience which occurred in the course of its transmission, see: Brian Berry, *The Human Consequences of Urbanization* (New York, 1973); Cyril Black, *The Dynamics of Modernization* (New York, 1966); Carlo Cipolla, *Before the Industrial Revolution: European Society and Economy, 1000–1700* (New York, 1976); Alan Dawley, *Class and Community: The Industrial Revolution of Lynn* (Cambridge, Mass., 1976); Jacques Droz, *Europe Between Revolutions, 1815–1840* (New York, 1967); Felix Gross, *Il Paese: Values and Social Change in an Italian Village* (New York, 1973); Carlton Hayes, *The Historical Evolution of Modern Nationalism* (New

York, 1931); E. J. Hobsbawm, *The Age of Capital, 1848-1875* (New York, 1975); Richard Hoggart, *The Uses of Literacy: Aspects of Working-Class Life, With Special References to Publications and Entertainments* (London, 1967); Hansfried Kellner, Peter and Brigitte Berger, *The Homeless Mind: Modernization and Consciousness* (New York, 1973); Daniel Lerner, *The Passing of Traditional Society* (New York, 1958); Karl Marx, *The Eighteenth Brumaire of Louis Bonaparte* (Moscow, 1963); John Merriman, *Consciousness and Class Experience in Nineteenth Century Europe* (New York, 1979); Jules Michelet, *The People* (1843; reprint ed., Urbana, Ill., 1973); Barrington Moore, *Social Origins of Dictatorship and Democracy: Lord and Peasant in the Making of the Modern World* (Boston, 1966); Charles Morazé, *The Triumph of the Middle Classes* (New York, 1968); W. E. Mosse, *Liberal Europe: The Age of Bourgeois Realism, 1848-1875* (London, 1974); Sidney Pollard, *European Economic Integration, 1815-1970* (London, 1974); Karl Polyani, *The Great Transformation: The Political and Economic Origins of Our Times* (Boston, 1957); Joan W. Scott, *The Glassworkers of Carmaux* (Cambridge, 1975); Richard Sennett and Jonathan Cobb, *The Hidden Injuries of Class* (New York, 1972); Peter Stearns, *European Society in Upheaval* (New York, 1967); Fritz Stern, *The Politics of Cultural Despair: A Study in the Rise of Germanic Ideology* (New York, 1961); J. L. Talmon, *Romanticism and Revolt: Europe, 1815-1848* (New York, 1967); Stephan Thernstrom, *Poverty and Progress: Social Mobility in a Nineteenth Century City* (Cambridge, Mass., 1964); E. P. Thompson, *The Making of the English Working Class* (New York, 1966); Eugen Weber, *Peasants into Frenchmen: The Modernization of Rural France, 1870-1914* (Stanford, Calif., 1976); Max Weber, "Class, Status, Party," in *From Max Weber* (New York, 1958); and Eric Wolf, *Peasant Wars of the Twentieth Century* (New York, 1969).

Modern progressive conscience in the twentieth century suffered a series of crises and reversals. These crises came in the form of war, mass culture, statism, totalitarianism, and a failure of confidence in all aspects of eighteenth-century Western bourgeois civilization. All older cultures—high, traditional, popular, and religious—increasingly were eclipsed, homogenized, and destroyed by mass national culture under the auspices of either commerical capitalism or centralizing statisms. Those who most suffered these unprecedented crises were the intellectuals whose conscience thus best reveals what we all in measure have come to suffer. For the twentieth-century intellectuals in crisis, see: R. Albérès, *L'aventure intellectuelle du XXᵉ siècle* (Paris, 1950); Raymond Aron, *The Opium of the Intellectuals* (New York, 1962), and Aron, *Progress and Disillusion* (Garden City, N.Y., 1968); Simone de Beauvoir, *Force of Circumstances* (New York, 1965), and de Beauvoir, *The Prime of Life* (New York, 1962); Victor Brombert, *The*

*Intellectual Hero: Studies in the French Novel, 1880–1955* (Philadelphia, 1961); Michel-Antoine Burnier, *Choice of Action* (New York, 1968); Albert Camus, *The Myth of Sisyphus and Other Essays* (New York, 1960), Camus, *Notebooks: 1935–1942* (New York, 1963), and Camus, *Notebooks: 1942–1951* (New York, 1965); David Caute, *Communism and French Intellectuals: 1914–1960* (New York, 1960); Roger Garaudy, *Perspectives de l'homme: existentialisme, pensée catholique, marxisme* (Paris, 1961); Peter Gay, *Weimar Culture* (New York, 1968); Erich Heller, *The Disinherited Mind* (New York, 1959); H. S. Hughes, *Consciousness and Society* (New York, 1961), Hughes, *Contemporary Europe* (Englewood Cliffs, N.J., 1961), and Hughes, *The Obstructed Path: French Social Thought in the Years of Desperation, 1930–1960* (New York, 1968); Martin Jay, *The Dialectical Imagination* (Boston, 1973); George Lichtheim, *Europe in the Twentieth Century* (New York, 1972), and Lichtheim, *Marxism in Modern France* (New York, 1966); Herbert Marcuse, *Reason and Revolution* (Boston, 1960); Jean Louis Loubet del Bayle, *Les non-conformistes des années 30* (Paris, 1969); Maurice Merleau-Ponty, *Humanism and Terror* (Boston, 1969); Ernest Nolte, *Three Faces of Fascism* (New York, 1966); Roy Pierce, *Contemporary French Political Thought* (New York, 1966); Mark Poster, *Existential Marxism in Postwar France* (Princeton, N.J., 1975); A. W. Salomone, "The Risorgimento between Ideology and History: The Political Myth of 'Rivoluzione Mancata'" in *American Historical Review* 68 (October 1962); Rolland Stromberg, *After Everything: Western Intellectual History Since 1945* (New York, 1975), and Stromberg, *European Intellectual History Since 1789* (Englewood Cliffs, N.J., 1981); Micheline Tison-Braun, *La crise de l'humanisme: Le conflit de l'individu et de la société dans la littérature française moderne* (Paris, 1958); Eugen Weber, ed., *The European Right* (Berkeley, Calif., 1966); and Theodore Zeldin, *France: 1848–1945*, 2 vols. (Oxford, 1973, 1977).

American national culture, which was formed by and out of high eighteenth-century Western culture, embodies—perhaps as no other national culture—the premises of modern progressive conscience. For a discussion of American official culture and conscience facing the test of the post–World War II world, see: Richard Barnet, *Roots of War* (Baltimore, 1973); Robert N. Bellah, "Civil Religion in America," in *Daedalus* 96 (Winter 1967); Zbigniew Brzezinski, *Between Two Ages: America's Role in the Technocratic Order* (New York, 1970); Peter Carroll and David Noble, *The Free and the Unfree: A New History of the United States* (Baltimore, 1977); Noam Chomsky, *American Power, For Reasons of State* (New York, 1973); Carl Degler, *Affluence and Anxiety: America Since 1945* (Glenview, Ill., 1975); Daniel Ellsberg, *Papers on the War* (New York, 1972); James Finn, ed., *A Conflict of Loyalties* (New York, 1968); David

Halberstam, *The Best and the Brightest* (Greenwich, Conn., 1972); Richard Hammer, *One Morning in the War: Tragedy at Son My* (New York, 1970); Paul Hollander, "Reflections on Anti-Americanism in our Time," in *World View*, vol. 21, no. 6, (June 1978); Godfrey Hodgson, *America in Our Time* (New York, 1976); Doris Kearns, *Lyndon Johnson and the American Dream* (New York, 1976); Kenneth Keniston, *The Uncommitted* (New York, 1965); Richard King, *The Party of Eros* (New York, 1972); Christopher Lasch, *The Culture of Narcissism: American Life in an Age of Diminishing Expectations* (New York, 1978); William Leuchtenburg, *A Troubled Feast* (Boston, 1973); Robert J. Lifton, *Boundaries* (New York, 1976); Margaret Mead, *Culture and Commitment* (New York, 1970); Douglas Miller and Marion Nowak, *The Fifties* (New York, 1977); Hans Morgenthau, "What Ails America?" in *New Republic* (October 28, 1967); Richard Neuhaus, *Time Toward Home: The American Experiment as Revelation* (New York, 1975); David Noble, *Historians Against History* (Minneapolis, Minn., 1965); Connor Cruise O'Brien, "Politics as Drama as Politics," in *Power and Consciousness* (New York, 1969); Philip Slater, *Pursuit of Loneliness: American Culture At Its Breaking Point* (Boston, 1970); Pitirim A. Sorokin, *The Crisis of Our Age* (New York, 1957); Massimo Teodori, ed., *The New Left: A Documentary History* (New York, 1969); Ernest Tuveson, *Redeemer Nation: The Idea of America's Millennial Role* (Chicago, 1968); Irwin Unger, *The Movement: A History of the American Left, 1959–1972* (New York, 1975); Carl Van Doren, ed., *The Patriotic Anthology* (New York, 1942); Richard Walton, *Cold War and Counter-Revolution* (New York, 1972); W. Lloyd Warner, "An American Sacred Ceremony: Memorial Day and Symbolic Behavior," in *The American Life* (Berkeley, Calif., 1962); and Gary Wills, *Nixon Agonistes: The Crisis of the Self-Made Man* (New York, 1970), and *The Winter Soldier Hearing* (Boston, 1972).

For works I found essential in defining the fundamental dilemmas and possibilities of contemporary conscience, see: Hannah Arendt, *The Human Condition* (Garden City, N.Y., 1959); John Berger, *About Looking* (New York, 1980); Peter Berger, *Pyramids of Sacrifice: Political Ethics and Social Change* (New York, 1976); Fred Branfman, ed., *Voices From the Plain of Jars* (New York, 1972); John Brodley, *Victims of Progress* (Menlo Park, Calif., 1975); Albert Camus, *The Rebel: An Essay on Man in Revolt* (New York, 1956); Rachel Carson, *Silent Spring* (New York, 1962); Jacques Ellul, *The Political Illusion* (New York, 1967), and Ellul, *The Technological Society* (New York, 1964); Kurt Glaser and Stefan Possony, *Victims of Politics: The State of Human Rights* (New York, 1979); Betrand de Jouvenel, *On Power* (Boston, 1962); Barrington Moore, *Reflections on the Casues of Human Misery* (Boston, 1972); Lewis Mumford, *Technics and Civilization* (New York, 1934); Roderick Seidenberg, *Post-Historic Man* (Boston,

1957); Richard Sennett, *The Fall of Public Man: On the Social Psychology of Capitalism* (New York, 1978); and Aleksandr Solzhenitsyn, *The Gulag Archipelago*, 3 vols. (New York, 1976).

For three works whose influences, as contradictory as they are, imposed themselves constantly throughout the work, see: Henry Adams, *Education* (Boston, 1918); Mircea Eliade, *Cosmos and History: The Myth of Eternal Return* (New York, 1959); and Emmanuel Mounier, *Personalism* (Notre Dame, Ind., 1970).

# Index

Adams, Henry, 24, 41, 188, 195
Adams, John, 63
Affirmative action, 175
Agnew, Spiro, 173
*All Quiet on the Western Front*, 104
America. *See* United States
Arendt, Hannah, 5, 7, 21 n. 34, 63, 147, 148
*Argonauts of the Western Pacific*, 31
Aron, Raymond, 90
Auerbach, Erich, 52

Barber, Elinor, 60
"The Battle of the Cannon", xiii-xix
Baudelaire, 130, 133-34, 135
Beccaria, Cesare, 65-66
Becker, Carl, 56, 193
Becker, Ernest, 69
*Being and Nothingness*, 130
Benedict, Ruth, 42-43 n.8

Bentham, Jeremy, 62
Berger, Peter, 19-20 n.23
Black movements, 168-71; Black Panthers, 168, 173; blacks as victim judges of America, 168-69; in conflict with whites, 174; as a source of white guilt, 168, 183 n.62. *See also* Civil Rights movement
Bonhoeffer, Christian Dietrich, 125
Bourgeoisie: critique of its civilization by twentieth-century intellectuals and politicians, 122-24; as a new class with new values, 58-60, 91-92, 98, 124
Brée, Germaine, 135
Brombert, Victor, 132
Brown, Norman, 44 n.16
Brzezinski, Zbigniew, 11

*Cahiers de doléances*, 90
Camus, Albert, 71, 125

Cassirer, Ernst, 63-64
Chekov, Anton, 6
Christianity: as a shaper of
    Western conscience, 51-55, 189;
    vs. traditional conscience, 36-37,
    41
*The Chrysanthemum and the
    Sword*, 42-43 n.8
Cipolla, Carlo, 24-25
Civil Rights movement, 129, 158,
    167
Cleaver, Eldridge, 168-69
Cobb, Jonathan, 10-11
Cold War, 157
Collectivism, 23-24
Communist Party, 124-25, 127,
    129
Comte, August, 80 n.55
Condorcet, Marie Jean, 67
Conquest, Robert, 39
Conscience: collective, 11;
    condition of contemporary,
    11-16, 57-58, 197-202; defini-
    tions of, 49-51; as formed by
    class and nation, 83-85; new
    and ideal, 13-16, 196-99; tradi-
    tional, 35-41, 85-90. *See also*
    Christianity; Gratitude; Guilt;
    Humanity; Progress; Sympathy
Cottonwood, Minnesota, xiii, 177
Counterculture, 163-66

Diderot, Denis, 55
Dostoyevsky, Feodor, 31, 71, 130,
    149
Du Bos, René, 11-12
Durkheim, Émile, 32-33, 46 n.29,
    47 n.39

Eighteenth-century philosphers: as
    allies of the bourgeoisie, 58-60;
    as critics of Christianity and the
    supernatural, 60-63; as definers

of the new conscience, 48-49,
    55-58, 71-74, 82, 84-85, 124,
    144, 177-78, 188-89, 193-94,
    195; United States as the land of
    the Enlightenment and the
    philosophers, xvii, xx, 144
*Elementary Forms of Religious
    Life*, 32-33
Eliade, Mircea, 87
Eliot, T. S., 6, 187
Ellsberg, Daniel, 150
Ellul, Jacques, 191
England, World War I, 99
Enlightenment, 3, 48-49, 63, 70
*The Essence of Christianity*, 70
European political left, 123-24
*Evénéments de mai*, 129, 162
Existentialism, 4-5, 121-22, 128

Fair exchange, 26, 30-35, 37-38,
    41, 59. *See also* Reciprocity
Fanfani, Amintore, 59, 91
Fanon, Frantz, 135
Fascism, 101, 114 n.56; critique
    of the bourgeoisie, 122-23; as
    enemy of conscience, 104-5;
    manipulation of gratitude,
    101-7. *See also* Nazism
Fatalism, 196
Ferguson, Adam, 78-79
Feuerbach, Ludwig, 70
Flacks, Richard, 152
*Flies*, 132
*Fontamara*, 89, 125
Foucault, Michel, 138, 187, 203
    n.3, 203 n.6
Franklin, Benjamin, 63
Free Speech Movement, 157-59
*Freikorps*, 101, 103
Fremiat de Chantel, Saint Jane, 53
French Revolution, 66-67, 71, 89,
    90-92
Freudianism, 120-21; views of

guilt, 4, 17 n.6, 18 n.8, 44 n.16
Fromm, Erich, 5
Furer-Haimendorf, Christoph
    von, 34
Futurists, 121

Genealogy of Morals, 54
Germany, post-World War I, 102-7
Gerth, Hans, 20 n.26
Gide, André, 134
The Gift: Forms and Functions
    of Exchange in Archaic Society,
    31-32
Gifts, xviii-xx, 27-29, 31-35, 119;
    as a source of values, 87-88,
    100, 133, 155, 190
The God That Failed, 140 n.8
Goffman, Erving, 20 n.26
Gramsci, Antonio, 125
Gratitude: America as object of,
    xvi-xvii, 149, 171-72; Christian
    ideals of, 52-54; definitions of,
    xvi-xxi; vs. guilt, xviii-xxi, 117;
    to the nation, 38-40, 96-108,
    171-72; nature of, 26-35, 87; as
    official cult, 100-101. See also
    Ingratitude
Gray, J. Glenn, 11
Guilt: as bad faith, 131; of being
    American, 160-61; of being
    identified with Nazism, 147-48;
    of being white, 169; of class,
    83-85; collective, 7-9; 11-12; of
    consciousness, 130-31; as debt,
    44 n.16; definitions of, 16 n.1,
    44 n.16; diffuse, 117, 118-19,
    120, 123, 128, 131, 136-40, 190,
    198-99; diffusion from Europe to
    America, 146-50; diffusion of,
    12-13; vs. gratitude, xviii-xxi;
    guiltlessness, 5, 163-66; in-
    troductory remarks, xviii-xxi;
    metaphysical, 147-48; of nation,

83-85, 96-108; vs. shame, 4;
    types of, 4-16; of Vietnam War,
    197-98
Guitton, Jean, 137

Halévy, Élie, 62
Happiness, 36, 85-86, 89, 107, 108,
    197
Harrington, Michael, 153
The Heavenly City of the
    Eighteenth Century
    Philosophers, 193
Hegel, Georg Wilhelm, 70, 127,
    148
Heidegger, Martin, 121, 129, 149
Henry, Jules, 11
Herder, Johann Gottfried von, 65
Heroism: America as hero, 146,
    154; heroes as victims, 130, 135;
    as a value, xvii-xviii, 102. See
    also Sacrifice
The Hidden Injuries of Class, 10-11
Hitler, Adolph, 102, 103-7
Holbach, Baron von, 61
The Homeless Mind: Moderniza-
    tion and Consciousness, 20 n.23
Horkheimer, Max, 200
Hughes, H. S., 121
Hugo, Victor, 68
Humanism: in the contemporary
    world, 189-93; under Nazism,
    105; vs. traditional conscience,
    36-37, 41; types of, 190-91
Humanity, as a value, 66-70, 74,
    108, 117, 126-27, 144, 188
Hume, David, 61, 64
Humility, 200-201
Husserl, Edmund, 121, 129

Individualism, 23-24
Industrial Revolution, 67, 71,
    85-87, 89, 90, 92; ethical rela-
    tions and, 93-96

Ingratitude, xvii, 26-27, 44 n.18, 105, 130, 138, 172; charges fathers against sons, 158-59. See also Gratitude

Intellectuals, 68-70, 117-39; characteristics in the twentieth century, 119-24, 128; in the crisis period 1929-1933, 121, 122; as guilty, 136-40; as the heirs of the eighteenth-century philosophers, 123-24, 140; in the 1920s, 120, 121; as victims, 135-36. See also Eighteenth-century philosophers

Jackson State University, 171
Jaspers, Karl, 147, 149
Jefferson, Thomas, 63
Johnson, Lyndon, 150, 159-60
The Just Assassins, 126
Justice, in preindustrial order, 87-89

Kafka, Franz, 6-7, 149
Kant, Immanuel, 62
Kazantzakis, Nikos, 53
Kennedy, John F., 150, 155-56, 157, 171
Kent State University, 170-71

Labor: American working classes, 171-77, 185 n.78, 185 n.79, 185 n.80; struggle with fascism and veteran's groups, 101-2. See also Marxism; Work
Lamartine, Alphonse, 68
Lasch, Christopher, 23
Last Temptation of Christ, 53
Lefebvre, Georges, 90
Legionnaires, xiv-xix, xxii, 100, 101. See also Veterans
Lerner, Daniel, 9-10
Les evénéments de mai, 129, 162
Lifton, Robert J., 151-52

Lippmann, Walter, 13
Lord Russell War Crimes Trial, 129

Maine, Henry Sumner, 30
Malinowski, Bronislaw, 31
Malthus, Thomas, 92
Marcuse, Herbert, 116-17, 165, 182 n.49
Marin, Peter, 197-98
Martindale, Don, 10, 20 n.26
Marx, Karl, 70, 127. See also Marxism
Marxism, 94-96; as an ethical system, 95-96, 192. See also Marx, Karl
Mauss, Marcel, 31-32
Mazzini, Giuseppe, 69, 97, 193
Mead, Margaret, 151
Mein Kampf, 105-6
Memorial Day, xiii
Merleau-Ponty, Maurice, 128
Michelet, Jules, 69
Mickiewicz, Adam, 69
Mill, John Stuart, 44 n.18, 68
Mills, C. Wright, 20 n.26
Modernization, 86-87. See also Industrial Revolution
Moore, Barrington, 10, 88-89, 192
Morgenthau, Hans, 154
Mounier, Emmanuel, xvi, 200
Mussolini, Benito, 102, 103-4
My Lai Massacre, 170

Nation state, 117; as enemy of humanity, 127, 189-93; as a former of values, 96-101, 112-13 n.37; nationalism, 80-81, 85, 97-98; patriotism in a nuclear age, 154; in relation to militarism, 100; in relation to war, 107-8
National Socialism, 102-7, 114 n.65. See also Fascism; Nazism

Nazism: culture of, 104-5; enemy of conscience, 104-7; as source of Western guilt, 146-47, 148. *See also* Fascism
New Left, in the United States, 129, 130, 156-68
Nietzsche, Friedrich, 42, 54-55, 105, 121, 127, 149, 191, 200, 203 n.8
Nixon, Richard M., 150, 169, 171-73
Nuclearism, 153-54

Oglesby, Carl, 157, 170
Orwell, George, 106

Pacifism, 101, 104
Paine, Thomas, 61
Pentagon Papers, 170
Personalism, xvi
Philanthropy, 77-78 n.36, 78-79 n.38. *See also* Sympathy
Polanyi, Karl, 37
Posterity, as a value and shaper of conscience, 55-57, 74. *See also* Progress
Professors, vs. legionnaires, xiv-xxii
Progress, 55; as a value, 66-70, 74, 188-89, 190-91, 195. *See also* Posterity
Punishment, 30-31, 45 n.20

Reagan, Ronald, 194
*The Rebel*, 126-27
Rebellion, in preindustrial order, 89
Reciprocity, 22, 29-35, 37-38, 41, 42-43, 43-44 n.15, 59, 130. *See also* Fair exchange
Resentment, 102, 105-6, 111 n.26, 171, 172-75, 197
Revolutions of 1848, 71

Riesman, David, 20 n.26
Romanticism, 65, 68, 70-71, 91
Rousseau, Jean-Jacques, 127, 134, 136
Russell War Crimes Tribunal, 170
Russian Revolution, 124-25

Sacrifice, 94, 46 n.28, 46 n.31; conflicting views of, 101-2; as a fascist ideal, 122-23; and nationalism, xvii-xviii; nature of, 32-35; relegated in importance by eighteenth-century philosophers, 59; as a value, 87-88, 95-96, 98; 99-101, 125; as a working-class value, 173-74, 175. *See also* Suffering
Saint-Simon, Claude Henri, 69
Salomone, A. W., 118
Salvemini, Gaetano, 102
Sartre, Jean-Paul, 116-17, 127, 129-37, 149, 170
Schweitzer, Charles, 133
Seidenberg, Roderick, 72
Sennett, Richard, 10-11, 23
Shame, 4, 10, 131
Sièyes, Joseph, 91-92
"The Silent Majority," 172
Silone, Ignazio, 89, 124-25, 127
Simmel, Georg, 28
Skepticism, 199-200
Smith, Adam, 64-65
Solzhenitsyn, Aleksandr, 192
Sombart, Wiener, 91
Sorokin, Pitirim, 73, 145
Southwest Minnesota State College, xiv
Soviet Union, 39, 124, 129
*Stalhelm*, 103
Students for Democratic Society, 156-58, 159, 173
Suffering, 92-93, 138; as a value, 87-88, 94-96, 109 n.7, 173-75

Sumner, William Graham, 108-9
Surrealism, 121
Sympathy, 3, 63-66, 77 n.36,
   84, 196-97

*Theory of Moral Sentiment*, 64-65
Third Estate. *See* Bourgeoisie
Thompson, E. P., 89, 111 n.22,
   111 n.27
Tolerance, 199-201
*The Trial*, 6-7

United States: a matter of criticism
   and guilt, xv, 129, 146, 148-49,
   153-54, 157, 158, 164-65, 166,
   176; as the myth America, xv,
   xxii, 144-46, 172-73, 175,
   177-78, 188, 193-95, 202; in the
   1950s, 153; in the 1970s, 171-78;
   in the 1960s, xvi-xvii, 154-71,
   174; in 1968, 161-62; as object
   of gratitude, xvi-xvii, 149,
   171-72; in Second World War,
   145-46; servant of humantiy,
   154, 155, 156; as a value, 175;
   as war criminal, 157, 159-61
Ure, Andrew, 67
Utilitarianism, 44 n.18, 62-63

Valery, Paul, 122
Veterans: of First World War,
   100, 101-3; of the Vietnam War,
   170, 176, 197. *See also* Legion-
   naires
Victims, 130, 148, 198; an
   American debate, 175; of
   American history, 167. *See also*
   Black movements; Heroism
Vietnam War, 129, 149-51, 157,

159-62, 170, 172, 197-98. *See
   also*Veterans
Vigny, Alfred, 68
Voltaire, François Arouet de,
   61-62, 63

Watergate affair, 150
Weathermen, 170
Weber, Eugen, 47 n.38, 123,
   138-39, 192-93
Weber, Max, 91, 112 n.31
Werfel, Franz, 107
Whitman, Walt, 69, 71
Wills, Gary, 176
Words, 132-36
Work: as a value, 94-95, 174-75;
   values of American working
   class, 171-77, 185 n.78, 185
   n.79, 185 n.80. *See also* Labor
Working classes, 171-77; values of
   American working class, 171-77,
   185 n.78, 185 n.79, 185 n.80
World War I, 38, 83-84, 98,
   99-101, 120

Xenophon, 27

Yeats, William Butler, 101
Youth, 151-71; generational conflict, xv, 150-68, 175-77; generations in America, 151; as heirs
   of European culture, 164-65; as
   an insult to the workng classes,
   174-75; protesting in Europe and
   the United States, 152-53,
   156-68

Zeldin, Theodore, 139, 187

## About the Author

Joseph Anthony Amato II is Professor of History at Southwest State University in Marshall, Minnesota. He is the author of *Mounier and Maritain: A French Catholic Understanding of the Modern World.*